# The
# Relationship
# Cure

# The Relationship Cure

A Five-Step Guide for
Building Better Connections with
Family, Friends, and Lovers

## John M. Gottman, Ph.D.,
### and Joan DeClaire

Crown Publishers
New York

Published by Crown Publishers, New York, New York.
Member of the Crown Publishing Group.

Random House, Inc. New York, Toronto, London, Sydney, Auckland
www.randomhouse.com

Crown is a trademark and the Crown colophon is a registered trademark of Random House, Inc.

Printed in the United States of America

Design by Meryl Sussman Levavi/Digitext

Library of Congress Cataloging-in-Publication Data
Gottman, John Mordechai.
   The relationship cure : a five-step guide for building better connections with family,
friends, and lovers / John M. Gottman and Joan DeClaire.—1st ed.
   1. Interpersonal relations.  2. Interpersonal communication.  3. Social interaction.
I. DeClaire, Joan.  II. Title.
HM1106 .G68    2001
158.2—dc21        2001023115

ISBN 0-609-60809-6

10  9  8  7  6  5  4  3  2  1

First Edition

To my wife, Julie; my daughter, Moriah; my sister, Batia;
and my friend and colleague Bob.
Turning toward them continues to be rewarding.
—J.G.

To my parents, Orville and Frances DeClaire, for caring so deeply.
—J.D.

# Acknowledgments

This book has emerged primarily from three wonderful collaborations. The first is with my coauthor, Joan DeClaire, who has put a great deal of herself into this book and put up with many frustrations as we puzzled through the ideas in this work. It has been a huge creative effort, the scope of which we didn't understand when we began. Second is the collaboration I have had with my very dedicated and very talented student Jani Driver. She did the hard work of building the bids and turning system from our apartment-lab data. It has been great fun working with her and seeing her talents develop. An amazing scholar and an intuitive observer, she has the potential to become a fine scientist and clinician. The third is the collaboration with my wife, Dr. Julie Schwartz Gottman, who put aside all her many obligations to do the powerful drawings for this book. I greatly appreciate all of her energy and talent in completing these drawings. She also brings to my work a great intuition and sensitivity for people, and every year I keep being more amazed at her depth of understanding and compassion. Without Julie's vision, hope, optimism, and encouragement, my laboratory and my work would not be thriving today.

The research that has resulted in this book was made possible by the continuous support I have received from my core laboratory staff, Dr. Sybil Carrere, Catherine Swanson, and Sharon Fentiman. We have been together and friends for more than a decade, and somehow it all works smoothly and keeps getting better all the time. Whether we are doing a television show or running a major study, we continue to be a great team. I also need to thank Virginia Rutter, whose energy, creativity, and imagination have been great at helping me bring this work to the public's attention.

I want to thank the staff of the Gottman Institute, particularly Etana Dykan, Peter Langsam, Kelly Scandone, Shai Steinberg, and Linda Wright, for all their support in planning and running workshops.

Thanks also to the many students and staff who have taught me so much about relationships, particularly Julian Cook, Joann Wu Shortt, Angie Mittman, Jim Coan, Melissa Hawkins, Carole Hooven, Vanessa Kahen Johnson, Lynn Katz, Regina Rushe, Kimberly Ryan, Kristin Swanson, Amber Tabares, Rebecca Tyson, Beverly Wilson, and Dan Yoshimoto.

I would like to acknowledge the amazingly insightful integrative work of Jaak Panksepp, whose great vision about affective neuroscience formed the basis for our work on the emotional command systems. I've read Jaak's book three times and still have not tapped its great potential.

The National Institute of Mental Health, particularly Drs. Molly Oliveri and Carolyn Morff, have generously supported my work on relationships. Recently, Ron Rabin, executive director of the Kirlin Foundation, and Craig Stewart, executive director of the Apex Foundation, have provided enormous support and encouragement of my work. They have emerged from the darkness and shown me the light ahead.

And thanks to Mark Malone for his help with the manuscript.

J.G.

# Contents

# Preface

A very fundamental and simple idea has emerged from our research: We have discovered the elementary constituents of closeness between people, and we have learned the basic principle that regulates how relationships work and also determines a great deal about how conflict between people can be regulated. That basic idea has to do with the way people, in mundane moments in everyday life, make attempts at emotional communication, and how others around them respond, or fail to respond, to these attempts.

Those everyday moments are not very dramatic. They are easily overlooked, and unfortunately that is their usual fate. Nonetheless, they are very powerful. By becoming aware and mindful of such moments, we can give and receive the intimacy and support we all need from our closest relationships.

We can now integrate this basic idea about moments of emotional connection with the seven basic emotional command systems of the brain. These command systems make it possible for us to see directions and purposes for our emotions. Awareness of the emotions these command systems generate allows us to examine what may be missing in our lives, and also to examine mismatches between our needs and the needs of those who are most important to us. Awareness of our emotions within ourselves and the emotions generated within our closest relationships can provide a natural guide for our search for meaning, and can give us the direction in our lives that we are continually seeking.

This book is designed to provide the guidelines and skills for building that awareness.

# The
# Relationship
# Cure

# 1

# How We Connect
# Emotionally

*A* work team at one of Seattle's floundering Internet companies has a problem that's common in many workplaces:
They can't communicate with their boss. If you catch a few
team members at a local tavern after hours, you're likely to hear an
exchange something like this:

"Joseph is the coldest fish I've ever worked for."

"I know what you mean. The other day I saw this picture of a little boy on
his bulletin board and I said, 'Cute kid. Is that your son?' And he goes, 'No.'"

"And that was it?"

"Yeah. So I'm standing there wondering, 'Well, who is it then? Your
nephew? Your stepson? Your *love child?*'"

"He's just so out of it. And to think we were so jazzed when we heard he
was going to head the team, with that vaunted success record of his."

"He's smart, all right. But what good has it done us? We still haven't
launched the site."

"That's because he has zero people skills. Have you noticed how all the
other managers try to avoid him?"

"Yeah, that's what's screwing us up. We have no real standing in the
company. I was hoping he could take our ideas up the ladder and we'd finally
get the resources we need. But he never asks for our input. He never even
asks if you've had a nice weekend."

"Remember when we moved to the new building and he decided to do
away with private offices? He said we'd have an open floor plan to 'enhance
communication.' What a crock!"

"Stop it, you guys. I feel sorry for him."

"Sorry for him? Why? He's the one with all the stock options!"

"Well, I think he wants to be a better boss—he just doesn't know how."

"Oh yeah? How can you tell?"

"I don't know. It's just a guess. Maybe he knows how disappointed we all feel in him. And that makes it even harder for him. I can't read his mind, but I bet that's what's going on."

Next meet Kristine, age fifty-four, an advertising executive whose mother was recently diagnosed with Alzheimer's disease. Kristine would like to help with her mother's care, but Mom lives several states away, near Kristine's sister, Alice. Here's a typical phone call between the sisters:

"How's Mom?" Kristine asks tentatively.

"She'll be better once the insurance pays her hospital bill," Alice responds. "That's all she talks about."

"But that was last December. The insurance still hasn't paid?"

"No, not *that* hospital stay. I'm talking about this last time, when she had that seizure."

"What seizure?"

"Didn't I tell you?"

"Tell me what?"

"She was in the hospital last month after a seizure. They ran some tests."

"I can't believe you didn't tell me about this. Why didn't you call?"

"It was just so hectic. And it's impossible to get hold of you with your voice mail or whatever. Besides, there's nothing you can do from the East Coast."

"But, Alice! I've asked you to call me when these things happen!"

"Well, it really doesn't matter now. They put her on some new medicine and she's doing much better. We got through it fine. There's no need to worry."

But Kristine does worry. And she's angry as well. She tells herself that Alice isn't cutting her out of the loop on purpose; she's just caught up in her own concerns. But now that Mom's health is going downhill, Kristine and her sister have got to cooperate better than this. Otherwise, Kristine might miss her only chance to be there when Mom needs help most. And if that happens, she and Alice could hold grievances against each other for the rest of their lives.

Now meet Phil and Tina, a couple in their thirties who seem to have it all. Solid jobs, two beautiful kids, lots of good friends—and they love each other. Trouble is, they haven't had sex in six months.

Seated together on a small sofa in a therapist's office, the couple describes how the problem started.

"Tina's company was going through this big reorganization," Phil explains. "And every day she'd come home exhausted."

"It was a real drag," Tina remembers. "I was spending all day in these long, tense meetings, trying to defend people's jobs. When I got home, I couldn't shake the stress. I didn't want to talk to anybody. I felt so anxious. Phil tried to be nice, but . . ."

"I wanted to help her, to tell her it was going to be okay, but I couldn't do anything right. It wasn't like we had this huge, catastrophic breakdown or anything. It was more about the little stuff. I'd kiss her on the back of her neck or start to rub her stomach when we were in bed—things that used to get her attention. But now I was getting nothing in return. Zip. It definitely threw me off balance."

"And I felt that if I didn't get all hot and bothered the minute he touched me, he was going to be *wounded* or something," Tina explained. "It just made me so tense."

Phil got the point. "She has all these people leaning on her at work. And then she comes home to this guy who's feeling insecure, who's whining about *his* needs. It was such a turnoff for her."

So, to preserve his pride, Phil quit trying. "I got tired of the rejection," he explains to the therapist. "I don't know how long we can go on like this. It's tough to keep putting yourself out there only to be shut down all the time. Sure, I love her, but sometimes I'm afraid we're not going to make it."

"It's not working for me, either," Tina says through tears. Then, after a long silence, she adds, "I miss making love, too. I miss the way it used to be."

"Well, maybe that's a place to start," Phil says quietly. "Because you never told me that before. You never gave me that information."

Phil couldn't have said it better. Whether people are struggling to save a marriage, to cooperate in a family crisis, or to build rapport with a difficult boss, they usually have one thing in common: They need to share emotional information that can help them feel connected.

The disgruntled workers at the Seattle Internet company need to know that their boss shares their dream of launching a successful site. They need to know that he appreciates their work and ideas. But when they turn to him for this emotional information, he fails to respond. In fact, he can't even react sociably to their attempts at friendly conversation. He doesn't inspire confidence that they'll be able to achieve their goal. As a result, the team members feel demoralized and they doubt whether they can make the launch.

A similar dynamic is happening between the sisters whose mother is sick. Kristine has asked Alice to keep her informed about their mother's condition. But she's after more than medical information. She wants to feel as though she is part of the family, especially in this time of crisis. By failing to call when their mother is hospitalized, Alice shows that she doesn't really consider Kristine a part of the world she inhabits with Mom. Alice may blame the miles between their homes, but the emotional distance Kristine experiences seems even wider.

Phil and Tina are like many couples I see in marital therapy. Whatever conflicts the couples may have—sex, money, housework, kids—all of them long for evidence that their spouses understand and care about what they're feeling.

Sharing such information through words and behavior is essential for improving any significant relationship. This includes bonds with our kids, our siblings, our friends, our coworkers. But even our best efforts to connect can be jeopardized as a result of one basic problem: failure to master what I call the "bid"—the fundamental unit of emotional communication.

This book will show you five steps you can take to achieve this mastery and make your relationships work:

1. Analyze the way you bid and the way you respond to others' bids.
2. Discover how your brain's emotional command systems affect your bidding process.
3. Examine how your emotional heritage impacts your ability to connect with others and your style of bidding.
4. Develop your emotional communication skills.
5. Find shared meaning with others.

But first let's make sure you understand what I mean when I talk about bids. A bid can be a question, a gesture, a look, a touch—any single expression that says, "I want to feel connected to you." A response to a bid is just that—a positive or negative answer to somebody's request for emotional connection.

At the University of Washington, my research colleagues and I recently discovered how profoundly this bidding process affects relationships. We learned, for example, that husbands headed for divorce disregard their wives' bids for connection 82 percent of the time, while husbands in stable relationships disregard their wives' bids just 19 percent of the time. Wives headed for divorce act preoccupied with other activities when their husbands bid for their attention 50 percent of the time, while happily married wives act preoccupied in response to their husbands' bids just 14 percent of the time.

When we compared how often couples in the two groups extended bids and responded to them, we found another significant difference. During a typical dinner-hour conversation, the happily married people engaged one another as many as one hundred times in ten minutes. Those headed for divorce engaged only sixty-five times in that same period. On the surface the contrast may seem inconsequential, but taken together over a year, the additional moments of connection among the happy couples would be enough to fill a Russian novel.

We also found that this high rate of positive engagement paid off in tremendous ways. For example, we now know that people who react positively to one another's bids have greater access to expressions of humor, affection, and interest during arguments. It's almost as if all the good feelings they've accumulated by responding respectfully and lovingly to one another's bids form a pot of emotional "money in the bank." Then, when a conflict arises, they can draw on this reservoir of good feeling. It's as if something inside unconsciously says, "I may be mad as hell at him right now, but he's the guy who listens so attentively when I complain about my job. He deserves a break." Or, "I'm as angry as I've ever been with her, but she's the one who always laughs at my jokes. I think I'll cut her some slack."

Having access to humor and affection during a conflict is invaluable because it helps to de-escalate bad feelings and leads to better understanding. Rather than shutting down communication in the midst of an argument, people who can stay present with one another have a much better opportunity to resolve issues through their conflicts, repair hurt feelings, and build positive regard. But this good work must begin long before the conflict starts; it's got to be grounded in those dozens of ordinary, day-to-day exchanges of emotional information and interest that we call bids.

And what happens when we habitually fail to respond positively to one another's bids for emotional connection? Such failure is rarely malicious or mean-spirited. More often we're simply unaware of or insensitive to others' bids for our attention. Still, when such mindlessness becomes habitual, the results can be devastating.

I've seen such results in my clinical practice at the Gottman Institute, where I've counseled many people who describe their lives as consumed by loneliness. They feel lonely despite their proximity to many significant people in their lives—lovers, spouses, friends, children, parents, siblings, and coworkers. Often they seem surprised and greatly disappointed at the deterioration of their relationships.

"I love my wife," one client says of his faltering marriage, "but our relationship feels empty somehow." He senses that the passion is waning, that the romance is drifting away. What he can't see are all the opportunities for closeness that surround him. Like so many other distressed, lonely people, he doesn't mean to ignore or dismiss his spouse's bids for emotional connection. It's just that the bids happen in such simple, mundane ways that he doesn't recognize these moments as very important.

Clients like these typically have trouble at work, as well. Although they're often skilled at forming collegial bonds when they first start a job, they tend to focus totally on the tasks at hand, often to the detriment of their relationships with coworkers. Later, when they're passed over for a promotion, or when they discover they have no influence on an important project, they're baffled. And they often feel betrayed and disappointed by their colleagues and bosses as a result.

Such feelings of disappointment and loss also crop up in these clients' relationships with friends and relatives. Many describe peers, siblings, and children as disloyal, unworthy of trust. But when we dig deeper, we find a familiar pattern. These clients seem unaware of the bids for connection that their friends and relatives have been sending them. So it's no wonder that their loved ones feel no obligation to continue their support.

People who have trouble with the bidding process also have more conflict—conflict that might be prevented if they could simply acknowledge one another's emotional needs. Many arguments spring from misunderstandings and feelings of separation that might have been avoided if people would have the conversations they need to have. But because they don't, they argue instead. Such conflicts can lead to marital discord, divorce, parenting problems, and family feuds. Friendships fade and deteriorate. Adult sibling relationships wither and die. Kids raised in homes filled with chronic conflict have more difficulty learning, getting along with friends, and staying healthy. People who can't connect are also more likely to suffer isolation, as well as dissatisfaction and instability in their work lives. Any of these problems can create a tremendous amount of stress in people's lives, leading to all sorts of physical and mental health problems.

But our findings about the bidding process give me a tremendous amount of hope. They tell me that people who consistently bid and respond to bids in positive ways have an astounding chance for success in their relationships.

We've written this book to share these discoveries with as many people as possible. We hope that reading it will help you to form and maintain the kind of strong, healthy connections that lead to a happy, fulfilling life.

## Bid by Bid: How to Build Better Relationships One Step at a Time

Writer Anne Lamott tells the story of her ten-year-old brother agonizing over a school report he had to write about birds. Frozen by the size and complexity of the task, he turned to his dad for help. She writes, "My father put his arm around my brother's shoulder and said, 'Bird by bird, buddy. Just take it bird by bird.' "

So it is with our ties to friends, family, and coworkers. Complex, fulfilling relationships don't suddenly appear in our lives fully formed. Rather, they develop one encounter at a time.

If you could carefully observe and analyze those encounters—as my research colleagues and I have done—you would see how each one is made up of many smaller exchanges. There's a bid and a response to that bid. Like cells of the body or bricks of a house, such exchanges are the primary components of emotional communication. Each exchange contains emotional information that can strengthen or weaken connections between people. Here are some examples.

> *"Hey, Mom, when's dinner going to be ready?"*
> *"Stop nagging! As soon as I can get it on the table!"*

> *"Your monthly report is past due—again."*
> *"Why don't you look in your e-mail? I sent it to you last night."*

> *"Knock-knock."*
> *"Who's there?"*

> *"Are you busy tonight?"*
> *"Maybe . . . Maybe not . . ."*

Bids and responses to bids can be big, overblown, cathartic events such as those we see in the movies:
*"Will you marry me, Violet?"*
*"I will, Jack, I will!"*
Or they can be the small, mundane exchanges of everyday life:
*"Get me a beer while you're up, okay?"*
*"Sure, do you want anything else? Any chips?"*
Bids can be subtle: *"That's a pretty dress."*
Or they can be straight ahead: *"I want to make love to you."*
Bids can be fairly insignificant exchanges between strangers: *"Can you call me a cab?"*
Or they can be poignant secrets whispered between friends: *"You're not going to believe what happened to me last night!"*
Bids allow strangers to get acquainted: *"Do you mind if I sit here?"*
And they're essential for longtime friends or partners who want to stay close: *"I've missed you so much. Let's go somewhere and talk!"*
Positive responses to a bid typically lead to continued interaction, often with both parties extending more bids to one another. Listening to this kind of exchange is kind of like watching a Ping-Pong game in which both players are doing very well.
*"What are you doing for lunch today?"*
*"I brought a sandwich. Want to join me outside?"*
*"Sure. But I need to get something from the deli first. Need anything?"*
*"Yeah, get me a Dr. Pepper. Maybe I'll bring those pictures from my family reunion?"*
*"Sure, I'd love to see them. And we can plan the party for Peg."*
*"Yeah, we better get started on that."*
But a negative response to a bid typically shuts down emotional

communication. All bids cease. The game is over. People want to pick up their Ping-Pong paddles and go home.

*"What are you doing for lunch today?"*

*"Lunch? Who's got time for that?"*

*"Maybe some other time, then."*

*"Yeah, some other time."*

But our research shows that "some other time" rarely happens. In fact, the probability that a person will attempt to re-bid once an initial bid has been rejected is close to zero. That's not to say people need to accept every lunch date that comes along. But they can refuse specific invitations while still accepting the bid for emotional connection.

*"What are you doing for lunch today?"*

*"I wish I had time for lunch. I've got to finish this report. What are you up to?"*

*"I brought a sandwich. I thought I'd go sit outside. But I have to go by the deli for a Coke. Want me to bring something back for you?"*

*"That would be nice. Can you get me a ham on rye and a Dr. Pepper? Oh—and catch some rays for me while you're out there, okay?"*

*"Sure thing."*

Bids typically grow in intensity and frequency as a relationship grows and deepens. Think about the steps you might take in making a friend on the job. Your initial bid might be a software question on your first day. That leads to a joke—politically correct, of course—over cubicle walls. Your potential friend laughs and invites you to lunch. Conversation centers on fairly routine, work-related issues. But then one day, after you've had a few breaks together, you take the risk of asking him how he *really* feels about the boss. He tells you, and you end up asking him for some career advice. A few months later, when you find out that your favorite project has been canned, you're enraged! Where do you go to blow off steam? To his office, of course. You trust him. You can say whatever's on your mind. It won't come back to haunt you. As the years go by, you start getting together on weekends to watch the game. You have him and his wife over for dinner. He learns all about your family, your childhood, your passions, your fears. It's hard to remember what life was like before you met him. You always open his e-mail first. And now you tell him *all* your jokes.

How did it become possible? One small interaction at a time. And how do you keep it afloat? By continuing to make bids to one another for connection, and by continuing to respond to one another's bids, moment by moment, in positive ways.

While the process sounds simple, most people can think of many relationships in their lives that have gone awry because of failed bidding or failed responses to bids.

Below are a few "disaster" scenarios that may seem familiar to you. First you'll see an example in which the bidding process goes badly, resulting in interactions that hinder the development of the relationship. Then you'll read a bidding "makeover"—the same scenario, but with a few adjustments in key exchanges that take the conversation into new territory, leading the relationship into a more positive realm.

Let's start with Kristine and Alice, the sisters whose mom has Alzheimer's. Although it's been years since they've been involved in each other's lives, Kristine wants to get closer. It's going to take some effort, though, especially considering their contrasting lifestyles. Kristine, who moved to New York after college, remained single and childless. Her life centers on her career. Alice married right out of high school, stayed in Omaha, and had four kids. Her life is built around kids and family. Because they've made such different choices, each spends at least a little time wondering what the other thinks. And if there's anything they want from each other, it's probably a little validation, or at least some good-hearted, sisterly interest. Still, it's hard because they've got so little in common, as we see in this phone conversation:

"I'm fine, honey," Alice says, sounding surprised to hear from her sister on a Thursday night. "We're all fine. How are you?"

"I'm okay," Kristine answers. "Quite well, actually."

"So what's going on?"

"Well, I've been working a lot. Um . . . looks like I'm finally going to get that big account I've been after for so long."

"You mean that makeup thing?" Alice asks.

"No, no. I've had the cosmetics firm for years. This one is an ISP."

"A what?"

"Oh . . . an Internet service provider."

"Ah, computer stuff." Alice chuckles nervously. "Well, you lost me there."

"Yeah . . . well, that's what it is. It's . . . computer stuff."

"Oh."

"So is it hot there?"

"Yeah, in the nineties."

"And how are the kids?"

"Good. Danny's baseball team is going to state finals."

"Neat."

"Yeah. We're real proud."

"You must be."

"Yeah. Well, we are."

And so the conversation continues with each sister delivering facts about her life that the other just barely responds to. They seem to have no frame of reference for each other's worlds, so it's hard for them to pick up each other's cues. If this conversation is a Ping-Pong game, then these women have holes in their paddles and their balls just keep dropping off the table. It doesn't take too long before they run out of steam, become discouraged, and call it quits. You get the feeling it will be a long time before either of them phones the other again.

But consider how the conversation can go differently if the women start giving one another just a little more information, asking just a few more open-ended questions in ways that express interest in the other. Here's a makeover. We'll pick up the conversation where Alice realizes that Kristine is talking about "computer stuff."

"Yeah, it's computer stuff," says Kristine, chuckling herself. "There's so much jargon to keep up with."

"I don't know how you do it."

"Actually, I feel like I'm always behind the curve. I try to make myself read the technology section in the newspaper—as much as I can stand, anyway. I imagine it must be the same for you and Larry with the kids. Isn't Danny always asking for something new for his PC?"

"Yeah, seems like Larry's always ordering him a new computer game or gadget or something. Hey, did I tell you that Danny's baseball team made state finals?"

"No, that's great! When is it?"

"At the end of the month. It's in Lincoln. Larry's taking time off work so we can all go down there and cheer them on."

"What a trip! I should send Danny some kind of good-luck charm. Maybe a Yankees cap or something."

"Oh, he'd love that. He still talks about our trip to Yankee Stadium."

Feel the difference? The interest Kristine and Alice express in one another's lives is a stretch for both at times. But the effort each sister puts forth seems to encourage the other to try also. You get the feeling they want to be in this conversation and in this relationship.

Now let's take a look at a classic bidding scenario that seems ripe for disaster: the bid for a mate. Paul is a divorced guy in his late forties who hasn't dated in several years. In fact, it's been years since he's even asked anybody out because he hates how vulnerable it makes him feel. Besides, he tells himself, all the great women are already taken. But then he meets Marly at a friend's birthday bash. She seems fun, attractive—a little shy, maybe—but, to his surprise, unattached. He gets her phone number from his friend and stumbles through an invitation to coffee. Incredible as it seems, she accepts.

Marly, too, is surprised that she accepted. Just a few months out of a bad split-up, she had decided to take a break from dating. But Paul gets good reviews from Greg, their mutual friend. Still, there's nothing she hates worse than a first date. She's just no good at making small talk.

Paul arrives at the coffee shop fifteen minutes early. Marly's about ten minutes late. They make eye contact as soon as she walks in the door. She flashes a weak, strained smile and heads toward his table.

"Hi, there," he says as she takes a seat. He notices that she looks smaller than she did at the party. And awfully nervous as she pulls her raincoat close around her body.

"Hi."

"Did you have any trouble finding it?"

"No."

"Good." She looks toward the menu hanging over the counter.

"It's self-serve. Let me get you something."

"Thanks."

"What would you like?"

"Um. Just coffee. Black."

He returns and sets the Styrofoam cups on the table. "Here you go."

"Thanks."

"So . . . gee," Paul offers. "I had a great time at Greg and Susan's the other night."

"Yeah, it was nice."

"Greg's a great guy."

"Yeah. He's so funny."

"Susan, too."

"I don't know Susan as well."

"Do you live near here?" Paul asks.

"No. I live on the East Side," Marly replies.

"But you work around here?"

"Yeah. Sixth and Maple."

"That's where AltaGuard is."

"Right."

"So that's where you work?"

"Um-hmm."

"That's quite a commute."

"Yeah. But I'm getting used to it."

"AltaGuard is an insurance company, right?"

"Um-hmm."

"What do you do there?"

"Data entry."

And so it goes . . . like a bad job interview. "I figured she was shy, but this is ridiculous," Paul says to himself. "She's bordering on depressive. Then again, maybe it's me. Maybe she doesn't like bald guys. Maybe I should have met her at a nicer place. Maybe she's sorry she came." And as the grilling continues, Paul's interior monologue gets gloomier and gloomier. "This isn't working. I shouldn't have done this. Greg should have warned me. How do I get out of this?"

Good question. Let's see how this conversation—this bid for relation-ship—might go if Paul made just a few adjustments in his questions and if

Marly responded with a little more information. We'll take it from Paul's arrival with the coffee.

"Here you go."

"Thanks."

"So . . . gee, I had a great time at Greg and Susan's the other night."

"Yeah, it was nice."

"Greg and I go way back. I think I told you we were college roommates."

"That's right. At Ohio State."

"And how do you know them?"

"Greg and I used to work together."

"At that insurance company on the East Side?"

"Yeah. SafeCore."

"Right. I remember Greg hated that place! His boss was this real neurotic—oh no, don't tell me . . . you were his boss, right?"

Marly laughs. "No. Thank goodness. That was Roberta."

"Right! 'Her Royal Majesty Roberta!' So do you still work there?"

"No, I'm at AltaGuard now."

"So did you guys get T-shirts made that said, 'I survived the Reign of Roberta—1999'?"

Marly smiles. "No. But Greg and Susan took me out for a great lunch after I quit."

"What made you finally decide to leave?"

"I dunno. I just woke up one day and knew I couldn't take it one more minute. I called in sick and started applying for other jobs that same day."

"I bet it didn't take you long to find something."

"About a month."

"So what's your new job like?"

"It's okay. It's better than SafeCore."

"In what way?"

"The people are more real, for one thing."

"What do you mean by 'real'?"

"Well, you know . . . it's like if you're having a bad day, you don't have to fake it."

"For example?"

"Well, take last Thursday. I had just gotten my grades from last semester . . ."

"You're in school?"

"Yeah, I'm trying to get out of this insurance thing. You see, what I'm really interested in is anthropology—"

"That's so cool. I almost majored in anthropology!"

"You did?"

"But then I switched to business instead. Big mistake. But you were telling me about what you want to do."

"Yeah, because insurance, it's just so . . . boring. But if I can get a master's in anthropology, I figure . . ."

And they're off. What makes the difference? Paul's use of a little humor, for one thing. But more than that, it's the way he expresses interest in Marly's life. She's still shy initially, so he's still got to draw her out with lots of questions. But this time he's not asking for simple data. Because he uses open-ended questions that get to the heart of her values and dreams, she can't help but respond. His interest in the "real" Marly makes her feel more warmly toward him and he can tell. This raises his spirits and prevents him from becoming self-conscious and gloomy. Instead, he keeps his focus where it belongs, on Marly. And she's getting more interesting to him by the minute. It feels to him that he may get what he's bidding for—an emotional connection.

And finally, let's take a look at one of the most challenging pairings of all: the parent-teen relationship.

Roger is a salesman who spends a lot more time than he'd like on the road. Each time he comes home from a trip and greets his daughter, Hannah, now thirteen, she seems to have grown another inch taller.

Hannah believes her dad when he says "I missed you," because she used to feel that way about him, too. But ever since she started middle school, that feeling is fading. There are just so many things to think about—friends, school projects, the track team, high school next year. Sure, she loves her dad, but he's not the top item on her agenda anymore.

One night, as Roger's flying home, he reads an ad for Cirque de Lune— "an animal-free circus that blends the pageantry of the Big Top with the antics of street theater," the ad says. The ticket prices are sky-high, but Hannah would love it, Roger muses—especially the "animal-free" part. She's been talking a lot about animal rights lately. He tears out the ad and sticks it in his pocket.

At breakfast the next morning he says, "Hey, sweetie, have you ever heard about this show called Cirque de Lune?"

"Nope."

"Well, it's kind of like a circus."

"Daddy, you know how I feel about circuses."

"No, this one's different. No animals. More like theater. Lots of acrobats and costumes. It's supposed to be really something. I think you'd like it."

"Hmm . . . maybe."

"Go get the ad that's in my jacket pocket over there," he says, pointing. Hannah, intrigued now, does just that.

"Oooh. It looks cool," she says, as she peruses the description.

"So I'm thinking I should get tickets," Roger says. "Just you and me. Next Saturday night."

"Next Saturday?"

"Yeah. You got a hot date or something?" Roger says, teasing.

"Well, that's the night of Rachel Iannelli's slumber party."

"Oh, she probably has slumber parties all the time," Roger says, good-naturedly. "Besides, that's the only night I'm going to be in town while it's here."

"But I really wanted to go to Rachel's party . . ."

"Honey, you girls have these parties nearly every weekend."

"No we don't."

"Well, okay. Maybe not every weekend. But I thought this was something special you and I could do together."

"But I don't want to go that night."

"Because your friends are more important."

"No. It's just that this is Rachel Iannelli's party and she's never invited me to one before and—"

"Okay, if that's a higher priority for you, fine. Go."

"So now I'm in trouble."

"No, you're not in trouble. I'm just disappointed, that's all. We don't have all that much time to spend together."

"And that's supposed to be my fault?"

"No, it's not your fault. It's nobody's fault. Forget it. Forget I mentioned it. Go to your damned slumber party."

With that, Roger crumples up the ad, and Hannah leaves the breakfast table in tears—not exactly the scenario Roger had in mind.

Could it have gone differently? Let's take a look, picking up the scene where Hannah tells Roger about Rachel's slumber party.

"Oh, she probably has slumber parties all the time," Roger says, good-naturedly. "Besides, that's the only night I'm going to be in town while it's here."

"But I really wanted to go to Rachel's party . . ."

"Now, whose party is it?"

"Rachel Iannelli. She's this new girl who Dana's always hanging with. Dana thinks she's really cool."

"You mean Dana—your best friend Dana?"

"Yep. And Dana's always spending the night over there. Kelly and Laura, too."

"Oh. Is this the first time Rachel has invited you to one of these parties?"

"Yeah."

"So it feels kind of important to you to go because you really like hanging out with Dana and Kelly and Laura."

"Yeah. I was feeling like they didn't like me anymore or something. But I think Rachel just doesn't know me that well. I really want to go."

"And it's the same night as this show. I feel kind of disappointed about that."

"Me, too. Because the show looks really neat, Daddy. And it's so nice that you want to take me."

"I really do want to take you. But maybe we could think of something else to do together. Like during the day on Saturday, instead."

"Really?"

"Yeah. Then you could go to Rachel's party."

"And you could take Mom to this circus instead. I bet she'd really like it, too."

"I think you're right. That's a great idea. So you be thinking about what you want to do together next Saturday afternoon. Just the two of us, okay?"

"Okay, Daddy. Thanks."

So Roger didn't get to take Hannah to Cirque de Lune, but he did get what he was bidding for—an opportunity to spend time with his daughter. Not only that, but he got the chance to do something parents too rarely do: He got to show Hannah that he's interested in her world, and that he really does understand how she's feeling. That's called emotional connection.

## Turning Points: The Choices We Make in Responding to Bids

My insights into the process of bidding for emotional connection are a result of many years of observing human interaction in a variety of real-life settings. My research colleagues and I have studied the dynamics of friendships, parent-child relationships, adult siblings, and couples in all stages of marriage and child rearing.

The group with whom I've always been most fascinated is the one I call "marital masters"—folks who are so good at handling conflict that they make marital squabbles look like fun. It's not that these couples don't get mad and disagree. It's that when they disagree, they're able to stay connected and engaged with each other. Rather than becoming defensive and hurtful, they pepper their disputes with flashes of affection, intense interest, and mutual respect. Amazingly, they seem to have access to their sense of humor even when they're arguing. In this way, their conflict actually becomes fruitful—a resource for discovery and problem solving, another place to demonstrate the overriding passion and respect in their relationships.

How do they do it, I've wondered. It seemed that they must have some kind of secret weapon against elements like contempt, criticism, defensiveness, and stonewalling—the factors that we discovered could destroy all kinds of relationships. What is it that allows couples to continue to react with good humor and affection despite the typical stresses of family life? If I could find the answer to this question, I might have a key to helping people build and sustain better emotional connections, not only in marriage, but in all sorts of significant relationships. The answer came, in part, when I started to look at the link between conflict and bidding behavior among sixty married couples who volunteered to spend the weekend alone together at our family research facility on the University of Washington campus. Affectionately dubbed "The Love Lab," the place includes a small studio apartment in a parklike setting on the University of Washington campus. From the apartment's large picture window, couples can watch pleasure boats float through the Montlake Cut, a canal that connects Seattle's Portage Bay to Lake Washington.

The apartment is furnished like a comfortable weekend hideaway. There's a kitchen, a dining area, a hide-a-bed, a television, and a VCR. Study couples bring along groceries to cook, games to play, movies to watch. They're asked to simply relax and do whatever they would normally do during a typical weekend at home together. The only difference is that we have stationed scientific observers behind a two-way mirror in the kitchen to observe every interaction that takes place. Four video cameras mounted on the walls and microphones attached to the couples' clothes capture all their movements, all their conversations. The couples also wear sensors on their bodies to monitor signs of stress such as a rise in heart rate or increased sweating. (To preserve the couple's privacy, we don't monitor them between 9:00 P.M. and 9:00 A.M., nor do cameras follow them to the bathroom. They also get a half hour of privacy to walk in the park that surrounds the lab.)

We learned that people typically respond to another's bids for connection in one of three ways: They turn toward, turn against, or turn away. By correlating these three types of behavior with the status of their relationships ten years later, we were able to show how each of these types of behavior affect people's connections over the long term. In a nutshell, here's what we learned:

**1. Turning toward.** To "turn toward" one another means to react in a positive way to another's bids for emotional connection. One person makes a funny comment, for example, and the other person laughs. A man points to an impressive car as it passes by, and his friend nods as if to say, "I agree. That's quite a car!" A father asks his son to pass the ketchup, and his son does so in a kind, accommodating way. A woman muses about a vacation she'd like to take, and her coworker joins in. He asks her questions, adds his opinions, lends colorful details to a trip they imagine together.

What happens in relationships where people consistently turn toward one another's bids for connection? Our analysis shows that, over time, they develop stable, long-lasting relationships rich in good feelings for one another. Like the "marital masters," they also seem to have easier access to humor, affection, and interest in one another during conflict, a factor that allows them to stay connected emotionally, solve problems, and avoid the downward spiral of negative feelings that destroy relationships.

**2. Turning against.**  People who turn against one another's bids for connection might be described as belligerent or argumentative. For example, if a man fantasized about owning a passing sports car, his friend might reply, "On your salary? Dream on!"

Turning against often involves sarcasm or ridicule. In one instance in our marriage lab, a wife gently asked her husband to put down his newspaper and talk to her.

"And what are we going to talk about?" he sneered.

"Well, we were thinking of buying a new television," she offered. "We could talk about that."

But his next response was just as mean: "What do *you* know about televisions?" he asked. After that, she said nothing at all.

This woman's withdrawal is typical in situations when one person habitually turns against another, we discovered. After all, who wants to be ridiculed or snapped at? We also found that this pattern of hostility followed by suppression of feelings is destructive to relationships. Among married couples, the pattern leads to divorce later on. Among adult siblings, such behavior is linked to being emotionally distant from one another and having a less supportive relationship. In addition, studies show that such hostility is also harmful to relationships among friends, coworkers, and other relatives.

Interestingly, the married couples in our study who habitually displayed this behavior did not divorce as quickly as couples whose main habit of interaction was for one partner to turn away. But eventually the majority of them did split up.

**3. Turning away.**  This pattern of relating generally involves ignoring another's bid, or acting preoccupied. A person in these instances might comment and point to that impressive sports car, but his friend wouldn't bother to look up. Or he might look up and say something unrelated, such as, "What time do you have?" Or, "Do you have change for a five-dollar bill?"

In a study I once conducted of childhood friendships, I often saw small children turn away from each other in games of make-believe. "Let's pretend we're pirates and this is our ship," one would say. And the other child— without being belligerent—might respond, "I'll be the mom and we have to go to the grocery store." For obvious reasons, the game never takes flight.

In one poignant example from our marriage lab, the wife apologized to her husband for a mistake she made in preparing dinner that night. She raised the issue three times during the course of the evening, obviously wanting him to let her off the hook. But all three times the husband met his wife's comments with silence and looked away.

Another husband said, "Dinner's almost ready," while his wife divided her attention between reading and watching TV. She didn't respond. So he went over to the couch where she sat and said, "How's your book, hon?" She ignored him again. He then kissed her twice, and she was unresponsive to his kisses. "Is that book good?" he asked. Finally she said, "Yes, it has some nice pictures in it." That was their entire exchange.

Consistently turning away from one another's bids is clearly bad for relationships, our research has revealed. In our studies of children's friendships, for example, the young children who couldn't engage one another in shared fantasy failed to develop lasting bonds.

In our marriage studies, we found that turning away on a regular basis is actually destructive. Partners who displayed this pattern of interaction in the apartment lab often became hostile and defensive with each other— particularly when they discussed an area of continuing disagreement. This behavior typically results in early divorce among married couples.

Studies done on the dynamics of parent-child, adult friendship, adult sibling, and coworker relationships lead us to believe that it's destructive to other relationships as well.

## Unrequited Turning

What happens when someone in a relationship habitually turns toward the other's bids, while the other person habitually turns away or against? As might be expected, our studies show that this is not a healthy situation. Just imagine the frustration of being in any relationship where you're constantly in pursuit of somebody's attention, but that person is always eluding you, and in some cases even being hostile in response to your advances.

Our studies indicate that children whose parents consistently thwart their bids for connection often suffer long-term consequences as a result of constantly experiencing more negative emotions and fewer positive emotions. They have trouble developing the social skills to get along with friends, for example. They don't do as well academically, and they have more problems with physical health.

Unrequited turning is clearly destructive to marriage, as well. Even the couples in our studies who habitually turned away from each other found themselves to be more happily married than couples in which just one partner (usually the wife) was constantly turning toward and getting no response.

We also learned that once bidders are ignored or rejected, they usually give up trying to connect in the same way again. My colleagues and I were quite surprised by how quickly people seem to lose heart once others turn away or turn against their bids. I think we expected people to be more persistent with one another, demanding a certain level of attention and responsiveness. But this rarely happens. Instead, we see failing bidders who just give up in response to another's indifference or hostility. Among people in stable marriages, spouses re-bid just 20 percent of the time. In marriages that are headed for divorce, people hardly re-bid at all. Instead, they simply fade away from conversations, relinquishing their attempts to connect. Such reactions are a sobering display of what it means to lose your confidence and enthusiasm for a relationship.

In addition to these discoveries, we learned that frequency of bids makes a difference. For example, happily married couples bid for connection far more often than unhappily married couples do. As I mentioned earlier, an analysis of dinnertime conversations showed that happily married couples bid as many as one hundred times in ten minutes. This compares with a bid rate among unhappily married couples of just sixty-five times in ten minutes.

That's not to say that happily married spouses turned toward one another every single time their partners made a bid. Attempting to pay that much attention to a loved one would probably drive a person batty. But because these couples gave one another so many opportunities to connect, they seemed to have a much higher potential for creating satisfying relationships than did those who didn't bid as frequently.

Many factors influence a person's ability and willingness to turn toward the significant people in their lives—factors such as the way their brains process feelings, the way emotions were handled in the homes where they grew up, and their own emotional communication skills. We'll take an in-depth look at each of these factors in the chapters ahead. But first let's look at what happens to relationships when people fail to connect.

## Disconnected: The Consequences of Living Without Emotional Bonds

Whether people make bids for emotional connection to a relative, a spouse, a friend, or a coworker, they're usually seeking to satisfy one of three emotional needs common to all people. Everybody wants (1) to be included, (2) to have a sense of control over their lives, or (3) to be liked. When such needs are met, people experience feelings of well-being and a sense of purpose to their lives.

But what happens when people don't have the ability to bid effectively or to respond to others' bids? Such failure can prevent the development of emotional connections or cause existing connections to deteriorate. This can create serious problems for people of all ages, across all walks of life.

## When Parents and Children Fail to Connect

The importance of strong, healthy emotional bonds between parent and child can't be overstated, because these bonds serve as the foundation upon which all other life relationships are built. If a child doesn't learn how to connect emotionally with a parent (or with another caregiver who serves as a parent), that child will probably encounter difficulty in connecting to people in all sorts of relationships for the rest of his or her life.

Many factors affect children's ability to bid, respond, and connect to others, including the type of temperament they inherit. We're all born with certain personality traits—sociable or shy, intense or easygoing, and so on. To some extent, these traits determine how comfortable we feel in reaching out to other people or responding to others' requests for connection. Still, a large part of a person's knack for emotional connection is also determined by what happens in the home. Consciously or not, parents teach their children through interaction and example.

Every time an infant cries, that's a bid. If her parents turn toward those bids with soothing attention such as rocking, patting, and soft words, such exchanges eventually teach babies to soothe themselves. Through cuddling and baby-talk "conversations" with Mom or Dad, babies also learn all the complex, give-and-take processes of verbal and nonverbal emotional communication.

An infant born into a chaotic, neglectful, or abusive environment doesn't get the same chance. When parents consistently turn away, ignoring a baby's cries of distress, she doesn't get to practice exchanging emotional information with her caregivers. Some parents may even turn against the fussy baby, responding to her bids with impatience and anger. Such mistreatment or neglect creates a state of chronic stress for the baby, adversely affecting the development of her brain and nervous system. In fact, such treatment may adversely affect her ability to respond to stress for the rest of her life. She may become quite unfeeling, for example. After all, what good does it do to feel and express anger or fear when you have a remote, abusive, or neglectful parent?

It's easy to see how problems can snowball for children who don't learn to bid, respond, and connect with parents early on. Many have persistent problems throughout early childhood because they can't cope with emotional stress. Often they have difficulty focusing their attention or listening well to others. They have trouble controlling negative impulses and reading their playmates' social cues. Perceived as too bossy or too shy, they're labeled as bullies or nerds. They're the outcasts of the playground.

As they move into their middle-school and high-school years, these same children can find it difficult to unlock the unwritten codes of teenage social interactions. When it comes to the complex tasks of negotiating cliques, making and keeping friends, or getting a date, they may feel awkward or "clueless." Difficulties can range from fleeting feelings of sadness and alienation to serious mental health problems. For girls—who often turn their feelings inward—such problems typically result in depression. Boys may get depressed, too. But they often lash out as well, becoming belligerent, hostile, or even violent.

One of the most visible and tragic examples of such alienation occurred in the spring of 1999 at Columbine High School in Littleton, Colorado. That's where Eric Harris and Dylan Klebold killed twelve of their classmates and a teacher, injured twenty-three others, and then turned their guns on themselves. As I watched the news coverage in the days that followed, I was stunned by our society's lack of insight into what had turned these boys into mass murderers. Like the media coverage of previous school shootings in Jonesboro, Arkansas, and Springfield, Oregon, these stories focused on the shooters' fascination with violent movies and video games and their easy access to firearms. Such factors obviously contributed to their killing sprees. But, to my mind, one more element loomed much larger: the fact that these boys were emotionally disconnected from family, teachers, and friends. Those who were supposed to be the boys' most important allies seemed unaware of how much pain and torment they were suffering.

Fortunately, the events at Columbine are an extreme and rare example of the consequences of turning away from children. But they're also a reminder of the astonishing power we have to harm or to heal by our responses to children's bids for connection. Progress is possible at any point in a child's development if parents and other caregivers start turning toward the child's bids for connection on a consistent basis. This may require extraordinary patience and keen perception from parents. They may have to recognize and respond positively to a troubled child's bids even when those bids are hard to uncover. They may have to commit to helping even in the face of a child's stone-cold passivity or resistance. But over time, committed, attentive parents can and do earn their children's trust and willingness to connect.

## When Couples Fail to Connect

Problems with connecting don't end in childhood. They often carry over into the adult years, interfering with a person's ability to find and keep a mate.

It's easy to see how the bidding process relates to dating. In fact, one might argue that making successful bids for emotional connection is what dating is all about. People who are adept at reading a potential partner's cues and responding appropriately are usually more lucky in love than those who don't possess this skill. Recall that our studies show that happy, stable couples respond positively to each other's bids at a higher rate than those whose relationships are on the rocks. Still, the lovelorn should take heart. As we'll explore in chapter 6, emotional communication skills can be learned and perfected at any age.

The greatest test of these skills comes as a couple begins to seek a deeper level of intimacy and understanding in their relationship. If partners can continue to turn toward one another in mutually satisfying ways, their bond will grow stronger. But, as my studies reveal, if they begin habitually turning away or turning against one another, their relationship will disintegrate.

Based on our research, I believe that failure to connect is a major cause of our culture's high divorce rate. First marriages now face a fifty-fifty chance of divorce within a forty-year period. Divorce rates among second marriages are 10 percent higher.

The cost of unhappy and failing marriages is high. In addition to the emotional turmoil that couples in stressed marriages experience, they also suffer more physical illness than others do. Studies show that being unhappily married can raise your chances of getting sick by more than 35 percent and shorten your life by an average of four years. Living in a constant state of stress is part of the problem. Over time, such stress can contribute to physical problems such as high blood pressure and heart disease, as well as psychological problems, including depression and substance abuse. It can also affect the immune system, making you more susceptible to infectious disease and cancer.

Family stress caused by a couple's failure to connect can also affect the well-being of their children. Our studies show that children raised in homes with a high level of marital hostility have chronically elevated levels of stress hormones. When we studied these children in early childhood, we found that they had more bouts of infectious diseases like colds and flu. When we checked back with them at age fifteen, we found that these same kids had far higher rates of psychological and social difficulties as well— problems like depression, rejection by peers, and poor behavior—especially aggression. They were also more likely to get bad grades and skip school.

It doesn't have to be that way. Learning how to recognize and turn toward each other's bids for emotional connection can help unhappily married couples and their children to create a more stable, loving family environment. It can also help couples who decide to divorce. As divorced couples who share custody know well, the relationship doesn't end when you sign the divorce decree. By improving your ability to connect emotionally with each other and your children, you'll be in a better spot to solve conflicts and create a healthier environment for your kids.

## Trouble Connecting with Friends and Siblings

While we hear lots of advice about ways to nurture our marriage relationships and the bonds between parent and child, relatively little is said about strengthening some of the most potentially rewarding relationships in our lives—our relationships with adult siblings and friends.

Connecting with other adults is a challenge for many people, for a variety of reasons. Issues of competition and jealousy may loom large—

especially in sibling relationships. Also, matters of trust and intimacy can be sticky to negotiate, particularly when you're first establishing a relationship with a new friend.

One of the most common barriers to adult relationships these days, however, is a practical one: lack of time. More families than ever now include two wage earners. And workers spend an average of 10 percent more time at their jobs today than they did twenty-five years ago. Many working parents try to reserve whatever leisure time they have for their kids. They often have aging parents who require their attention, too. With so many demands on time, something's got to give, and for most of us, that something is the time we have for friends and adult siblings.

But there's a price to pay for cutting ourselves off from relationships with other adults in our lives. Studies show that people with good friends usually have less stress and live longer. They have better health, higher resistance to infection, and stronger immune functioning, and they recover more quickly from illness. Indeed, some research suggests that longevity is determined far more by the state of people's closest relationships than by genetics. The quality of our bonds with others and the amount of kindness we can gather around us may be the most important factors.

A study of people living in Alameda County, California, for example, showed that people who had close friendships and marriages lived longer than those who didn't. This was true independent of such factors as diet, smoking, and exercise. Another study, of 2,800 men and women over age sixty-five, showed that those with more friends had a lower risk of health problems and recovered faster when they did develop them. In addition, a study of 10,000 seniors at Yale University showed that loners were twice as likely to die from all causes over a five-year period as those who enjoyed close friendships.

The simple fact is, having a community of close, supportive friends and relatives can make life's good times even better. And then when tough times hit—crises such as divorce, job loss, a serious illness, or a death in the family—being surrounded by people you can count on makes a big difference in your ability to weather the storm and recover.

Still, sustaining such relationships over the long haul can be challenging. For siblings, problems can be exacerbated by knowing so much about one another's past. Perhaps you've been striving to grow and develop in new ways over the years. If that's the case, the history you share with your siblings may serve as a constant reminder of all your imperfections, past and present. Also, differences in age, birth order, gender, personality type, or other traits may give you different perceptions of the same childhood experiences—differences that are hard to reconcile. At the same time, however, a sibling's point of view can be enlightening, helping you to see the past in new ways.

If we can connect with our siblings around our shared history, we may find that it draws us together, especially as we reach our middle years and seek to find deeper meaning in our life stories. And if we can connect with a sibling around our current life circumstances, it's a bonus; we've got a friend who knows not only where we're going but where we've been.

## Trouble Connecting on the Job

Much has been written in recent years about the importance of "emotional intelligence" at work—how getting ahead requires more than the kind of intelligence measured by standard IQ tests. Emotional intelligence has been defined in different ways, but I believe that it consists largely of our ability to bid and to respond to another's bids for emotional connection. This type of connection makes it possible for coworkers to get along, to see issues from one another's points of view, to solve problems together, and to invest in others' visions of the future.

Such skills become increasingly important with advances in technology. We're spending increasingly less time on mundane tasks better suited to computers and robots. To be successful in today's workplace, we need to excel in areas such as communication, collaboration, motivation, and adaptation to constant change. All these skills require the ability to understand and connect well with other human beings.

What happens when people habitually fail to connect on the job? The same thing that happens when connection fails in families and marriages. Individual workers or entire work teams may begin to feel alienated, passive, or hostile. Employees may feel cut off from vital information or from important sources of control and power. Whole departments may feel isolated or "at war" with other parts of an organization. Supervisors may lose touch with their workers while front-line employees feel misunderstood or disrespected by management. People at lower rungs of the organization may fail to see how their assignments contribute to the big picture, while folks in the executive suite scratch their heads at reports of low morale and high turnover.

It's hard for me to make a purely economic case for fostering better emotional connections within organizations. I've seen too many cases of employers making huge profits by dismissing the human needs of their workers. And on an individual level, I've seen too many people grow rich by focusing only on work and ignoring their own feelings and the emotional needs of their families.

But I do believe that employers and individuals who place a high value on encouraging better emotional connections within their organizations can reap significant benefits aside from financial rewards. These benefits include the creation of a less stressful work environment with lower turnover, increased productivity, and a higher quality of life.

Much depends on the dominant leadership style within the organization—a factor over which individual workers have little control. But each of us makes daily choices that affect the quality of relationships we create and sustain at work. How you manage these relationships can determine not only the kind of experience you'll have on the job today, but also the direction your career may take in the future.

## The Good News About Connecting

Failure to connect can hinder your career. It can interfere with friendships. It can weaken your relationships with relatives, including your kids. It can even ruin your marriage.

But here's the good news: Connecting is *not* magic. Like any other skill, it can be learned, practiced, and mastered. And there's never been a better time to master these skills. Recent scientific discoveries about the emotional brain, along with the latest observational studies of human interaction, have helped us to form a body of scientifically proven advice for connecting with one another and improving the quality of our lives.

That's not to say that connecting more effectively will solve all our problems. I'm reminded of a woman who came to me for marriage counseling shortly after a major career change. The problems she faced were significant: She had new financial pressures, anxiety about the future, and she dearly missed the friends she used to work with. But when I asked her about her marriage—which was to be the focal point of our session—she said, "That's what puzzles me. My husband and I are doing fine. So why do I feel so anxious and depressed?"

At that point I had to tell her, "Feeling connected to your husband isn't going to fix all your problems. It won't fill your bank account, it won't land you the perfect job, and it won't make you stop missing your friends. But it will make the two of you feel closer as you go through this transition together. And that's as good as it gets."

That's the beauty of feeling emotionally connected to others. Whatever you're facing—serious illness, divorce, job loss, grief over the death of a loved one—you don't have to face it alone. Sharing your experience with other people who express understanding and empathy may be helpful in ways we're only beginning to understand. Consider, for example, studies of survival rates among cancer patients who participate in peer support groups. With all other factors equal, those who take part in the group support typically outlive those who don't.

As healing as connecting can be, it doesn't happen automatically. Even when people are highly motivated, it takes a certain amount of conscious effort and diligence. A good example is the communication that typically takes place between mother and infant. In one study, researchers found that mothers misread their fussy babies' bids 70 percent of the time. The mother might think the baby is hungry when he's not, for instance. Or she might start to bounce the baby, only to find that the stimulation upsets him more. Consequently, the mother must switch strategies, trying something different to meet her baby's needs. As she does so, both she and the baby learn more about each other's cues. Her willingness to keep trying, even when things aren't going well, ensures that the relationship will get better over time.

So it is in relationships between spouses, friends, relatives, and coworkers. If both parties are willing to hang in there, pay attention, and change direction when they make mistakes, chances are they can improve the relationship. Having to apologize, make adjustments, or "patch things up" is not necessarily the sign of a bad fit. It's a sign that people value one another and are willing to work through the rough spots to stick together. It's by weathering conflicts that marriages, families, friendships, and work teams grow strong.

In the next chapter you'll get an in-depth look at the first step toward mastering emotional connection: analyzing the way you bid and the way you respond to others' bids. You'll see what typically happens when people turn toward, turn away, or turn against each other. In addition, you'll also have a chance to evaluate how well you and others in your life send and receive bids.

Chapter 3, Six Bid Busters and How to Avoid Them, shows you how to steer clear of some of the most common obstacles to emotional connection.

Chapters 4 through 6 cover the next three steps—each of which addresses a key factor that affects an individual's ability to successfully make and respond to bids for emotional connection. These factors are your brain's unique emotional command systems, your emotional heritage, and your emotional communication skills. You'll learn about the way those factors influence your own style of bidding, as well as the styles of those around you. You can then use those insights to become better at bidding and connecting with others.

Chapter 7 covers the final step: finding shared meaning through the exploration of one another's dreams and visions, as well as shared rituals.

Chapter 8 will help you apply all we've learned to improve relationships with spouses, children, friends, adult siblings, and coworkers.

Building better emotional connections is like any other valuable life goal, in that it requires attention and sustained effort. But I'm certain that few other endeavors can promise a reward as rich as connecting does. Through it, we learn to know, express, and understand the shared meaning we find in one another's experience.

# *2*

# Step One: Look at Your Bids
# for Connection

ne of the biggest surprises of my career came shortly after my colleagues and I opened our apartment lab at the University of Washington in 1990. For years I had been pursuing the question, What makes marriages succeed or fail? Many psychologists at the time agreed with theorist Sydney Jourard that the key to good relationships was self-disclosure—a person's willingness to reveal his or her most guarded, personal thoughts and experiences to another person. Now that I could spend hours observing our study couples from behind one-way mirrors in this natural, homelike setting, surely I would see many profound examples of this behavior. I'd be able to analyze couples' conversations, shedding light on how people achieve this intense, intimate level of connection.

Boy, was I wrong. After collecting and viewing hundreds of hours of videotape, I found very few examples of self-disclosure. There were few heart-to-heart exchanges about broken dreams, hidden fears, or unfulfilled sexual desires. Instead, I had endless hours of people engaged in exchanges like these:

> *"Get me a cup of coffee, will you, honey?"*
> *"Sure. As soon as I turn these pancakes."*
>
> *"Did you call your sister? She seemed real down last time."*
> *"No, I haven't. What do you suppose is wrong with her?"*
>
> *"Here's a funny comic strip . . ."*
> *"Will you please be quiet? I'm trying to read."*

*"Wow! Did you see that double play?"*
*"Yeah, that was incredible!"*

*"Listen to this one. A guy goes to a psychiatrist with a duck on his head . . ."*
*"Yeah, okay. So then what?"*

Even couples who scored high on surveys of marital satisfaction spent most of their time talking about such scintillating topics as breakfast cereals, mortgage rates, or the baseball game.

"What a waste of time," I thought to myself. "Here we've gone to all this effort, and all we're collecting is junk."

But after many months of watching these tapes with my students, it dawned on me. Maybe it's not the depth of intimacy in conversations that matters. Maybe it doesn't even matter whether couples agree or disagree. Maybe the important thing is *how* these people pay attention to each other, no matter what they're talking about or doing.

I asked my graduate student, Jani Driver, to take a closer look at the videotapes with this idea in mind. And sure enough, she saw couples facing a certain set of choices at every turn.

The wife reads a funny tidbit from a magazine to her husband. Will he look up and smile? Will he ignore her? Or will he snap at her to be quiet?

The husband points to an ad in the paper for stereo equipment. Will she acknowledge his interest? Will she look past it to the ad for women's shoes? Or will she frown in disapproval?

The wife tells her husband he put too much dressing on the salad she just made. Will he wink playfully and say she made the salad too small? Will he sulk in silence? Or will he tell her it was a lousy salad anyway?

The topic of conversation hardly mattered in these couples' willingness to connect. Some seemed determined to ignore their spouses, no matter how riveting or mundane the subject at hand. For example, we watched one wife completely ignore her husband as he tried to tell her about the harrowing military coup he had witnessed in Spain. In contrast, another couple seemed utterly entranced by one another's descriptions of how their mothers made bread.

Once Jani started coding these interactions and comparing them with other tests of marital satisfaction we had collected, it was clear that these were definitive moments in the couples' marriages. By choosing to turn toward, turn away, or turn against each other's bids for connection—no matter how ordinary or small—they established a foundation that could determine the future success or failure of their relationships.

We also discovered the importance of playfulness in people's bids. For years I have wondered why some couples are able to make jokes and express affection for each other—even in the midst of an argument. It's an important question because our research shows that such emotional "repair tools" lead to the development of happier, stronger relationships. But I couldn't figure out how some pairs were able to melt each other's hearts with a playful gesture or an apologetic smile, while others didn't even try.

Once we started studying bids and responses to bids, however, the answer was clear: People who make playful bids and turn toward one another's bids enthusiastically during everyday conversations have more access to humor later on, when they get into an argument. In other words, responding with good humor has become such a habit in their relationships that it's always at the top of their bag of tricks. So when disagreements arise—as they do in all relationships—these playful bidders have a full supply of goodwill and affection handy. And when they apply it to the argument at hand, it helps to soothe hurt feelings, leading to better problem solving and a more harmonious relationship.

In this chapter you'll get a closer look at the anatomy of this very fundamental unit of emotional communication—the bid and the response to the bid. You'll see how the bid is used in a variety of situations, including marriage, friendship, parent-child, sibling, and coworker relationships. You'll learn how making and responding to bids successfully contributes to the development of strong, healthy bonds. You'll see how it can be used as a way to immunize relationships against the kind of aggressive negative interactions that can harm them. You'll also have a chance to evaluate how you and the important people in your life bid and respond to bids. Then you can apply all of these lessons to your own relationships, discovering better ways to connect with others.

## How Bids Work

People make bids because of their natural desire to feel connected with other people. Such needs can be quite fleeting—like the impulse to exchange pleasantries with a friendly grocery clerk. Or they can be quite profound—like the longing to share comfort with a close friend when a mutual loved one dies.

Everybody experiences emotional needs in his or her own way. The kind of relationships that are most important to you may not matter as much to somebody else. And the needs that are most important to you today may not be so significant several years from now. But regardless of how much you value certain types of relationships over others, you probably have some hierarchy of needs in your mind. Here's an example of how one man might rate his various needs for emotional connection on a scale of 1 to 10, with 10 being the most important:

**1.** My need to feel respected by the sales clerk when I'm out shopping
**2.** My need for friendly conversation with neighbors at my bus stop
**3.** My need to fit in with the other guys playing basketball at the gym
**4.** My need for recognition from my coworkers when I do my best work
**5.** My need to feel accepted by the members of my church
**6.** My need to feel appreciated by my sister when I call her on holidays
**7.** My need for affection from my kids when I tuck them into bed at night
**8.** My need for empathy from my best friend after a bad experience at work
**9.** My need for sexual intimacy with my spouse
**10.** My need to feel forgiven by my spouse after I apologize for losing my temper

As you can see from this list, this man looks to the people who are closest to him—his spouse, his best friend—for the needs that are the most important. His expectations of relationships with neighbors and sales clerks aren't nearly as high. That's typical with bids for connection. The closer we feel to others, the more intense, frequent, or demanding our bids for emotional connection with them may be. (You'll want to keep this hierarchy in mind as you read about ways to enhance your own bidding process. For example, exercises that require high degrees of intimacy and trust may be appropriate to do with your spouse or close friend, but not with your new coworker.)

People also tend to follow a certain hierarchy when they make bids within a particular close relationship, such as friendship or marriage. Although they may not be aware of it, they typically ask first for help with matters that require the least time, attention, risk, or intimacy. Then, once their initial bids are fulfilled, they may up the ante, asking for more in terms of the intensity of their demands. A typical ladder of needs within a friendship might look like this:

**1.** Light conversation or "small talk"
**2.** Humor
**3.** Friendly gossip
**4.** Affection
**5.** Support
**6.** Problem solving
**7.** Connection around heartfelt subjects like future goals, worries, values, meaning

Using such ladders allows you to establish a base of connection with low-risk bids before moving up the hierarchy of needs. In other words, you can test the waters to decide whether the climate is right before you bid for more intense needs.

## What Do Bids Look Like?

Imagine if people made all their bids for connection in the form of standard written invitations. All our expectations and feelings would be spelled out in vivid detail. Nothing would be left to speculation. You'd never have to grapple with questions like, Is this person flirting with me or not? Am I going to get work from this client again? When will my spouse get over the argument we had last night? All the answers would be spelled out in engraved letters before you. There'd be no more tension, no more guesswork.

For better or worse, human communication is much richer and more complicated than that. Bids for connection come in an infinite variety of styles—some that are easy to see and interpret, others that are nearly indecipherable. Bids can be verbal or nonverbal. They can be highly physical or come totally from the intellect. They can be sexual or nonsexual. They can be high- or low-energy, funny or dead serious. Bids may include questions, statements, or comments, the content of which might involve:

- Thoughts
- Feelings
- Observations
- Opinions
- Invitations

Some bids are nonverbal, including:

- **Affectionate touching,** such as a back-slap, a handshake, a pat, a squeeze, a kiss, a hug, or a back or shoulder rub
- **Facial expressions**, such as a smile, blowing a kiss, rolling your eyes, or sticking out your tongue
- **Playful touching,** such as tickling, bopping, wrestling, dancing, or a gentle bump or shove
- **Affiliating gestures,** such as opening a door, offering a place to sit, handing over a utensil, or pointing to a shared activity or interest
- **Vocalizing,** such as laughing, chuckling, grunting, sighing, or groaning in a way that invites interaction or interest

When we make our bids clearly and boldly, there's little doubt what we're after:

- *"Robert, I want to come work for your company."*
- *"Harvey, I think it's time you asked me out to dinner."*
- *"Hey, Wendy, want to go with me on a bicycle tour of France?"*

Usually, however, our bids are much subtler, requiring those around us to guess our intentions and pick up their cues:

> RICHARD: So, Wendy, what's your idea of a great vacation?
> WENDY: I've always dreamed of sailing in the Caribbean. Why do you ask?
> RICHARD: Oh, I was just wondering . . .

> DAVE: I've been reading about your company, Robert. What an exciting venture!
> ROBERT: Yeah, it's been a great year. We can barely keep up with demand.
> DAVE: So you're hiring in many different areas, I suppose . . .

> GAIL: Did you want to ask me something, Harvey?
> HARVEY: Yes, but I can't seem to remember what it was.
> GAIL: Well, try to think hard, Harvey, and maybe you'll remember.

## What Causes Fuzzy Bidding?

Why do we dance around issues like this? For many reasons, the most common of which is to avoid emotional risk. Openly bidding for connection can make us feel vulnerable. In career and mating situations especially, our hearts and egos are on the line. We can reduce such feelings of vulnerability by making bids ambiguous or fuzzy. Humor and double entendre are common. ("When she said, 'I like it spicy,' was she talking about the spaghetti sauce or *what?*") If the other person responds positively to an ambiguous or humorous bid—smiling coyly or offering another pointed pun, for instance—that's great. But if the intended recipient fails to respond, the bidder loses no pride.

Such "trial balloons" are common even in long-term love relationships. Imagine, for example, that Mary and Jeff are sitting on opposite ends of the couch, reading. Mary wants to cuddle with Jeff. And if cuddling leads to sex, she wouldn't mind that, either. But Jeff has been agitated today, and Mary's afraid that if she moves toward him or says, "Would you hold me for a while?" he'll push her away. So, rather than making an overt pass, she says, "It feels kind of cold in here, don't you think?" She's hoping he'll say, "Come over here and warm up a bit." But she also knows he might respond by handing her the sofa blanket behind his back. The downside of Mary's subtle approach is obvious: Jeff may never get the message that Mary wants cuddling and perhaps sex. But, for the time being, Mary would rather take that chance than to risk that Jeff might blatantly reject her advances.

Kids often learn to soft-sell their bids as well, especially if they're raised in an environment where clear expressions of desire are discouraged. "Annie's mom fixes Annie's hair in French braids every morning," a child might say. But what she'd really like to tell her harried mom is, "I wish you'd pay more attention to me in the morning."

By the time people reach adulthood, they've typically mastered the subtle dynamics of bidding, making all sorts of challenging social situations easier to negotiate. How often, for example, have you heard someone offer a vague invitation like "Let's get together sometime"? By extending this type of bid, the person receiving the bid can slip out of it gracefully if needed. And the bidder retains his or her dignity regardless of the response received. Here's an invitation to a business lunch accepted:

> JAY: We should have lunch sometime.
> GARY: That would be great. How about next week?
> JAY: Monday works for me.
> GARY: Monday's fine. Say about noon?

And here's the same one when it's declined:

> JAY: We should have lunch sometime.
> GARY: That's a great idea. But you know, I am so swamped these days.
> JAY: I understand completely. Give me a call when your schedule opens up.
> GARY: Great. I'll do that.

Because Jay doesn't try to get a specific commitment from Gary, it's easy for him to feel comfortable with either of Gary's responses. There's a drawback to this approach, however: Jay can't tell how Gary really feels about his bid. Is Gary really that busy, or is he just saying so as an excuse to avoid having lunch with Jay? Will Gary call him for lunch in the future? Jay's not certain; only time will tell. Still, he may prefer this outcome to what could happen if he extended a more specific bid:

> JAY: How about getting together for lunch—say next week sometime?
> GARY: Oh, I'm sorry, Jay. I'm busy next week.
> JAY: That's too bad. How about the following week, then?
> GARY: No, the following week won't work, either.
> JAY: Well, what's a good time for you?

GARY: You know, I'm really swamped. How about if I give you a call
  when things lighten up a bit?
JAY: Okay. That would be great. Give me a call.

See how Jay loses power in this exchange? And Gary is made to look difficult. That wouldn't have happened if Jay hadn't been so determined to pin
Gary down. That's not to say you never want to try this approach. Insisting
that people respond to your bid may be useful and necessary—especially in
instances when you absolutely need a commitment. ("This is the third time
I've waited for you, and you didn't show up and you didn't call. If you don't
show more respect for me, it's over between us." Or, "You've been promising
me a raise for two years. If it doesn't come through this time, I'm going to
have to start looking for a new job.") But such conversations are far from
low-risk propositions.

Of course, not all camouflaged bids are vague by intention. Sometimes
they're just a matter of poor communication. A husband may tell his wife,
"We've got to plan a vacation," when he's actually thinking, "I want some
time alone with you." But because he doesn't state his need in a specific way,
she may think he's talking about the family reunion in Minnesota. Or an
office worker may tell her boss, "I'd like some new challenges," when she
wants to join his sales team. But because she's not explicit, he misunder-
stands her interests and enrolls her in classes on database management.

Sometimes people state their bids in such a negative way that it's
unlikely the recipient will respond at all. One husband I know often
expressed how much he missed his wife during the day this way:

HUSBAND: How was your day?
WIFE: Hectic, as usual.
HUSBAND: So you wouldn't even think of calling me, would you?

A simple adjustment, however, can turn what sounds like a complaint
into a simple statement of need:

HUSBAND: How was your day?
WIFE: Hectic, as usual.
HUSBAND: I missed you a lot. It would be nice to talk on the phone.
WIFE: Just call me when you feel like that.
HUSBAND: I know how busy you are.
WIFE: Still, it would feel good to touch base during the day.
HUSBAND: That's nice. I'll call more often.

Bids can also be hard to decipher when the bidder doesn't acknowledge
his or her own needs for connection. When that happens, bids can get dis-
guised as something else—usually anger or sadness. This is particularly

common among children, who can sense when something's missing from their relationships with parents, teachers, friends, and family. But, because they're children, they don't have enough life experience to name the problem, or enough power to fix it. Consequently, they start misbehaving in response to stresses such as changing schools, moving to a new home, or their parents' marital problems. Temper tantrums, crying fits, belligerence, and sassiness may be bids for connection in such situations. What these children are looking for is an emotional bond with people who can help them to feel more secure amid the stress and confusion. It's as if the children are saying, "Talk to me about what I'm feeling and thinking, please."

Adults may express their need for connection in the same confused way—particularly if they don't learn to recognize and pay attention to their own emotional needs. That's how it was for Sarah, who recently came to the Gottman Institute for therapy with her husband.

Clearly unhappy, Sarah talked in our sessions about her longing for a peaceful, attentive relationship with Rick. But according to Rick, her behavior engendered just the opposite. During their time together, she often acted sullen and withdrawn, he said. "Then I do one little thing that she doesn't like—like pick up a golf club or turn on the television—and she flies off the handle! She acts like I can't do anything right—that I never do enough to please her."

In our sessions, we discovered that Sarah rarely feels entitled to bid for the kind of moment-by-moment attention it takes to make a marriage work. Her reluctance may be related to the way she was raised. One of seven kids in a family with an alcoholic father and too few resources, she learned that her own needs were the least of her family's concerns. Only people with severe problems deserved any attention, if at all.

Sarah carried these beliefs into her marriage to Rick. Instead of making the kind of ordinary bids for connection that happily married couples do, she kept her longing for affection and attention to herself. Even though she felt resentful when Rick worked overtime and came home too tired to talk, she would say nothing. When he went out with his coworkers on Friday night without inviting her, it made her even angrier. Still, she kept a lid on her feelings. She tried not to complain on the weekends when he went to the driving range, turned on the baseball game, or sat down at the computer. But every few weeks, after she had amassed enough pain, she would finally let it blow.

"How much of this am I supposed to take?" she'd yell. Righteously indignant, she'd run down her entire list of grievances from the past few weeks— all the times she'd felt slighted, all the times that Rick had shut her out.

Overwhelmed by her sudden barrage, Rick would simply retreat. Sometimes he'd leave the apartment. But if that wasn't possible, he'd just go to another room, turn on the television, or put on a headset—anything to escape the storm. Of course, Rick's withdrawal would further infuriate Sarah, making her feel more justified than ever.

As we talked about these interactions in therapy, Sarah's intent was clear to all of us. She wanted to feel closer to her husband. But the way she was bidding for that connection made it impossible to achieve. So our goal in therapy became twofold: One was to help Sarah understand that she didn't need to stockpile her complaints before making a bid for connection. She could simply and gently talk to Rick about her needs as they occurred to her. The second goal was to help Rick see the longing behind Sarah's anger. In this way he could view her anger as a bid for connection with him. Unacceptably expressed? Yes. Unpleasant? Certainly. But it *was* a bid, nevertheless. And once he recognized her anger as such, he was more willing to work with her, to help her to learn more loving and effective ways to express her longing.

That's how it is once you begin to recognize the many idiosyncratic ways that people can make and respond to bids for connection. If you can see past a person's anger, sadness, or fear to recognize the hidden need, you open up new possibilities for relationship. You're able to see your coworker's sullen silence as a bid for inclusion in decisions that affect his job, for example. Or you can recognize that your sister's agitation says she's feeling alienated from the family. You can even see the bid in your three-year-old's temper tantrum: He not only wants the toy you can't buy for him, he wants your comfort in a frustrating situation, as well.

To summarize, there are lots of reasons for fuzzy bidding. These include:

- Making ambiguous bids on purpose to avoid vulnerability or emotional risk
- Unintentionally poor communication, such as using inexplicit language
- Framing bids in negative ways that are hard for others to hear or accept
- Failing to acknowledge your needs in the first place

Does this mean that to read one another's bids, we have to read one another's minds? Obviously not. That's impossible. Nor does it mean that we have to tolerate abusive expressions of rage or frustration just because they can be interpreted as bids for connection. But our research shows that a little understanding can go a long way toward uncovering the bids for connection that often lie beneath people's masks of anger, sadness, or fear. And once a bid is recognized, we can start the work that brings people together— the work of turning toward.

As we've discussed, people typically make one of three choices in response to a bid for connection. They can:

**1.** Turn toward the bid:
   BID: How was your vacation?

RESPONSE: It was all right. The slopes at Sun Mountain are magnificent, but the ski conditions were lousy. Have you ever been there?

**2.** Turn away from it:

BID: How was your vacation?

RESPONSE: Have you got any messages for me?

**3.** Turn against it:

BID: How was your vacation?

RESPONSE: As if you really cared.

The table below shows the many variations of each type of turning behavior. In the next several pages we'll take a closer look at each type of response, how to recognize it, and how it affects your relationships.

## Three Ways to Respond to Bids

| | Turning-toward responses | Turning-away responses | Turning-against responses |
|---|---|---|---|
| How they might appear | Nearly passive: *Nods, "uh-huh"* | Preoccupied: *No response* | Contemptuous: *Put-downs, insults* |
| | Low-energy: *"Okay," "Sure"* | Disregarding: *Irrelevant response or no response* | Belligerent: *Provocative, combative* |
| | Attentive: *Validation, opinions, thoughts, feelings, questions* | Interrupting: *Introducing unrelated information or a counterbid* | Contradictory: *Arguing, with or without hostility* |
| | | | Domineering: *Controlling, overbearing* |
| | High-energy: *Full focus, enthusiasm, empathy* | May be "mindless" or intentional | Critical: *Character attacks, blaming* |
| | | | Defensive: *Fake helplessness, "victim" stance* |
| How it often affects relationships | More bidding and responding | Less bidding | Less bidding |
| | Growth and development of relationship | Increased conflict | Avoidance of conflict |
| | | Hurt feelings, loss of confidence | Suppressed feelings |
| | | Relationship ends sooner rather than later | Relationship ends, but it may take a while |

## Choosing to Turn Toward Bids for Connection

The scope of turning-toward behavior is broad. It can include the following:

- **Nearly passive responses,** such as a one- or two-word comment, or a mild shift in behavior with no verbal response. The person responding may not stop what he or she is doing to interact with you, but at least you know that you've been heard.

  PARENT: How was school today, honey?
  CHILD: Okay.

Sometimes there's no verbal response at all, but only a gesture.

  FRIEND A: I can't believe it's raining again!
  FRIEND B: *(Shakes head in disgust.)*

- **Low-energy responses,** involving a few words or a question to clarify the bid.

  WORKER A: They loved my presentation in Chicago.
  WORKER B: That's good.

  HUSBAND: Do you think I look okay in this outfit?
  WIFE: Sure.

  FRIEND A: What are you doing Saturday?
  FRIEND B: This Saturday?

- **Attentive responses,** often involving opinions, thoughts, and feelings.

  SISTER A: Look what I found on sale.
  SISTER B: That's nice. It's just the right color for you.

Attentive responses are often validating.

  WIFE: What an awful day I had. The phones never stopped.
  HUSBAND: That must have been hard. You look exhausted.

These responses can be funny.

  CHILD: Will you make me a sandwich?
  DAD: Poof! You're a sandwich!

They can include pointed questions.

> BROTHER A: I saw Dr. Rogers this afternoon.
> BROTHER B: Did you find out the results of your tests?

They may involve action as well.

> CHILD: Good night, Daddy.
> DAD: *(A kiss on the forehead, while tucking in covers.)* "Good night, cowboy."

> WIFE: My back itches!
> HUSBAND: *(Scratches bidder's back.)*

If the bidder tells a joke, an attentive respondent will laugh, or at least smile, even if the joke isn't that funny. The respondent isn't interested in judging the bidder's talent as a standup comic; he or she simply wants to express pleasure with the bidder's effort.

- **High-energy responses,** involving full attention with good eye contact. High-energy responses are usually enthusiastic.

> FRIEND A: Donna and I are getting married next fall.
> FRIEND B: That's great news! Congratulations! I'm so happy for you!

They often involve humor, kidding, or affection.

> MOTHER: Hi, there. It's your mother.
> SON: Mother? Mother who?

> WORKER A: This guy walks into a bar . . .
> WORKER B: *(Anticipatory smile, delighted at the very idea of another "guy walks into a bar" joke.)*

Or they may involve sincere empathy.

> FRIEND A: I'll never understand how that guy could have fired me.
> FRIEND B: It was totally unfair. You're such a terrific accountant. I think he must have felt threatened by you.

High-energy responses often involve broad physical gestures like big hugs, ceremonious kisses, enthusiastic handshakes, or mock sparring. If the bidder tells a joke, an enthusiastic respondent laughs heartily. In fact, the respondent may appear ready to laugh as soon as the joke-telling begins.

Of all the three possible responses to bids, turning toward has the most positive results. It tells the bidder:

- I hear you.
- I'm interested in you.
- I understand you (or would like to).
- I'm on your side.
- I'd like to help you (whether I can or not).
- I'd like to be with you (whether I can or not).
- I accept you (even if I don't accept all your behavior).

When you turn toward a bid, it helps the bidder to feel good about himself or herself, and about the interaction you're having. Consequently the bidder welcomes more interaction, typically leading to more bids and more positive responses from both sides.

I like to compare such exchanges to an improvised jazz duet. Neither musician knows exactly where the piece is going, but they get their cues by tuning in to one another. One musician's set of notes is a bid that stimulates musical ideas in the other musician. On his own, neither could create the magic that happens as a result of their collaboration. The music they create together takes on a life of its own, born of their positive, willing interaction.

Turning toward leads to the growth and development of healthy partnerships in all kinds of relationships. Children who habitually turn toward their playmates form friendships more easily. Siblings who turn toward one another early on are more likely to stay close for life. Coworkers find it easier to collaborate on projects. Married couples and other pairs have fewer conflicts.

Turning toward leads to fewer conflicts, because the partners in a relationship are having the conversations they need to have—the conversations where they demonstrate their interest and concern for each other. With such high levels of interest expressed, there's simply less static in the air. People see evidence that their friends, coworkers, and loved ones are there for them and care for them. They have fewer problems to fight about.

Our research into the emotional lives of families shows that parents who have fewer conflicts create better environments for their children. Kids from such families are likely to be more attentive and do better in school than kids whose families don't have these habits. They're more apt to soothe themselves when upset, get along better with other children, and have fewer bouts of colds and flu.

A study of young-adult siblings, conducted in our labs by Joann Wu Shortt, showed that brothers and sisters who turn toward one another in conversation are more likely to maintain close, supportive, satisfying relationships.

Studies like these conducted in the workplace show that coworkers who consistently turn toward one another form more productive work teams, with higher morale.

We saw many delightful examples of couples turning toward one another in the marriage lab. Sometimes the bids were quite playful. One husband bopped his wife gently with a rolled-up newspaper, saying, "I've been meaning to do that all day." She reciprocated by rolling up her own paper bat and chasing him playfully around the couch. Another wife charmed her husband by copying a particularly silly gesture he made during dinner. The man had picked up an artichoke leaf, bit off the edible part of it, and then slammed the remnant down on the table. "I'm drinking shots," he said playfully. Without any prodding, his wife picked up a leaf and did the same thing, eliciting a broad smile from her husband. Then he took another turn, acting as if he'd been challenged. "Slap 'em down!" he said. She followed suit, saying, "Chew 'em up! Slap 'em down! Rawhide!" And the two ceremoniously continued to eat the entire artichoke this way. The game they had invented was totally original, spontaneous, and fun.

As stated earlier, such playfulness is extremely good for relationships. What does it require? A willingness to turn toward another's sense of silliness, give oneself over to the moment, and have a little bit of fun.

While baking cookies, your ten-year-old reaches for a canister of flour from the top shelf and accidentally spills it, covering himself and much of the kitchen in a cloud of white stuff. Delighted at his own snowmanlike appearance, he starts to laugh. Now you've got a choice. You can express irritation at the mess or you can turn toward his silliness and share the laugh.

You and a coworker are discussing a serious work-related problem when she realizes that, without meaning to, she's just made a truly funny pun. This seems like no time for frivolity, and yet she appears to be having a pretty good time. You can stop working for a moment and laugh with her. Or you can forge seriously ahead, focusing exclusively on the problem at hand.

Making the second choice—that is, turning toward one another's sense of humor in everyday situations—bolsters your relationships while making life together a lot more fun.

One husband in our studies appeared to have just the opposite inclination, but he surprised me. He was an engineer with a very staid, serious personality. But he adored his wife and would go to extreme lengths to tickle her funny bone. In fact, he once trained his pet beagle to sit on its haunches and duck its head so that it looked just like the *Peanuts* cartoon dog, Snoopy, posed on top of his doghouse as a vulture. Then, one Sunday morning, before his wife came down for breakfast, the man propped the dog on top of the refrigerator, crawled up there with him, and, clad only in his underwear, struck a similar pose. When his wife entered the kitchen and saw her beloved and his dog hovering near the ceiling like buzzards, she literally fell on the floor laughing. That, in my opinion, was the ultimate in playful bids. Not all playful bids have to be this elaborate, of course. But the more you can tap in to each other's sense of humor and joy, the stronger your relationship becomes.

Of course, not all bids for connection are so good-natured and playful. As we stated earlier, people sometimes camouflage their bids in expressions of anger, fear, and sadness. Rather than invitations to play, these bids are more likely to come in the form of a complaint, criticism, or lament. Such negative bids are hard even to recognize, much less respond to. And once you recognize them, you've got to muster the patience, creativity, and trust it takes to turn toward the bidder with a helpful response.

But if you want to build solid, long-term relationships, you've got to be willing to turn toward each other's bids in all sorts of circumstances. That's why marriage vows include phrases like "for better or worse." That's why people shun the idea of a "fair-weather friend." We long for relationships with people who will stick by us even when we're tired, crabby, fearful, depressed, or frustrated.

Remember, our research shows that the less people turn toward one another, the less satisfying their relationships are.

People can turn toward, turn away, or turn against all sorts of bids for connection—even those bids that appear hostile or off-putting. Take a look at the examples in the chart on page 55. As you read these responses, you may think turning toward is a great ideal to strive for, but it would be impossible to do all the time, especially given all the pressures so many of us face. True, we all face competing demands: the coworker who could use your ear at exactly the same time you're supposed to pick your kids up from the babysitter; the sister who calls with a marital crisis just as you're leaving for that long-planned romantic weekend. Nobody has the emotional stamina to turn toward other people's needs twenty-four hours a day, seven days a week.

Realizing the limits of our time and attention, I'm reminded of a story told by a couple who participated in one of our research studies. Although they described their marriage as happy, they experienced some stress after the birth of their second child.

"One day I was lying in bed," says Allen, "and I realized that there were two people between me and Becca. Literally two whole bodies—our two-year-old and our newborn. And that made me really depressed. I missed Becca. I just wasn't getting enough of her."

A few days later, when he and Becca were sitting on the couch with the kids, she asked, "What's the matter?"

"I'm having a pity party," Allen confessed. "I feel like you and I never do anything together anymore—just the two of us. You're always busy with the kids. I can't seem to get any of your attention."

How did Becca react? "I blew up!" she recalls. "Here I was with one little kid crawling all over me and this infant hanging on my teat. Then I've got this other big baby telling me I'm not paying enough attention to *his* needs! It really made me angry. I told him, 'I can't deal with this situation, either. *You've* got to do something about it!'"

What did Allen do? "He was great," Becca says. "He got up off the couch and he took the two-year-old to the park. And it wasn't just that afternoon. He did the same thing every day for the next month. They went to the zoo, the aquarium, McDonald's. Everywhere. And I finally got to spend some time alone with the baby, which is what *I* really needed. For the first time since he was born, I started to relax."

As for Allen's needs: "It took a few weeks," says Becca, "but after a while I was able to say, 'Okay, let's get back to your pity party. What can we do about your feelings?'"

"Waiting awhile was fine," Allen explains. "What's important is that Becca came through. She always does."

The point of the story is that Allen had a valid need to connect with Becca and he stated his bid in the gentlest of ways. But Becca was in no position to turn toward his bid at that time. In fact, she not only turned against his bid—she upped the ante by demanding that he do something for her instead! Still, everything worked out, and here's why: Allen and Becca had a long history of turning toward one another. That history gave them the confidence to ride out the crisis, knowing that eventually they'd get back to even ground.

My advice, then, is this: If you want to build a deeper emotional connection with somebody, turn toward that person as often as you can. This will vary, of course, depending on how comfortable each of you feels with the level of independence and intimacy in your relationship. You typically have more chances to turn toward your child than toward a work colleague, for example. And opportunities for turning toward a spouse are usually more abundant than for turning toward an adult sibling. But in general, if you can turn toward any significant person in your life—even when you're angry, frustrated, complaining, or sad—your relationship will grow stronger. Then, if you face a time when turning toward one another is impossible, the goodwill you've accumulated will be enough to see you through to better times.

For adult-child relationships, keep in mind that children are often less reciprocal than adults, and that's natural for their stage of emotional development. In other words, parents and teachers may feel that they're doing *all* the turning toward and that the child is giving little back. My advice is to be patient and keep responding positively to the child's bids for attention, because *it will pay off* in the long run. Your consistent response tells the child that you can be trusted. It also serves as an important model for positive relationship-building. Over time, the child will begin turning toward you more often.

Also, make it a point to turn toward people with fun-loving, high-energy responses when you can—responses that include kidding, affection, and humor. Our studies show that this type of enthusiastic, positive response has an impact on people's ability to access humor during conflict situations. When you regularly feel enthusiastic support and affection from somebody, you're more comfortable cracking lighthearted jokes in the midst of arguments with them. And humor is key to unlocking even more interest, affection, support, and empathy in relationships.

## Choosing to Turn Away from Bids for Connection

Turning away is what happens when you fail to pay attention to another's bid for attention.

Turning away typically occurs in one of three different ways:

- **Preoccupied responses,** in which the respondent is often involved in an activity, such as reading or watching television. Here are some examples:

    WORKER: Excuse me, Mr. Brady. I was wondering if we might talk about . . .
    BOSS: *(Staring at his computer, and waving his hand in the air as if to say, "Not now.")*

    MOM: Hey, you guys . . . dinner's ready.
    CHILDREN: *(Staring at the television, motionless. No response.)*

    HUSBAND: *(Wraps arms around her waist. Kisses her amorously on the neck.)*
    WIFE: *(Pushes him away. Continues to make the family's sack lunches.)*

    FRIEND A: It says here that interest rates are going up.
    FRIEND B: *(Reading the paper; no response.)*

- **Disregarding responses,** in which the bid is completely ignored or the would-be respondent focuses on insignificant details of the bid.

    FORMER HUSBAND: We need to talk about Megan's spring break. Is she going to spend it with me or with you?
    FORMER WIFE: *(Silence.)*

LOVER A: It's my great-grandmother's wedding ring. I thought you'd really like it.
LOVER B: *(Silence.)*

MOM: What do you want for dinner—tuna noodle casserole or tofu patty melts?
CHILD: *(Silence.)*

WORKER A: I need some volunteers for the cleanup committee. Anyone?
WORKERS B, C, AND D: *(Silence.)*

FRIEND A: What did you think of my manuscript?
FRIEND B: I like the way you double-spaced the pages.

- **Interrupting responses,** in which the respondent introduces unrelated matters or counterbids:

DAD: Who's going to say grace tonight?
CHILD: Pass the salt.

CUSTOMER: I am really upset about the way you handled my account.
SERVICE REPRESENTATIVE: We've been so busy this month.

CHILD: Dad, Barney got out of his pen. I can't find him anywhere!
DAD: Look at your shoes! You're tracking mud all over the house.

WORKER A: Who's going to respond to the complaints I'm getting from Customer Service?
WORKER B: Let's set a time for the next staff meeting, shall we?

WIFE: What a beautiful sunset!
HUSBAND: Did my sister ever call?

When people turn away from one another, it raises the question: Are they being intentionally disregarding, or are they simply being "mindless"? Our research shows that it's usually the latter. People rarely intend to be malicious or mean-spirited when they turn away. Rather, they're operating on "automatic pilot," unaware of how their behavior is affecting those around them. Perpetually late for appointments, the harried manager rushes into the office each morning without greeting his staff. After several months of this, the staff begins to feel that he doesn't care about them at all. Preoccupied with friends and school, the busy teen rarely stops to chat with her parents about anything other than her allowance or borrowing the car. So, unless her parents are astute enough to make her slow down for connection, they may find their daughter drifting further and further away from the family.

Problems of mindlessness can usually be remedied if people become more conscious of their interactions, a topic we cover in more detail in chapter 3.

But sometimes people are turning away for a reason: Consciously or unconsciously, they want to gain more autonomy in a relationship. In these cases, turning away helps us to regulate the balance between freedom and interdependence, an important task in any relationship, including those between friends, lovers, family members, or coworkers. It's usually best to aim for a level that's comfortable for both people in the relationship, and finding this balance can take some time. Also, the balance may change over time as we grow and change. Expectations get out of balance, with one person wanting consistently to connect while the other consistently turns away.

If you find yourself in a relationship where either one of you is regularly turning away, look carefully at your intentions. If both of you are committed to having a close relationship, you can take steps toward becoming more aware of each other's needs so you can turn toward one another more often. But if you feel that either of you is turning away in order to gain more autonomy in the relationship, it's important to talk about your relative needs for independence. To avoid this discussion simply leads to hurt feelings and the eventual dissolution of the relationship. That's because it hardly matters whether a person turns away consciously or unconsciously, on purpose or with little intent; the message to the bidder is pretty much the same:

- I don't care about your bid.
- I want to avoid your bid.
- I'm not interested in your interests.
- I've got more important things on my mind.
- I'm too busy to pay attention to your bid.
- Your bid is not worth my time.
- I want to be more independent than you want me to be.

How do such messages affect the bidder? That depends on the person. But our research has revealed some common patterns. First, most people feel hurt—"more upset than I ever thought I had a right to be," some have told us. They may experience feelings of loneliness, isolation, and rejection. It may sound extreme, but imagine the emotions of a child who's told, "No, you can't play on our team. We don't want you. You're no good at this." There's a little kid inside all of us that feels that way when our bids are ignored or dismissed.

Indeed, a person may feel so distressed that he becomes hypervigilant, or oversensitive to insult. He goes into a state of mind that University of Oregon psychologist Bob Weiss calls "negative sentiment override." This means that he has an overwhelming negative feeling about the relationship that overrides positive events happening in the moment. It may become difficult for him to determine objectively how others are reacting to his bids. ("Did Sol really give me the bum's rush this morning, or am I just being paranoid?") To get a clearer idea, the disregarded bidder starts consciously searching for solid evidence that people are treating him badly. And because he's got his sensors so finely tuned, he's likely to find that evidence. ("I'm not just imagining it. Sol held an impromptu meeting about the proposal in his office this afternoon, and they didn't bother to call me. Something's up.")

A bidder's reaction to turning away is typically much different than to an outward attack (turning against); in the latter case, the bidder may feel so enraged that he or she is energized by the interaction. In contrast, when somebody turns away from a bid, the bidder loses confidence and self-esteem. In our observational studies, we see how people almost seem to "crumple" when their partners turn away. The bidders don't get puffed up with anger; they don't get indignant; they just seem to fold in on themselves. On video, we can see their shoulders sag slightly as if they've been deflated. They feel defeated. They give up.

In children the effects can be much worse. Kids look to their mothers and fathers for emotional cues. They need their parents to validate their feelings and guide them. When parents fail to do this, kids begin to doubt themselves. They begin to feel lonely in their emotions, internalizing problems and wondering, "What's wrong with me that I feel this way?"

Feeling discouraged once their bids for connection have been rejected or ignored, people rarely re-bid. I was surprised to find that even in satisfied relationships—where you might expect people to confront one another about behavior that upsets them—couples hardly ever repeat a failed bid. It's as if something inside the bidder says, "Why bother? It's no use." And if this hopeless attitude becomes dominant, there's less bidding, less opportunity for connection.

My research shows that habitually turning away can eventually destroy relationships. Even if the bidder doesn't act hurt or angry at the moment his or her bid is rejected, there seems to be some internal mechanism that keeps score. By watching relationships over time, my colleagues and I have seen that the dismissed bidder typically gets fed up. He or she starts complaining to and criticizing the person who turns away, leading to a pattern of attack and defend. And once this attack/defend pattern becomes ingrained in a relationship, it can start a downward spiral of interaction that eventually ends in the dissolution of that bond. The initial stages of this dynamic were dramatically demonstrated by Anna and Frank, a couple who discussed their marital problems with me as part of a profile on *The Oprah Winfrey Show*.

The parents of twins, Anna and Frank were under considerable stress when their babies were small. Anna stayed home with them all day while Frank worked at a commercial art job he hated. At the end of a hectic day, Frank liked spending just a little time alone on his own computer-generated art. The problem was that this was often the same time that Anna most needed help with the twins. Sometimes Frank would get so preoccupied at his computer that he disregarded Anna when she called him for help. Sure, he heard her, Frank admitted, but he knew that if he could just hold her off for a few minutes, she'd solve whatever problem she was having and leave him alone. Using this tactic successfully one night, Frank finished his project, then got up, fixed himself a snack, and proceeded to turn his attention to the babies.

But that's not the end of the story, because later that same night, Anna walked into the kitchen, where she saw something that sent her into an absolute rage. There, lying on the counter, was the mayonnaise-covered knife Frank had left when he made his sandwich. Anna picked up the knife, started screaming at him for leaving such a mess, and threw the knife across the room.

"All the while, I'm thinking, 'Why am I doing this?'" Anna recalled. "'Why am I being such a witch?' It was just a little mayonnaise. It was such a trivial thing. I could easily have just picked up the knife and put it in the sink."

"Yes," I told them, "you could easily have taken care of the knife. But no, it's not a trivial thing."

That's because, at that moment, that knife was charged with all the anger and contempt Anna felt for Frank because of the way he had turned away from her earlier. This high-energy rage, which seemed to originate from nowhere, was actually linked to her loneliness and the lack of connection she felt. She needed him, but in his mindlessness, he had turned his back on her.

This dynamic is seen in children all the time—especially in those whose parents are distracted by their jobs or in the throes of a crisis such as family illness or divorce. Adults in the family don't mean to neglect their kids or cause them harm, but they're so consumed by their own problems that every interaction with their kids amounts to telling them to be quiet or go away. The trouble is, kids are designed by nature to get adult attention any way they can—even if that means becoming increasingly rebellious or belligerent. And so they do, causing more stress in the family.

That's how it was for Amy, a divorced mother of two preteen boys, whose life changed when she got accepted to law school. In retrospect, Amy sees that she lost a lot of ground in her relationship with the boys during her first year of study. "They'd come to me for help with homework, or because they were having some silly argument, and I was just so overwhelmed with work that I couldn't deal with them. I'd say, 'Let's talk about it later,' or 'You guys are going to have to settle this one on your own.' After a while they stopped bothering me."

But then, one day in the spring, Amy got a call from the boys' middle school because her older boy, Josh, had been involved in a fight. "When I went to pick him up, this teacher took me aside and started telling me about all these changes she'd seen in him—how his grades were falling and how sullen he'd become," she remembers. "It really shook me up."

Driving home, Amy started peppering Josh with lots of questions, and for most of the ride he didn't say a thing. "But then suddenly he blew up and said, 'What the hell do you care? All that matters to you is studying. You don't care about us anymore.'

"I was devastated. Of course I cared about them. That's why I was working so hard—so we could get ahead." But later that night, as she thought about it, she realized that she never *talked* to her boys anymore. "All we did was argue—about homework, chores, TV—you name it. And I felt so sad, because we used to get along so well."

Amy decided to see a family therapist so they could get back on track. The therapist was encouraging, telling her that the most important thing for her to do was to start paying more attention to the details of her boys' lives: to make a concerted daily effort to offer them praise for the things they were doing right, and to be absolutely certain to ask them about their activities—not in a nagging way, but in a way that showed she was really listening. It's been challenging for Amy—especially with the demands of law school. But she says she's finding small niches of one-on-one time daily for each boy, even if it's just to drive one to football practice or to sit and play a short video game with the other. Her relationship with the boys is slowly improving as a result. "The biggest change is that I don't think of them as a negative distraction anymore," says Amy. "The breaks I take from my work to be with them are my reward."

These stories show what we're finding in our observational research—that the more people turn away from one another, the more conflict they'll have to contend with later on. But the more they turn toward one another's bids, the less contentious their relationships will be.

That's not to say that an occasional missed bid spells disaster. Everybody drops the ball sometimes. And if you're happy in a relationship, there's often enough positive interaction happening between you that one missed bid won't affect the overall quality of the relationship. But you can't make a habit of turning away and expect the relationship to survive.

There are two more observations my colleagues and I have made about turning away that merit special attention. The first is that interrupting does not seem to be as harmful to relationships as the other two types of turning-away behavior: being preoccupied or ignoring the other person. Psychologists used to think that interrupting was a sign of trouble in a relationship. They'd look for a struggle for dominance between partners. They'd suspect that one person was trying unfairly to silence the other. But I believe that interrupting can also be a sign of people's enthusiasm for interacting with each other. A pair may have so much to share that they literally can't wait for their partner to stop talking before they jump back into the conversation. When interrupting happens in this way, and neither partner seems to be irritated by the disruptions, it may not be so harmful.

My colleagues and I also found some interesting differences in the way that being preoccupied relates to marital dissatisfaction in husbands and wives. Wives who turn away because they are preoccupied with other tasks are more often dissatisfied with their marriages than are husbands who do the same thing. It's hard to say for certain what accounts for this difference, but I believe it may be related to differences in the meaning these women and men attach to turning their attention away from the relationships. Women may see turning away as an act of hostility, so when they do it, it's a conscious expression of dissatisfaction with their spouses. But men may turn away without even acknowledging it consciously, and with no hostility intended. In other words, if a woman ignores her husband's bids while she's watching TV, she's doing it to send a message that she's mad at him. But if a man ignores his wife while he's watching TV, he's not trying to send any message; he's doing it without even thinking about how it might affect his relationship with his wife.

Regardless of a person's intentions, however, ignoring or turning away from another's bid for connection makes the bidder feel bad. And if turning away becomes a habit, it can have a harmful effect on most any type of relationship.

## Choosing to Turn Against Bids for Connection

Turning against a bid for connection means responding to it in a negative way. In our studies, we've seen many ways of turning against:

- **Contemptuous responses** that entail hurtful, disrespecting comments aimed at the person bidding for connection. Such put-downs are often delivered with an air of superiority, as if the speaker wants to put some distance between him- or herself and the bidder, and intentional insults will do the trick. Here are some examples:

  CHILD: I don't understand this math homework at all.
  DAD: Of course you don't. You take after your mother and all her lame-brained relatives.

HUSBAND: Do you want to go have some lunch?
WIFE: Is that all you ever think about—eating?

WORKER A: I enjoyed your presentation this morning. I learned a lot.
WORKER B: Well, that's surprising. It wasn't really aimed at your demographic.

- **Belligerent responses** that are provocative or combative. You get the sense that the speaker is looking for a fight. He or she would argue with whatever the bidder says, regardless of content. Belligerent responses often involve unfair teasing or a dare.

CHILD: Here's an interesting article . . .
MOM: Can't you see I'm trying to read?

SISTER A: Would you get me a napkin while you're up?
SISTER B: Get it yourself.

HUSBAND: Do you want to watch TV tonight?
WIFE: So that's all you think I'm good for, right? Sitting in front of the tube watching mindless TV shows all the time?
HUSBAND: Of course not. What would you like to do? Maybe you'd rather go see a play instead.
WIFE: Oh, like that's supposed to make me feel better? *(Mocking)* "Maybe you'd rather go see a play instead."

PARENT: I'm so frustrated with you, I don't know what to do.
CHILD: Why don't you just hit me and get it over with? I know that's what you're dying to do.

- **Contradictory responses,** in which a person seems intent on starting a debate or argument. This is less hostile than a belligerent response, but it still blocks the bidder's attempt to connect.

FRIEND A: Would you like a tangerine?
FRIEND B: That's not a tangerine. It's a Satsuma orange.

WORKER A: I'd love to have your comments on this report by Friday.
WORKER B: Why Friday? Isn't Monday good enough?

- **Domineering responses** that involve attempts to control another person. The respondent's goal is to get the bidder to withdraw, retreat, or submit. You often hear a parental message in these responses, whether the speaker is a parental figure or not.

BROTHER A: Do you know where I'd love to go someday? India!
BROTHER B: Don't be ridiculous! You'd hate it there, with all its poverty and overcrowding. Scandinavia—now there's a place you'd really love!

FRIEND A: My car's in the shop. Can you give me a lift?
FRIEND B: I suppose. But only if you're ready at five P.M. sharp.

CHILD: Aw, Mom. Please don't call me "Angel" in front of my friends.
MOM: But that's who you are—my littlest angel. And that's who you'll always be.

- **Critical responses** that are broad-based attacks on a bidder's character. They're different from a complaint, which focuses on a particular event or specific behavior. When people are being critical, they frequently speak in global terms, saying things like "you always . . ." and "you never . . ." Often you'll hear statements of blame or betrayal in these responses:

WIFE: I'm feeling really tired. I need some time alone this afternoon.
HUSBAND: That figures. You're always so lazy and self-centered. All you do is think about yourself.

WORKER A: Have you got a minute? I've got some questions about this procedure.
WORKER B: Okay, but make it quick. I can't afford to hold your hand all the time.

CHILD: Can we pull over soon? I've got to use the bathroom.
DAD: Why don't you ever go before we leave the house? You never learn, do you?

- **Defensive responses** that create a sense of separation by allowing the speaker to relinquish responsibility for matters at hand. If the bidder is upset about something, the respondent may act like an innocent victim of misplaced blame.

HUSBAND: What a day I had! I'm exhausted.
WIFE: So you think my day was a picnic? I worked my tail off, too!

WORKER A: The three-hole punch is missing. Has anybody seen it?
WORKER B: Don't look at me!

WIFE: I'm worried about the bills.
HUSBAND: It wasn't my idea to buy the new car.

Unlike turning-away responses, which are more mindless than mali-cious, turning against has a bite to it. It's hard to hear such responses with-out thinking, "That's mean," or "That was uncalled for." Still, I doubt that most people who turn against their loved ones really intend to cause as much harm to their relationships as they do in these exchanges. Rather, they may simply have developed a personal style of relating that's charac-teristically crabby or irritable. This type of prickliness may result from many factors, such as having too many demands on your time, not enough peace of mind, or the lack of a satisfying purpose or direction for your life. Often it's a spillover of self-criticism that has its origins in the distant past. The problem may also be a biologically based irritability that is chemically related to depression.

Regardless of its origins, however, habitually turning against another's bids for connection is hard on relationships. This type of behavior says:

- Your need for attention makes me angry.
- I feel hostile toward you.
- I don't respect you.
- I don't value you or this relationship.
- I want to hurt you.
- I want to drive you away.

Even more than turning away, these responses can make the bidder feel hurt and rejected. If the respondent holds a position of power over the bid-der—a boss, teacher, parent, or dominating spouse, for example—the bid-der may even become anxious or afraid, which leads to suppressing feelings and avoiding conflict. Such reactions make sense when you're in a relation-ship with somebody who habitually responds to you with contempt, bel-ligerence, and other attacks; you find a way to start dodging those bullets. Take the employee whose boss constantly responds to her low-level bids with anger and irritability, for example. Once she catches on, she's not likely to take the chance of discussing her most heartfelt dreams with him. Whether the worker is conscious of it or not, she may feel, "This guy is scary enough when I ask him to sign my time sheet. There's no way I'm going to tell him what's really on my mind."

It's not unusual for people to remain in such suppressed, conflict-avoiding relationships for an exceptionally long time. In the case of parent-child or childhood sibling relationships, there's no way for a child to leave voluntarily. Unhappily married couples in this state may put off talking about separation or divorce indefinitely, despite their misery. Disgruntled employees may stay in their jobs much longer than they should. But all the while, it's as if some radar inside is keeping track of incoming assaults. And once the radar registers a certain threshold, that's it. The bidder says, "Why bother? I'll only get hurt." All bids cease, and partners drift apart. Although they may stay in the relationship, many quit interacting with each other altogether.

## Exercise: Create an Emotion Log

An Emotion Log can be a way to document your progress toward improving emotional communication, including the ways you bid and respond to bids. Think of it as the kind of logbook an explorer might keep during a journey of great discovery. As an explorer, you may make observations and jot down notes on various topics, whether such details prove to be significant later on or not. What's important is to get it all down on paper so that you can see interesting patterns emerge.

Choose whatever kind of blank book fits your style. Some people like to use a fancy bound journal, while others simply jot down notes in a spiral notebook. People with an artistic flair might want to use a drawing pad for sketching people's facial expressions or illustrating insights. Others may want to scribble notes on napkins and receipts, and then stuff them all in a folder.

Regardless of your style, you can start by making entries about the bids and responses to bids you're noticing each day. You might want to answer one or more of the following questions:

- What did you notice today about the way you made bids for connection with important people in your life?
- How did you feel about the way people responded to your bids?
- Did you notice anybody turning toward? Turning away? Turning against? What did that behavior look like?
- Was there anything about the way you made your bid that might have affected their choice in turning? Is there anything you might do differently next time?
- What did you notice today about the way you responded to other people's bids for connection?
- Did you notice yourself turning toward, turning away, or turning against other people? What did that behavior look like?
- Was there something about the way that person made his or her bid that affected your choice in turning? Can you imagine making a different choice? Can you imagine how that might have affected the next thing that happened in the conversation?

## Examples of Various Turning Responses

| Bids for connection | Turning-toward responses | Turning-away responses | Turning-against responses |
|---|---|---|---|
| "I finally finished painting the kitchen." | "What a big job. I bet you're glad it's done." | "Have you seen my glasses?" | "It took you long enough." |
| "Would you like to have dinner with me?" | "I'd love to, thanks." Or, "That's a nice invitation. But I can't. I've got to get home to my boyfriend." | "No. Sorry. I'm busy." | "No, I'm cleaning the lint out of my clothes dryer tonight." |
| "I can't believe you're going out again tonight!" | "Yeah, I've got to meet Brian at eight. But it sounds like you're mad. Do you want to talk about it?" | "Yeah, I've got to meet Brian at eight. I'll see you later." | "Well, you don't have to believe it, because it's none of your business." |
| "I'm going to be a little late to the party, but I'll get there as soon as I can." | "That's great! I really appreciate that you're coming." | "I still haven't decided what to wear." | "And I suppose you expect me to hold off serving the meal just for you." |
| "I don't suppose you'd even think of asking me to go for a walk." | "I might. Hey, I've got an idea: Do you want to go for a walk?" | "No, it hadn't occurred to me." | "You're right. I wouldn't ask you—not with that attitude." |
| "I heard this great joke last night." | "What?" | "When did you get home?" | "Don't blow the punchline again." |
| "This stupid computer! I'm sick of this job!" | "Sounds like you need a break. Go get a cup of coffee and I'll find you that number for tech support." | "Hmmm. Do you have any floppies I could borrow?" | "If you'd read the manual sometime, you wouldn't have these problems." |

*(continued)*

| Bids for connection | Turning-toward responses | Turning-away responses | Turning-against responses |
|---|---|---|---|
| "Mom, I'm bored." | "I don't like being bored, either. Let's brainstorm some things you can do." | "And I'm busy." | "Whose fault is that?" |
| "I hate teachers like you!" | "Whoa! That's a strong statement. Let's back up. Is there something else you wanted me to understand about what you just said?" | "I'm not even going to respond to that." | "Yeah, well, I hate students like you, too!" |
| "Here, I saved you a seat." | "Thanks. That was nice of you." Or, "Thanks. That was nice of you. But I already have a seat next to Kim. Would you like to join us?" | "Did you get a program?" | "Why do you always have to sit in the front row?" |
| "I love that song!" | "I've never heard it before. Who's singing?" | "Can you turn it down just a bit?" | "You've got to be kidding!" |

## The Difference Between Men and Women

Many factors influence the way people bid and respond to bids, and gender is certainly one of those factors. A few key points of difference, which emerged from our studies of husbands and wives, merit special attention.

First, we learned that husbands in happy marriages turned toward their spouses with much greater frequency than husbands in unhappy marriages did. But wives turned toward their partners with the same frequency whether their marriages were happy or not.

We can conclude from this that men may hold a significant key to determining whether or not their marriages will succeed. While wives' attention to their husbands' needs is always important, it's the additional benefit of the husbands' mindfulness that puts the relationship over the top, giving the couple a much better chance of a long, happy marriage.

That's not to say that the wife's contribution is inconsequential. Our studies show that the wife's sense of humor, interest, and affection can have a big impact on the husband's ability to remain calm during conflict—a factor that ultimately predicts stability in a marriage. In this regard, it's the wife's positive expression that makes a bigger difference than the husband's. But what allows a wife access to these attributes when she's engaged in a conflict? Our research reveals that it's the practice she gets constantly turning toward her husband in everyday interaction.

We also found that in partnerships where spouses *turned away* from each other's bids, husbands and wives were equally likely to get hostile with one another during disagreements. But in marriages where partners *turned against* each other, the husbands typically suppressed their feelings or became hostile. Their wives, on the other hand, usually reacted in just one way: They simply suppressed their feelings.

It's hard to say for certain why this gender difference exists in marriages where spouses turn against each other. One reason may have to do with the balance of power in relationships. Many women whose husbands consistently turn against their bids may simply feel too frightened by their spouses' anger to react with hostility during an argument. So they shut down and try to avoid or suppress their negative feelings.

Another theory might be that, under stress, men tend to become more irritable and critical than women do. In fact, a recent study on differences in stress among men and women showed that while men tend to respond with a "fight or flight" reaction, women are more likely to "tend and befriend"— i.e., to seek support from and affiliation with others. While suppressing one's feelings is not exactly seeking affiliation, at least it's not antagonistic in the way that a hostile reaction would be.

## Exercise: What's Your Style of Bidding and Responding to Bids?

To take this test, think about a person who's important to you—perhaps a partner, friend, child, parent, sibling, or coworker with whom you're currently having some conflict or discomfort.

If you have a high level of intimacy and trust with this person, you might ask him or her to take the test as well. That way, you can share the results, which may lead to a better shared understanding of how you can interact in ways that will strengthen your relationship.

If you don't feel that you can ask this person to take the test with you, taking it alone may still benefit your relationship—especially if it helps you to see the relationship from the other person's perspective.

Here's what you do:

**1.** Complete each item, indicating the extent to which you agree or disagree with each statement about yourself in this relationship. For each item, circle the alternative that best fits.

**SA** = strongly agree
**A** = agree
**N** = neutral
**D** = disagree
**SD** = strongly disagree

**2.** If you're doing this exercise with another person, talk about the results and what you've learned from them. If you're doing the exercise alone, complete each item again, this time pretending to be that other person. This can help you to see your relationship from the other person's perspective. Either way, consider what you've learned and areas in which you might want to improve your bidding and responses in the future.

## *Bidding*

**1.** I sometimes get ignored when I need attention the most.
**SA   A   N   D   SD**

**2.** This person often doesn't notice me.
**SA   A   N   D   SD**

**3.** This person usually doesn't have a clue to what I am feeling.
**SA   A   N   D   SD**

**4.** I try, but am not successful in obtaining the social support I need in this relationship. **SA   A   N   D   SD**

**5.** I think that this person should know what I need without my saying so explicitly. **SA   A   N   D   SD**

**6.** I often have difficulty getting a meaningful conversation going with this person. **SA   A   N   D   SD**

**7.** I have trouble getting emotionally close to this person.
**SA   A   N   D   SD**

**8.** If this person can't tell what I need, I typically withdraw.
**SA   A   N   D   SD**

**9.** I often find this person too busy to be emotionally available to me.
**SA   A   N   D   SD**

**10.** It's hard for this person to tell what I need or want from him or her.
**SA   A   N   D   SD**

**11.** This person often takes the focus off me and puts it onto him- or herself. **SA   A   N   D   SD**

**12.** I often feel excluded by this person.   **SA   A   N   D   SD**

**13.** My needs are neglected in this relationship.   **SA   A   N   D   SD**

**14.** I get mad when I don't get the attention I need from this person.
**SA   A   N   D   SD**

15. When I feel let down by this person, I let him or her know it in no uncertain terms. **SA** **A** **N** **D** **SD**
16. I can take just so much of being ignored by this person, and then I blow up. **SA** **A** **N** **D** **SD**
17. I believe in strongly and assertively asking for what I need from this person. **SA** **A** **N** **D** **SD**
18. I often find myself becoming irritable with this person.
 **SA** **A** **N** **D** **SD**
19. I get so frustrated because I have to demand what I need from this person. **SA** **A** **N** **D** **SD**
20. I get angry because I don't get the emotional support I need from this person. **SA** **A** **N** **D** **SD**
21. I often feel irritated that this person isn't on my side.
 **SA** **A** **N** **D** **SD**
22. I have to let this person know that he or she isn't being a team player.
 **SA** **A** **N** **D** **SD**
23. I just can't seem to get close to this person.
 **SA** **A** **N** **D** **SD**
24. I have trouble getting this person to listen to me.
 **SA** **A** **N** **D** **SD**
25. I have trouble getting this person to talk to me.
 **SA** **A** **N** **D** **SD**
26. I have trouble getting this person to trust me. **SA** **A** **N** **D** **SD**
27. I find it difficult to get this person to open up to me.
 **SA** **A** **N** **D** **SD**
28. This person won't share his or her true feelings with me.
 **SA** **A** **N** **D** **SD**

### SCORING

For all items, calculate your score as follows:

**SA** = 2
**A** = 1
**N** = 0
**D** = −1
**SD** = −2

First, consider items 1 to 12, which show how reticent you are at bidding. If you scored 6 or greater, you're bidding in a way that tends to keep your needs hidden and unknown. You have a tendency to be unclear in stating what you need from this person. This can be a problem in the relationship because the other person may feel he or she has to be a mind reader to understand what you need. A score lower than 6 means that you're more direct. This is better for your relationship, because you have the ability to state clearly what you need from this person.

Next consider items 13 to 22, which reveal how forceful you are at bidding. If you scored 6 or greater, you may be expressing so much anger in your bidding that you're pushing the other person away. This could be the result of your past frustration with this relationship, or it could be an enduring characteristic of your personality. Either way, this can be a problem in the relationship because your bids may sound more like criticism or righteous indignation. A score lower than 6 means that you are not overly forceful in expressing what you need from this person. This is better for your relationship because it's easier for the other person to hear and understand what you need.

Finally, consider items 23 to 28. These items concern the issue of trust, which can be an area of concern in any relationship, but may be particularly relevant to adult-child relationships. If you scored 4 or more on these six items, you may need to do more to win this person's trust. One of the best ways to do this is to concentrate more on responding to the other person's bids, rather than trying to get the other person to respond to you. If you scored less than 4, you probably have a high level of trust in this relationship.

## Responding to Bids

1. My need for independence is such that I find this person cloying and smothering. **SA A N D SD**
2. I often feel like running away when this person asks for my attention. **SA A N D SD**
3. I really find it hard to sit and listen to this person. **SA A N D SD**
4. My mind wanders when this person talks. **SA A N D SD**
5. When this person gets overly emotional, I don't want to be with him or her. **SA A N D SD**
6. I think that if this person is feeling sad, he or she should keep it private. **SA A N D SD**
7. I wish that this person took care of his or her own needs more and relied on me less. **SA A N D SD**
8. When I am busy, I resent being interrupted by this person. **SA A N D SD**
9. I need my own personal space without this person expecting me to take care of him or her. **SA A N D SD**
10. I often resent being bothered by this person when I am trying to concentrate. **SA A N D SD**
11. I will avoid this person when he or she is overly needy. **SA A N D SD**
12. I don't usually notice what this person is feeling. **SA A N D SD**
13. I seem to be continually disappointing this person. **SA A N D SD**

**14.** I never seem to know what to say to this person when he or she approaches me. **SA  A  N  D  SD**
**15.** I have a lot of trouble emotionally supporting this person.
**SA  A  N  D  SD**
**16.** I try to notice this person's emotional state. **SA  A  N  D  SD**
**17.** I will often ask this person questions about how they are.
**SA  A  N  D  SD**
**18.** I generally like meeting this person's needs. **SA  A  N  D  SD**
**19.** I enjoy listening to this person talk. **SA  A  N  D  SD**
**20.** It is important for me to be there for this person.
**SA  A  N  D  SD**
**21.** I am usually responsive when this person needs my time and attention. **SA  A  N  D  SD**
**22.** I can tell when this person is upset and I respond to it.
**SA  A  N  D  SD**
**23.** When this person is worried or scared I am usually comforting.
**SA  A  N  D  SD**
**24.** When this person has suffered a setback or loss I am understanding and helpful. **SA  A  N  D  SD**
**25.** When this person wants to just talk I am usually available.
**SA  A  N  D  SD**
**26.** When this person asks for my time and attention, I tend to be annoyed. **SA  A  N  D  SD**
**27.** Lately I tend to feel crabby when this person is near me.
**SA  A  N  D  SD**
**28.** I get stressed out by this person's constant need for attention.
**SA  A  N  D  SD**
**29.** I often feel critical of this person's behavior. **SA  A  N  D  SD**
**30.** I find myself being angry when this person wants to have long conversations. **SA  A  N  D  SD**
**31.** This person tends to make me impatient with him or her.
**SA  A  N  D  SD**
**32.** This person needs too much from me. **SA  A  N  D  SD**

**SCORING**

For all items, calculate your score as follows:

**SA** = 2
**A** = 1
**N** = 0
**D** = −1
**SD** = −2

For items 1 to 15, a total score of 8 or more means that you typically turn away from this person's bids. A score of 7 or lower means that you do not typically turn away from this person's bids, nor are you put off by this person's expressed needs.

For items 16 to 25, a total score of 6 or more means that you typically turn toward this person's bids. A total score of 5 or less means that you do not typically turn toward this person's bids.

For items 26 to 32, a total score of 4 or more means that you typically turn against this person's bids. A total score of 3 or less means that you do not typically turn against this person's bids.

## Exercise: Create a Love Map for People Close to You

This exercise is based on a similar activity for spouses that appears in my book *The Seven Principles for Making Marriage Work*. "Love map" is a term I use for that part of your brain where you store all the relevant information about a loved one's life. It's based on the idea that being familiar with the details of one another's lives can help you have happier, more stable relationships. I believe this is true in marriage as well as other close relationships. Whether you're relating to your spouse, children, friends, relatives, or coworkers, the more you know about their daily experiences, feelings, and preferences, the easier it will be to turn toward them and connect emotionally.

The goal of this exercise is to answer the following questionnaire as the other person would. In this way, you create a love map for somebody to whom you're close or would like to be closer. You can do it alone, but it's also fun to do together, with the other person completing a map of your life as you complete a map of his or hers. Don't think of the exercise as a competition— that's not helpful. Instead, think of it as a game you can play together to benefit your relationship.

If either of you has trouble answering particular questions, circle those items. Then, when you're done with the questionnaire, ask one another about the items you couldn't answer. You'll probably have lots of items to discuss, which is a good thing. Fostering communication is the whole point.

You may also want to return to this exercise at times over the course of your relationship. You could do it each year on one of your birthdays, for example, to help you stay up-to-date with important changes you're both going through.

1. Favorite meal:
2. Special hobbies and interests:
3. Two closest friends:

4. Worst enemy or rival:
5. Two people most admired:
6. Favorite movie:
7. Favorite TV shows:
8. Favorite kind of animal:
9. Ideal vacation destination:
10. Favorite sports to watch and follow:
11. First thing this person would buy if he or she won the lottery:
12. One thing this person would like to change about you:
13. One thing you could do to improve your relationship with this person:
14. Favorite types of clothes to wear:
15. Least favorite relative:
16. Favorite relative:
17. Favorite holiday:
18. Least favorite holiday:
19. Ideal job:
20. Favorite way to spend evenings at home:
21. Favorite kind of books:
22. Favorite musical group, composer, or instrument:
23. Favorite ways to spend weekends:
24. Toughest problem this person has faced:
25. Favorite restaurants:
26. Favorite magazine:
27. Places or events this person would find most uncomfortable:
28. Most comforting pastime when sick:
29. Saddest life event:
30. Worst life event:
31. Happiest life event:
32. Favorite way to exercise:
33. Ideal birthday present:
34. Two worst fears or disaster scenarios:
35. Best recent day:
36. Worst recent day:
37. Two things that make this person very angry:
38. Current stresses or worries:
39. Best parts of this person's current job or school life:
40. Worst parts of this person's current job or school life:
41. Favorite way to spend time with friends:
42. Favorite way to get over being sad:
43. Best vacation this person ever had:
44. Favorite way to get your attention:
45. Two reasons this person is proudest of himself or herself:
46. Gift this person would give to you for your birthday:

**47.** Fondest unrealized dream:
**48.** Activity that makes this person feel most competent:
**49.** Personal improvements this person wants to make in his or her life:
**50.** Secret ambition:

## Better Bids Ahead

Once you become more conscious of your bidding process and how it works in particular relationships, you'll notice opportunities for connection that you've never seen before. You may also become more aware of missed opportunities—times when you wish you could connect emotionally, but it's just not working out.

Through years of observational research, my colleagues and I have been able to pinpoint several common behavioral patterns that keep people from forming closer bonds. We've also identified ways to change those patterns and make your bidding more successful. That's what you'll read about in chapter 3.

# 3

# Six Bid Busters
# and How to Avoid Them

hrough my observational research, I have learned a great deal about the way people succeed and fail in their bids for emotional connection. In this chapter you'll read about six key problems I call the "bid busters." These are patterns of behavior that repeatedly show up among those who have trouble bidding or responding to bids for connection. See if you recognize these habits as barriers to connection in your own relationships. If so, you can try some of the simple, practical remedies I recommend for overcoming these obstacles.

## 1. Being Mindless Rather Than Mindful

Most people don't get married, have children, make friends, or take jobs with the intention of allowing these relationships to fail. And yet that's what often happens—simply because people don't pay enough attention to the emotional needs of others. They're not acting mindlessly because they want to be mean; they're just temporarily caught up in their own concerns and not focusing on the people around them.

But if you don't pay attention, you don't connect. And if you don't connect, you wind up operating on the principle that your partner, your friend, or your coworker is not going to be there for you. That, in turn, starts a cascade of negative interactions—including criticism, defensiveness, attacking, and withdrawing—all of which eventually destroy the relationship.

Being mindful, on the other hand, leads to the formation of stable, satisfying relationships. When you're mindful, you notice other people's bids and you respond to them. You can shift attention from your own concerns to the concerns of others. In doing so, you learn to understand what other people are feeling, and you're able to feel those same emotions at the same time. You can be "in the moment" with another person, focusing on your shared awareness and your shared experience. You have the sense that you're on a journey of discovery together. It's a creative process of revealing your life stories to each other. These stories unfold every day when people are mindful of one another.

Such encounters are akin to the type of "optimal experience" that the psychologist Mihaly Csikszentmihaly describes in his book *Flow* (Harper & Row, 1990). During such experiences, "concentration is so intense that there is no attention left over to think about anything irrelevant or to worry about problems," he writes. "Self-consciousness disappears and the sense of time becomes distorted. An activity that produces such experiences is so gratifying that people are willing to do it for its own sake, with little concern for what they will get out of it."

Sounds a bit like falling in love, doesn't it? Perhaps that's because romance is the kind of bond to which people are most willing to apply this type of mindful focus. But achieving a comparable kind of connection is possible with friends, relatives, and coworkers as well—as long as you're willing to give your full attention to another person and his or her feelings.

What typically prevents people from achieving such mindfulness in their relationships? I believe it's the choices they make to focus instead on other priorities. For example, a husband and wife may be putting so much thought into keeping the kids busy, remodeling their home, and acquiring stuff that they have no energy left for the primary relationship in their lives. It's not that they don't talk to one another. It's that all their conversations concern things like the kids' soccer schedule, the basement remodeling project, and how to get the best price on a new SUV. There's never time in their day to just check in with each other; their minds are always focused on the family's agenda of accomplishment and acquisition.

I've also seen people's career identities get in the way of their ability to be present in their relationships. It's a problem particularly common among people in professional roles that reward them for their objectivity, intellectual prowess, and emotional distance. While such qualities may be highly valued in boardrooms and surgical suites, they can be obstacles to emotional intimacy. A neurosurgeon I had as a client is one example. All day long in his professional life, people relied on him for his highly objective, clinical analyses of life-or-death situations. And when he came home at the end of the day, he found it hard to shed this persona. I once heard his wife ask him, "How do you think we're doing—as a couple?" And he responded with a long-winded, highly accurate evaluation. Trouble was, he had misread her question. She wanted his reassurance, support, and affection—not a clinical assessment. Consequently, she burst into tears and ran from the room, which left him clearly puzzled. "I can never do enough to please her," he told me.

This man's problem wasn't incompetence, however. In previous evaluations (including use of the Emotional Communication Game on pages 202–205), he had shown himself to be quite skillful at reading her emotions. His problem was that he was so stuck in the role of the objective, professional expert that he was oblivious to her emotional need in that moment. He was operating on automatic pilot. He wasn't being mindful of what her bid was all about.

What's the antidote to such mindlessness? Simply put, it has to do with goal setting. You have to ask yourself: What is my main goal in this relationship? Is it to accomplish tasks and acquire things? Is it to prove that I'm always right? Always powerful? Or is it to build intimacy and understanding—that is, emotional connection? If your goal is emotional connection, the steps we've outlined throughout this book will help. But you've also got to bring your willingness to focus on being with each other's feelings in the moment. You've got to be willing to ask, "What am I after *in this moment?* Faced with the choice of turning away, turning against, or turning toward, which choice will take me closer to my goal?"

One way to enhance your mindfulness in relationships is to become a "collector of emotional moments." It's a term I first learned from my friend Ross Parke, a psychologist and the author of many books on child development. Over an exceptionally fine dinner conversation one night, Ross explained to me that he had come to think of his life as a string of pearls in which each pearl was a moment just like the one we were having—where we felt totally present and were connecting with each other on a deep and meaningful level. He said that he had decided to make a conscious effort to collect moments like these. By doing so, he was becoming more mindful in his relationships and they were growing stronger as a result.

I have since learned that each of us can become a collector of emotional moments. The key is to look for and celebrate those moments in which you connect with another person on a feeling level. Such moments usually begin by noticing an emotional expression as a bid for connection. You hear something a person says, or you see a facial expression or gesture, that reveals their happiness, sadness, anger, fear, contempt, or disgust. Once you notice it, you let this person know with your words, expressions, or gestures that you understand how they're feeling. Your demonstration of understanding provides a bridge for emotional connection and paves the way to a deeper, more meaningful relationship. It's that simple. Emotional moments can be shared with your spouse, family members, friends, coworkers—even the checker at the hardware store.

Let me give you an example of an emotional moment I had with my ten-year-old daughter, Moriah. My wife, Julie, was away for a few weeks on a trek to Nepal, and I was aware that Moriah might be missing her mom. I asked her from time to time, "How are you doing? Are you feeling a little lonely for Mom today?"

"Nope," she would usually reply. "I'm okay. I'm just fine."

But then, one evening after I told Moriah to get ready for bed, she came downstairs dressed in Julie's bathrobe.

If I had been operating in a less mindful mode (which *all* parents, including me, do from time to time), I might have ignored this gesture or even gotten irritated. "What were you doing in your mother's closet?" I could have said. "You're not supposed to get into her things."

But because I was watching for a chance to connect emotionally with Moriah, I recognized her behavior as a sign that she was finally ready to talk about her feelings.

"You're wearing Mom's robe," I said, acknowledging the obvious.

"Yeah," she replied, "it's really nice."

"Does it feel kind of comforting to put it on?" I asked.

"Yeah, it kind of smells like her," she said. "It's kind of like she's here a little bit, so I don't miss her so much."

Julie called on her satellite phone later that night, and although she and Moriah could only talk for two minutes, Moriah seemed happy when she went to bed. As I tucked her in, I said, "I bet Mommy could tell you missed her and put on her robe. That's why she called. She loves you and she'll be home soon."

Moriah said, "Yeah, I know."

You can become a collector of emotional moments by consciously looking for opportunities to connect with others. Doing so allows you to take a proactive role in the development of stable, meaningful relationships. The following exercise, when practiced on a daily basis, is designed to help you fine-tune this skill.

## *Exercise: Become a Collector of Emotional Moments*

Many people start the day with certain goals in mind—to exercise, to eat a healthy diet, to meet a performance standard at work, and so on. Try adding this one to your list: "Collect at least three emotional moments." Then, at the end of the day, look back and see how you did. You may want to write about your moments in your Emotional Log. As you describe them, consider the following questions:

- Was there a bid for emotional connection? What need was behind that bid?
- How did you first notice that this person was feeling an emotion? Did this person reveal his or her feelings through words, facial expressions, gestures, or in some other way?

- What emotion did you perceive this person was feeling? Was it happiness, sadness, anger, fear, contempt, disgust, or some other emotion?
- What did this person need from you? (Examples: just to be there, to listen, emotional support, understanding, humor, a bit of fun, conversation, etc.)
- How did you communicate to this person that you understood what he or she was feeling or needing? If you used words, what did you say?
- How did this person react to your acknowledgment of his or her feelings?
- What effect do you think your interaction had on this person? On your relationship with this person?
- What effect did this interaction have on you? On your feelings about yourself?
- Other insights?

After a few days of collecting emotional moments, don't be surprised if you become more mindful in your relationships and if your bonds with others become a bit more emotionally satisfying. Doing this over time could make a big difference.

## 2. Starting on a Sour Note

Have you ever launched a conversation only to wish you could rewind it like videotape and start again? This happened to me recently. It was after dinner and my wife, Julie, had gone downstairs to her office to answer some e-mail. My daughter and I both felt a little disappointed because we'd been looking forward to spending the evening with her.

So I yelled down the stairs, "Hey, Julie, stop working! It's family time!"

My harsh tone put Julie on the defensive, so she answered back in an angry tone. "I can't! I've got to get this done!"

The result? She felt criticized and misunderstood and I felt more distant from her than when our exchange began.

Imagine (as I did the next day) how I might have started this conversation with Julie differently. I might have said something like, "Hey, Julie, we miss you. Come upstairs as soon as you can, okay?"

Instead, our exchange was a classic example of what I call "harsh startup": You want to connect with somebody, so you make a bid for that connection. But because your bid begins in such a negative, blaming, or critical way, you get just the opposite of what you're after: You drive the person away.

Harsh startup can sabotage perfectly valid bids for connection in all sorts of relationships. Take George and his boss, for example. George had been concerned about a whole host of troubles on his job at the warehouse—problems like safety issues and a new vacation policy. But mostly he was worried about a new automated inventory system that would be installed within the year. He and his coworkers wondered how many jobs might be lost as a result. So he decided that the next time he saw the warehouse manager in the lunchroom, he would corner him for answers. Trouble was, George brought up the most contentious issue first—the vacation policy. And he told the boss just exactly what he thought of it— not much. This critical attack made the boss feel defensive, so he told George he didn't like his "attitude"—a word that always triggered George's anger. Rather than having a productive conversation, the two men ended up in a heated argument, after which George felt more frustrated and insecure than ever. But imagine how differently the conversation might have gone if he had started the conversation by telling his boss how much he cared about his job and how concerned he was about the impact of automation.

Then there's Karen, whose teenage daughter, Courtney, has been running with a new crowd and staying out too late at night. Worried that she's losing all parental influence, Karen knows she needs to talk with Courtney about the matter. She wants to feel more connected to her daughter, but at breakfast one morning, she starts the bid in a way that automatically raises the girl's defenses.

"What time did you get in last night?" she asks in a critical, accusing tone.

"You know what time I came in," Courtney says with a sullen stare. "Your bedroom light was still on."

"That's right," Karen says. "It was two o'clock."

"So then why did you ask me?" Courtney replies, obviously baiting her mother—and it works.

"Don't use that tone of voice with me," Karen snaps.

In just this short exchange, the two have managed to make one another so angry that there's little hope for any meaningful conversation. Karen never gets a chance to tell her daughter that she's worried about her and why. And Courtney never gets a chance to tell her mom what's been happening in her life.

When bids for connection start on such a negative, blaming, or critical note, it's fairly easy to predict what will happen next. In fact, my studies of married couples show that 96 percent of the time, you can predict the outcome of a fifteen-minute conversation based on what happens in the first three minutes of that interaction. And if the first three minutes include a lot of negativity, blame, and criticism, the outcome is not going to be very good.

What's the solution? One answer is to start your bids on a softer note. The chart below provides some tips, along with examples of harsh startups and soft startups.

## Harsh vs. Soft Startup

| Tips for soft starts | Don't start like this: | Start like this instead: |
|---|---|---|
| Begin with something positive. | "We never have fun together anymore. Why don't we ever do anything adventurous?" | "Look at this article about a couple who hiked the Pacific Crest Trail. It reminds me of how much fun it is to have adventures with you. Let's plan something now." |
| | "I'm fed up with this job. I feel like you expect me to perform miracles and it's not going to happen." | "Remember when we talked about my performance goals last month? That was really helpful. Can we discuss them again?" |
| Express appreciation and gratitude. | "I never hear from anybody anymore. The only time the family contacts me is when somebody dies." | "It was great to be invited to Uncle Henry's surprise party last year. I'd love to know when the family plans another get-together." |
| | "Why do I have to ask to see these reports? They should have sent me a copy of this." | "Thanks for letting me see this report. This information really helps. Who can I contact to get a copy for myself next time?" |
| Start with "I" instead of "You." | "You could have called. You made me stay up all night worrying about you." | "I was so worried when you didn't call that it kept me up all night." |
| | "You're not keeping me informed about the project. From now on, we need to meet every Wednesday morning." | "I want to stay more informed about this project. How about if we meet every Wednesday morning?" |

*(continued)*

| Tips for soft starts | Don't start like this: | Start like this instead: |
|---|---|---|
| Don't stockpile complaints. | "I didn't want to say anything, but I can't take it any-more. You haven't asked for sex in over six months, and I feel like you don't love me anymore." | "I like it when you make the first move, but it's been a while. Can we talk about it?" |
| | "You haven't spent any time with your little brother in ages, your grades have been slipping since October, and you haven't helped me with chores in six weeks." | "I'm worried about your report card. You've dropped a grade in every subject." (Address the other issues one at a time as they come up.) |

Another solution when things have gone awry is to revisit the episode with that person later on. You can begin by saying something like, "I feel bad about that short conversation we had yesterday. I didn't handle it very well. So I want to say I'm sorry and I'd like to make things better between us." Of course, you have to gauge how receptive the other person might be to this. I believe that most friends, siblings, love partners, and kids are responsive to such attempts at fixing failed bids.

In fact, children often benefit greatly from a parent's willingness to admit errors. It gives children permission to make mistakes without feeling bad about themselves.

Colleagues at work may also be open to genuine attempts to repair mis-communication, particularly if you already share a high level of trust. But if your bonds with coworkers aren't that strong, be cautious. They may or may not view your attempts to revisit and fix the interaction as appropriate.

## 3. Using Harmful Criticism Instead of Helpful Complaints

Conflict is inevitable whenever people come together around common activities or goals. How you express your position in a conflict makes a tremendous difference in your ability to connect with others.

Here's the basic rule of thumb: Complain when you must, but don't criticize. What's the difference? A complaint focuses on a specific problem, addressing the other person's behavior, not his or her perceived character flaws. Criticism, on the other hand, is more judgmental and global; it frequently includes such phrases as "you always . . ." or "you never . . ." Criticism attacks the other person's character, often with negative labels or name-calling. It often assigns blame.

"You said you would deliver the package and you didn't do it" is a complaint. "You forgot to deliver the package! That's irresponsible!" is a criticism.

Complaints can be difficult to say and hear at times. But they're generally worth the trouble because they help people to understand one another and to solve problems. Criticism, however, does just the opposite. It hurts people's feelings, leading to increased tension, resentment, and defensiveness in relationships. People don't communicate well when they feel defensive. They tend to shut out new information. They're not open to others' influence. All of this gets in the way of emotional connection.

## Criticism vs. Complaint

| Tips for good complaining | Criticism | Complaint |
|---|---|---|
| State your needs without attacking or blaming the other person. | "What's the matter with you? All you ever think about is golf. You never think about me and the kids." | "I need your help with the kids on the weekends. But for the past three Saturdays, you've been playing golf." |
| | "You never call me. You'd never think to send me a card or anything. You're self-centered." | "I wish that you'd call me more often. When I don't hear from you, I feel like you don't care about me." |
| | "How could you change the procedure without asking me about it? You're such a space case. You're going to mess the whole thing up!" | "I'm irritated because you changed the procedure without asking my opinion. I know the process better than anybody else." |
| Describe your side as your perception, not "the absolute truth." | "People who don't respond to their e-mail are not team players. Everybody knows you should treat e-mail like a phone call." | "When you don't respond to my e-mail, I feel like you don't care about our project." |
| Focus on specific behavior, not global judgments. | "You're always so cold toward me." | "At night, when I try to snuggle with you, I can feel your body get tense." |
| | "If you don't tell me that you've got too much work, how will I know? You don't have to play the martyr, you know." | "If you don't tell me that you've got too much work, how will I know? I don't want you to have to work such long hours." |

## 4. Flooding

In troubled relationships, discussions of conflict can trigger intense emotions that sometimes lead to "flooding." This means you feel so stressed that you become emotionally and physically overwhelmed. You're no longer able to think clearly, or to participate in the conversation in a fruitful way. You'd rather be anywhere else than right here with this person. Obviously, this reaction gets in the way of sending or receiving bids for emotional connection.

Physical signs of flooding include a pounding heart, sweaty hands, and irregular or shallow breathing. Rather than focusing on what the other person is saying, your mind races with defensive thoughts like "I can't handle this anymore," or "I've had just about all of this I can take." You may feel like an innocent victim, cornered into a conversation from which you just want to flee.

When you're in this state of mind, it's as if you're not capable of hearing new information or accepting influence. The other person may even make attempts to apologize or placate you, but it's as if you can't hear them. Although flooding can happen to anybody in an emotionally intense situation, studies show that it occurs more often among men than among women.

What's the best thing to do when you feel flooded? I recommend that you take a break from the conversation and do something that you find soothing for at least twenty minutes. That's the amount of time it typically takes the body to recover from emotional stress. You might want to read a magazine, watch television, or go for a run. But whatever you do, try to think about something other than the conflict during this break. Don't focus on thoughts of being righteously indignant or an innocent victim. Doing so is counterproductive and will just maintain your distress. Many people find that it's helpful to use this time to meditate or to do a relaxation exercise (see below). Once twenty minutes have passed and you feel more relaxed, try to get back to discussing the problem, or schedule another time to discuss it soon.

### *Exercise: Relax*

Here are a few simple steps you can take to soothe yourself when you're feeling emotionally agitated, overwhelmed, or "flooded."

1. Sit or lie in a comfortable position.
2. Close your eyes and think about your breathing. Take several slow, deep breaths, finding a comfortable, regular pace. Ten deep breaths a minute is a good choice.
3. As you continue to breathe slowly and evenly, mentally scan your body, looking for any areas of tension. The face, jaw, neck, shoulders, and back are common trouble spots. When you find an area that's tense, deliberately tighten the muscles in that area, hold the tension for a few

seconds, and then release them. Do it again—tighten, hold, and release. This will leave your muscles feeling more relaxed than when you began.

4. Now relax each of those areas of your body by imagining that it's very heavy. As you envision gravity's pull, let your muscles relax and let the tension dissipate.

5. Next, imagine that each of those muscle areas is very warm. Imagine that you're basking in the sun or sitting near a warm, relaxing fireplace. As you grow warmer, even more tension will flow away.

6. Continue to relax by envisioning a place that's especially safe and restful to you. Maybe it's a warm beach, a quiet mountaintop, or a secluded forest. Stay in this place for a few minutes, noticing the details of your surroundings, enjoying its peace and solitude. Each time you do this exercise, your image of this setting will come more easily to you. Soon, simply thinking of it may help you to automatically relax.

## *Exercise: Avoid Emotional Flooding*

You can also take steps to prevent flooding from happening in the first place. This exercise includes questions to ask yourself about the times when you've felt flooded. Answering them may give you insights about the things that set off, or "trigger," this reaction and how to avoid such triggers. You may also discover new ways to soothe yourself when you're feeling emotionally overwhelmed. Don't do this exercise right after you've experienced feeling flooded. Wait until you're relaxed and feeling calm.

Begin by considering the following questions, thinking about recent situations in which you felt flooded. If possible, discuss your answers with a person with whom you've had conflicts in the past. The discussion may help the two of you to talk about problems in the future. If you feel that you can't discuss these issues with that person, then answer the questions on your own and discuss them with a trusted friend or write about them in your Emotion Log.

- What typically happens just before you start to feel flooded?
- Are there particular words, actions, or topics that seem to "trigger" you to flood?
- What would allow you to stay in an intense conversation without flooding?
- How are upsetting subjects introduced into your conversations?
- Does either of you bring up these subjects in a harsh way?
- Are there ways that either of you could introduce these subjects so that you might stay calmer?
- Does either of you tend to "store up" problems and try to deal with them all at once?
- Can you do a better job of handling your problems one at a time?

- What can you do to soothe yourself when you feel irritable, scared, or angry?
- What can you do to soothe each other?
- What signals can you develop for when either of you feels flooded?
- Can you take breaks?
- What can you do during these breaks to calm down?
- How can you make sure that you get back to the problem later on?

## Exercise: Give Me Just One Word

Here's another exercise designed for two people who are having conflict and who want to improve their relationship. It's based on a technique used by sports psychologists to help athletes perform better under pressure. The idea is that people often find it hard to remember complex instructions in the heat of competition. So their coaches give them just one word that summarizes the most important concept they need to remember in order to win. Then, just before the competition, the athletes focus on that word. If they get confused, agitated, or "flooded" during the game or match, the coach can repeat the word, helping them to get back on track. A boxing coach, for example, can tell the boxer, "Dance!" during the short break between rounds. A soccer coach might tell his player, "Aggress!" And this one word helps him to get his drive and concentration back again.

All of this can be applied as well to people who want to improve their relationships. When you're in conflict with somebody and you become flooded with fear or anger, all your best intentions can go out the window. But if you can remember just one word that might help you to focus on what the other person needs during these conflicts, you'll have a better chance of finding common ground and connecting. Here's what each of you should do.

**1.** Read the list of words that follows. As you look at each one, think about what you usually feel you need from this other person during a typical conflict.

**2.** Circle the five words that best describe your needs.

**3.** Now share your list of five words with each other. Tell the other person what each word on your list means *to you,* and how you would like to see him or her display this behavior or characteristic during your conflicts.

**4.** Listen carefully as the other person describes the words on his or her list. Avoid getting into a debate about the correct meaning of a particular word. This is not a vocabulary lesson. Your goal is to try to understand what that word means to that person, and how you might personify it. Ask questions about any points that seem unclear.

**5.** Keep talking until you can determine together how each of you can best display the characteristics on each other's lists.

**6.** Write all the words down and keep them in a place that's easily accessible to both of you.

**7.** The next time you get into a conflict with this person, remember the words that were on your list. Say the one that best describes what you need from this person in that moment. Think of yourself as an encouraging coach who only wants the best for both of you.

**8.** When you hear your partner offer his or her word, stop and remember what he or she needs in the moment. Think of this person as an encouraging coach who only wants the best for both of you.

**9.** Try to use this exercise consistently over a period of several weeks. The more you use it, the better you'll learn it, and the more effective it will become.

## Words to Use

| | | |
|---|---|---|
| Empathize | Expand | Accept |
| Respect | Endure | Watch |
| Nurture | Accept me | Cooperate |
| Court me | Tenderness | Stand up for me |
| Dignity | Teamwork | Honesty |
| Start over | Cherish | Hold me |
| Listen | Caress | Talk |
| Love | Be silly | Conscience |
| Fun | End the chaos | Connect |
| Company | Emote | Compromise |
| Validate | Be strong | Feel |
| Touch | Don't whine | Feedback |
| Affection | Let it in | Faith |
| Forgive | Include me | Explain |
| Help | Don't go | Experiment |
| Honor me | Take charge | Abandon |
| Notice | Know yourself | I was wrong |
| We | Kiss me | You may be right |
| Boundaries | Laugh | I see your point |
| Symbiotic | Defend me | Humor |
| Believe | Stop | Heal |
| Soften | Stay | Grow |
| Begin again | Create | Give in |
| Surprise | Courage | Stand by me |
| Assert | Cope | Spontaneity |
| Ask questions | Kindness | Stand up |
| Summarize | Follow through | Sorry |
| Say yes | Breathe | Energy |
| Strength | Accept influence | Compassion |

| | | |
|---|---|---|
| Commitment | Think | Careful |
| Us | Optimism | Responsibility |
| Yield | Soften | Relax |
| Hug me | Sense | Reason |
| Yes | Sensation | Protect |
| Taste | Gentleness | Principles |
| Soothe | See my point | Calm down |
| Solidarity | See | Pleasure |
| Unity | Say maybe | Peace |
| Understand | Romance | Repair |
| Trust | Restore | Patience |
| Treasure | Rest | Open |

## 5. Practicing a Crabby Habit of Mind

Comedian George Carlin used to say there were only two kinds of drivers in the world: the "maniacs" who drove faster than he did, and the "idiots" who drove slower. We all laughed at the joke because it poked fun at a common human weakness: the crabby habit of mind.

Everybody feels irritable on occasion, but when you have a crabby habit of mind, you feel this way just about all the time. You constantly scan the world for evidence to justify your feelings. And in this imperfect world, that evidence is not hard to find. ("Damn it! You left the milk out on the counter—again!" "Look at that yard! Are those people ever going to mow their lawn?" "Politicians! Their double-talk gets on my nerves!")

When you have a crabby habit of mind, you often try to correct imperfect situations and you get overly concerned about other people's faults. Consequently, you may do more than your fair share of turning against others' bids for connection, and your relationships may suffer as a result.

What can be done to transform the crabby habit of mind? I believe a small percentage of people who feel chronically angry or irritated have a chemical imbalance that can be treated with antidepressants like Prozac. If you believe this may be true for you, you'll want to talk to your physician or a mental health practitioner about it.

But I also believe that most crabby people can change by making a conscious choice to react to the world in a different way. The key is to scan your environment regularly for things and people to appreciate rather than to criticize. In so doing, you create a new climate of praise and gratitude in your life. Instead of getting bogged down in people's faults and mistakes, you get swept up in a fruitful search for reasons to say "thank you."

I have seen this transformation happen among couples I've counseled as well as in my own life. Let me give you an example. Several years ago, I joined a new synagogue, and on my first Saturday, I observed a man who was leading the prayer and singing. He had a beautiful voice, but instead of appreciating that, my first reaction was to think, "What a show-off!"

When I got home, I realized how my response was directly opposed to the whole reason I had gone to synagogue. The Sabbath is supposed to be a celebration of compassion and understanding, of letting go of your judgments of other people. And here I was, harshly criticizing a man I didn't even know. That made me think about how critical and impatient I had become in so many areas of my life. I was turning increasingly irritable with my wife, my coworkers, and my friends. Like a crow gathering bits of debris for a nest, I kept looking around for faults I could use to build my case against other people. I wanted evidence to justify the low-level irritability I was feeling. So, like George Carlin, I started to believe that my world was populated by maniacs and idiots!

I decided that day that I would make a conscious effort to change. Instead of looking for people's faults, I would look for their strengths and take the opportunity to praise them if I could. The first time I was introduced to the man who sang at the synagogue, I said, "I really enjoyed your singing today." It was the honest truth and the beginning of a lasting friendship.

Taken individually, such statements seem like no big deal. But when you decide to make praise and appreciation a habit in your life, it can have a profound impact on your relationships. Our research shows that married couples who regularly express their appreciation for each other have much happier, stronger marriages. And in our laboratory studies with parents and their children, we observed significant differences in the ways children reacted when their parents criticized or praised them. In one study, for example, parents were asked to teach their children a new task. Those children whose parents focused mainly on their errors made more mistakes. But those whose parents emphasized what they were doing right improved their performance.

We also observed that children whose parents did not get involved in their mistakes turned toward their parents when they had a problem. This is a significant lesson for critical parents who may wish that children would view them as wise and discerning advisers. Our research shows just the opposite: Children with critical parents turn away from their parents in times of trouble. But children with parents who consistently praise them for their accomplishments turn toward their parents for support, even when things go wrong.

This same principle holds true in all kinds of relationships. Regularly expressing praise and appreciation can change the whole emotional climate of your home, your workplace, and your various circles of family and friends. People grow closer in the knowledge that they can count on one another for support in good times and in bad.

The following exercise can help you to transform a crabby, critical habit of mind to one that praises and appreciates.

## Exercise: Thanksgiving Every Day

A steady diet of gratitude is one of the best-known cures for a crabby habit of mind. Here's how the diet works.

**1.** Each day for one week, keep track of the times you feel like criticizing somebody important in your life, such as your spouse, a relative, a friend, or a close coworker. Try to come up with at least five incidents each day, and write them down in your Emotion Log.

**2.** After you've described the critical feelings and the incident that preceded it, find a way to counter that criticism with praise and appreciation. You may feel some resistance to doing this, especially if you feel that your criticism was justified. But try to ignore that resistance. Just set aside the faults you perceive in that person and look instead for reasons to value him or her. The list of qualities provided may be helpful as you consider these reasons.

**3.** Each day, make a point to share those five bits of praise or appreciation with the people who earned it.

**4.** Notice what effects these offerings have on your relationships, and write about them in your Emotion Log.

### Examples

- **Criticism:** You're sitting there thinking that Jack the bartender's habit of whistling drives you up the wall.
- **Praise or appreciation:** You notice that the customers really seem to like Jack's sense of humor, and that's good for business. You tell Jack what you're thinking.
- **Effects of praising him:** Jack laughs and seems to be in a good mood all night. You think maybe it's made him whistle more, but folks are hanging around and he's selling lots of drinks.

- **Criticism:** Your daughter forgot to fold the laundry as you asked her to do. You think, "She's so thoughtless," but you say nothing. You start looking around for something about her to appreciate.
- **Praise or appreciation:** You see why she forgot about the laundry: She has so much homework to do. At least she's diligent about her studies. She gets good grades, and she's learning so much. You decide to praise her for being so good about her homework.
- **Effects of praising her:** She seems calm and peaceful, content to keep studying. You realize how proud of her you are.

- **Criticism:** Your brother is so opinionated. He acts like such a know-it-all. You don't say anything. Instead you try to think of qualities you like about him.

- **Praise or appreciation:** You realize that he takes such good care of your mom. He's conscientious and responsible. You don't know what your family would do without him. You've never told him how much you value this about him. You decide to do so now.
- **Effects of praising him:** He seems to understand how genuinely grateful you are. You notice that he becomes a little easier to be around. It seems that he's not trying so hard to prove himself. Maybe he just needed a little appreciation.

## Qualities to Praise and Appreciate

| | | |
|---|---|---|
| Loving | Cheerful | Nurturing |
| Sensitive | Coordinated | Warm |
| Brave | Graceful | Virile |
| Intelligent | Elegant | Kind |
| Thoughtful | Gracious | Gentle |
| Generous | Playful | Practical |
| Loyal | Caring | Lusty |
| Honest | A great friend | Witty |
| Strong | Exciting | Relaxed |
| Energetic | Thrifty | Beautiful |
| Sexy | Full of plans | Handsome |
| Decisive | Shy | Rich |
| Creative | Vulnerable | Calm |
| Imaginative | Committed | Lively |
| Fun | Involved | Assertive |
| Attractive | Expressive | Protective |
| Interesting | Active | Sweet |
| Supportive | Careful | Tender |
| Funny | Reserved | Powerful |
| Considerate | Adventurous | Flexible |
| Affectionate | Receptive | Understanding |
| Organized | Reliable | Totally silly |
| Resourceful | Responsible | |
| Athletic | Dependable | |

## 6. Avoiding the Conversation You Need to Have

When things go wrong in a relationship, people often ask, "Was it something that I said?" Well, maybe. But more often it's the things people *don't* say that harm their relationships. According to the psychologist Dan Wile, many arguments spring from issues that people need to discuss but never do. In the resulting tension and confusion, quarrels erupt, leading to hostility, defensiveness, and withdrawal.

For example, Harry comes home in a foul mood after a terrible day at his business. He feels that he's been putting out fires for the past two months, and today there seemed to be a crisis a minute. He's exhausted and discouraged. His sales are off, and he's worried that this year may be a disaster. He's not sure why this is happening. What's worse, he's doesn't even like his work. He's been thinking for some time that he'd like to go back to school and get a certificate to teach high-school math. But that would radically lower the family's income, and he suspects that his wife, Jane, won't go for it. So he doesn't even mention it to her.

Entering the house, Harry feels he needs some time alone just to think about his future, particularly to brood about potential disasters. But Jane has also had a terrible day, and she wants to talk. She's been very worried about their oldest boy, who's been having behavior problems and is failing in school. She and the boy had a nasty argument after school, when she confronted him about his grades.

Jane is feeling incompetent as a mother, and she wants Harry's help. But for the past year or so, he's been overworked, depressed, and withdrawn from her and the children. Every time she tries to talk with Harry, he puts her off, so she winds up handling things alone. By now she's starting to feel very lonely. They haven't made love in months. Their relationship, however, can wait. Tonight she's determined to talk to Harry about their son. And she's determined that she's going to get some help from Harry right now.

How does Harry react to her demands? He explodes. "I've been dealing with one crisis after another all day," he growls. "All I want is a little window of peace when I get home so that I can read the newspaper and unwind. Is that too much to ask?"

"Yes, it is," Jane tells him. Especially considering that he's been absent from the family for quite some time, she thinks. "You've become a working machine. And if you don't care enough about me and the kids to deal with this, then why don't you just move out of here and live at the office?"

After a few more mean-spirited exchanges, Harry and Jane storm off to separate corners of the house to eat their dinners in a tension-filled silence.

Clearly there's an important conversation—or two or three—that Harry and Jane need to have. But because they haven't had that conversation, they had this fight instead.

If you're in a relationship where there seems to be an inordinate amount of conflict, you may want to take a look at the issues that *aren't* being discussed. Perhaps one person is making repeated bids for connection around a particular matter, only to have those bids ignored or dismissed. As we described in chapter 2, consistently turning away from one another's bids often leads to the type of hostility that destroys bonds. Or perhaps both of you are avoiding a hot issue because you believe that talking about it will just cause more problems. Trouble is, you're experiencing conflict and discomfort over the issue anyway. But if you talk about it, you open the possibility of breaking down the barrier that's growing between you.

As Wile explains, you typically have three choices when faced with an interpersonal conflict:

1. **Attack and defend.** This happens when you decide the other person's faults or inadequacies are to blame, so you lash out at that person, driving him or her away. If you're the recipient of such an attack, you get defensive, which also leads to alienation.
2. **Avoid or deny.** Here, you try to ignore or minimize your negative feelings about the problem. You tell yourself, "It's silly to feel this way," or "I just won't think about it and maybe it will go away." As the problem persists, however, it gets harder and harder to hold this position.
3. **Self-disclose and connect.** You can discuss how you feel about the problem and work on common understanding. Even if you don't find the perfect compromise or solution, you've at least established an emotional connection.

When you're tired of attack-and-defend, and you find that avoid-or-deny isn't working, then you're left with just one viable option—self-disclose and connect. Although talking about your feelings sounds simple, we all know that often it's not. If it were, you probably wouldn't have these problems in the first place, right? But my research and experience tell me there's a great place to start: *Focus on your feelings in the moment.* Also, know that you can talk about those feelings without acting on them. You can say:

- *"I feel so angry I want to yell at you."* But you don't have to yell. You can just talk about the feeling of wanting to yell. You talk about your anger.
- *"I feel so defensive that I just want to lash out at you."* But you don't have to lash out. You can talk about the feeling of wanting to do so. You talk about feeling defensive.
- *"I feel so upset I want to leave."* But you don't have to leave. You can stay and talk about the feeling of wanting to withdraw. You talk about being upset.
- *"I feel so scared that I want to ignore this problem and pretend it will go away."* But you don't have to ignore it. You can talk about how the problem makes you feel afraid. You can talk about your fear.

Talking about your feelings in this way doesn't make all your problems go away, nor does it solve conflicts. But it does create an opportunity to connect with that other person. You're not attacking and you're not withdrawing. Instead you're extending yourself and making a bid for understanding. If the other person can turn toward your bid, then you won't feel isolated anymore. You won't feel as if you're facing off at opposite ends of a boxing ring. You'll feel that you're together in the problem. You'll feel you can support one another emotionally as you work it out.

Let me give you an example. Kyle and Jessica are a couple who came to the Gottman Institute for help with sexual problems in their marriage. As a child, Jessica had been sexually abused by a close relative. Consequently she had a hard time feeling safe and relaxed in her sexual encounters with Kyle. His advances often made her feel terribly anxious, so she would push him away. Sometimes she'd feel so desperate to make him leave that she'd tell him that he wasn't good enough—that his body wasn't sexy or that his technique was all wrong. She knew this was untrue and unfair, and she felt terribly guilty about it. But at times it seemed the only way to protect herself from an anxiety that would overwhelm her. In doing so, Jessica was choosing option 1 from Wile's list: She was dealing with the problem by *attacking* Kyle.

Kyle felt there was little he could do about Jessica's anxiety. And he was getting tired of being hurt by her every time he wanted to get close. So after a while he simply stopped trying to touch Jessica sexually. He started focusing more on other things that bolstered his ego—his job, his friends, his hobbies. He was choosing option 2: He was dealing with the problem by *avoiding* Jessica.

Of course, neither option was good for Jessica and Kyle's marriage. So, in therapy, I persuaded them to start working on option 3: self-disclosure and connection. Instead of attacking Kyle when he tried to get close, Jessica would work on simply telling him how tense she was feeling in the moment when he touched her. And instead of withdrawing, Kyle would work on staying with Jessica in her tension and telling her how he was feeling in the moment as well. He wouldn't try to push her into having sex; he'd just listen, encourage her to talk about her feelings, and let her set the pace. But he wouldn't give up and walk away, either.

In one of our sessions, I asked them to close their eyes and imagine an encounter, talking through their emotions as they surfaced.

"I feel anxious," Jessica said after a few minutes of silence.

I asked her to talk about the physical sensations she was feeling.

"It's hard to breathe," she said. "I feel this tightness in my jaw."

I asked Kyle how he felt.

"Like I don't need this. I just want to bag it. I just want to walk away," he replied.

"Can you tell Jessica how you're feeling?" I asked. After a pause, he said softly, "I feel like forgetting it. I feel like you just want me to leave you alone, so . . . I don't want to be here."

"I know," Jessica said, just as softly. "Part of me wants you to leave, to push you away. But that's not what I really want." Then, after a long silence, she added, "It just feels tense, that's all. You know, like it always has."

I told them both to breathe, to stay present, and to keep talking about how they were feeling in the moment.

"I feel edgy," Jessica said. "In my muscles, in my skin."

"I feel bad, like you're going to say I'm a loser, that I can't get it right," Kyle said.

"No, it's not that. I know it's not your fault. It's me. I'm just . . . tense. I feel tense."

"I feel . . . sad. Like I want to help you, but I can't," Kyle said.

"I know," Jessica said. "But it's okay."

"All right. I can't do anything, but I'll just stay here, okay?"

"Okay. I don't want you to leave," Jessica said, breathing deeply. "It's okay."

"I'll just stay here, then, and be with you," Kyle said, breathing deeply as well.

And so the conversation went as the couple continued to breathe together, to express their feelings, and to soothe one another. As we used the technique in subsequent sessions, they got increasingly better at focusing on their current feelings and describing them. I discouraged them from blaming one another, or from rehashing the history of their problem. Whenever they started to lose their way, I would remind them, "You have three choices—attack, avoid, or disclose. Make the third choice and tell one another how you feel right now."

Self-disclosure was not always the easy choice. Jessica didn't always want to stay with her anxiety. And Kyle didn't want to face his feelings of being hurt and rejected. But they were willing to keep working on the exercise because they saw how it was drawing them together and healing their relationship.

Over time, as Jessica and Kyle learned to use the technique at home, they built a foundation of emotional connection that allowed Jessica to relax. She stopped pushing Kyle away, and eventually started enjoying his sexual advances. As Kyle started feeling more confident, he grew more content in the relationship and quit withdrawing from Jessica.

This technique of focusing on your current feelings can help in all sorts of situations where people are avoiding the conversations they need to have:

- A single mom comes home after a bad day at the office to find her two school-aged kids clamoring for her attention. She feels so exhausted that it's hard to respond to their demands for dinner and homework help. She can (1) blow up and tell them to leave her alone; (2) lock herself in the bathroom without a word; or (3) tell them how she's feeling and ask for their support: "Hey, you two, I had a terrible day and I feel drained. Let me go soak in the tub for twenty minutes, and when I get done, I'll do my best to help you." With this she helps the kids to understand why she's acting so down. They know they're not to blame; in fact, they can be part of the solution. It may not be the response the kids want to hear, but it provides a way for them to understand what their mother is experiencing. It's the conversation they need to have.

- A woman who's been battling depression wants to talk with her older brother about a traumatic incident they survived together as children. Her brother, who has never been comfortable talking about the incident, tries to dodge the conversation time and time again. Sometimes he teases her, telling her she ought to write a sappy memoir. At other times he brushes off her concerns and says, "Quit feeling sorry for yourself." The woman feels hurt that her brother doesn't care enough to talk seriously about the issue. In her disappointment, she can (1) lash out at him and tell him he's an insensitive jerk; (2) give up and let her resentment become a wedge between them; or (3) tell her brother how it feels in the moment when he dismisses her attempts to talk about the matter: "I feel hurt that you don't care more about my problems." Then she might invite him to share how he's feeling in the moment: "You seem to feel uncomfortable talking about this and I wish I understood why." She could even take a chance at trying to help him to identify his feeling. "Is it hard for you to talk about this because it's painful to remember what happened?" Or, "Maybe it makes you feel sad to talk about this because you wish you could have protected us both." He may or may not respond to this invitation. But if he does, it may help them to develop a deeper, richer relationship. It could be the conversation they need to have.

While these types of self-disclosing, trusting conversations are extremely valuable, you can't have them unless both parties are willing to work on the relationship. If only one person talks about his or her feelings, engaging in a conversation like this may feel like too much of a risk for that person. But if each person can take even the smallest steps toward self-disclosure, it can make a tremendous difference. Even when you feel as though you can't talk about an issue, expressing those feelings of fear, reluctance, or anxiety is a sign of willingness and trust. And that small step can move the relationship in the right direction.

## Looking Ahead

Improving your ability to bid and respond to bids is not going to solve all your problems. It will not banish all negative feelings. It will not solve all conflicts. But it will help you to get along better with people, to share life's burdens, and to build better connections with significant people in your life.

You can improve your skills in this area by discovering more about the basics of human emotion, which is the focus of the next three chapters of the book. In Step Two: Discover Your Brain's Emotional Command Systems, you'll learn about the latest discoveries in brain physiology, which show that each of us has a unique configuration of brain-based emotional command systems. These systems affect the way we experience emotions, and thus affect our personalities and the way we bid and respond to others. You'll see, through a series of questionnaires, which command systems are the most dominant in your life and how they may impact your bidding interactions and contribute to your current sense of emotional well-being.

In Step Three: Examine Your Emotional Heritage, you'll take a look at your past, discovering how previous experiences may affect your bids. You'll learn, for example, how your unique family history may have created enduring vulnerabilities that influence the way you now think about feelings and deal with other people's feelings. This, too, can color your bids and the way you respond to others' bids. Becoming more aware of these influences, however, helps you build stronger bonds with friends, family, and coworkers.

Then, in Step Four: Sharpen Your Emotional Communication Skills, you'll read some very concrete, practical advice for improving your skills at sending and receiving emotional information in the bidding process.

These three steps—understanding aspects of brain physiology, examining emotional heritage, and sharpening communication skills—are presented together because of the way they interact to define who we are emotionally. Research scientists are continually discovering how neurophysical pathways in the brain influence the way we behave. At the same time they are learning that the way we behave affects how those neurophysical pathways develop. The implications of such research are clear: As organic, living human beings, we have the capacity to grow and develop continually. With insight and skill-building, we can create in our lives an upward spiral of better emotional awareness and better relationships.

# 4

# Step Two: Discover Your Brain's Emotional Command Systems

*I*magine that a group of seven old friends meets for a reunion at a wilderness resort. They've been looking forward to the trip for weeks, and upon arriving, each person has a clear vision of how to make the gathering a success. Because they're such a well-rounded group, these visions vary quite a bit. And within an hour, each friend is bidding for connection around his or her top priority. Take a look.

*Christopher could be dubbed the **Commander-in-Chief.** He's the one who planned the gathering and chose the site. He likes the place because there are no distractions. Everybody can concentrate on the activities he planned for the group—hiking, river rafting, and rock climbing. He figures he may get resistance about the rock climbing, but he's not worried. He'll bring the dissidents around. Christopher's first bid? He wants help unloading the gear and getting organized.*

*Merrill is the **Explorer.** As soon as she arrives, she drops her suitcase in the cabin, and grabs a topographical map and a compass. She's so excited to be out here in the great unknown, she can hardly contain herself. She feels compelled to check out every trail, every stream, every mountain peak. "Anybody up for a quick hike?" she asks. Finding no takers, she heads out on her own.*

*Carlos is the **Sentry.** He's the one who spotted the notice about grizzly bear attacks when the group stopped at the general store on their way in. In fact, he picked up some little bells for everybody to attach to their backpacks; if you don't surprise the bears, he said, they'll keep their distance. He's distributing the bells when he realizes that Merrill's gone. "She took off without a bell?" he asks, dismayed. "We'd better go find her."*

*Katie is the **Energy Czar.** Her first order of business is to review the schedule, the menu, the supplies. "Let's see, if we're going to hike twelve miles tomor-*

row and then go rock climbing the day after, we're going to need lots of nourishment and lots of rest. Did we bring enough trail mix and water bottles?"

Darrin is the **Sensualist.** His initial inspiration is to reconnect with Merrill. It's been years, but he hasn't forgotten the terrific fling they had in their junior year at college. He's pleased to see that she still wears her hair in that sexy French twist. And that walk of hers . . . Of course, Katie's not looking too bad, either.

Peter is the **Jester.** His first task is to hang the porch swing and set up a game table nearby. He's not concerned about the food, the schedule, or the bears. For him, the most important thing is to relax, have some laughs, play some games, and enjoy the surroundings.

Shelby is the **Nest-Builder.** She's got her eye on everybody else. After she helps Christopher unpack, she pitches in to assist Katie. Then she sits with Peter on the swing to swap a few jokes. She spots the kerosene lamp near the window. "Perfect," she says. "It will feel so cozy when we gather around the lamp after dinner. I just can't believe it—at last, everybody's here!"

Interesting mix of folks, don't you think? Now imagine yourself among them. Does any one character remind you of how you might behave in a similar situation? How about your spouse or other loved ones? What about your coworkers? Do you see them in the scenario? Perhaps you can see yourself or others in two or three of these characters. That wouldn't be surprising, since we created them based on seven distinct "emotional command systems" believed to be present in each person's brain.

These seven specific systems were first described by neuroscientist Jaak Panksepp, a researcher at Bowling Green State University. We have given them labels like "Commander-in-Chief," "Sensualist," and so on to help people understand how each system functions. Each one coordinates the emotional, behavioral, and physical responses needed for certain functions related to survival (rest, procreation, self-defense, etc.).

According to this theory, people differ in how much they like to have these systems stimulated. Identifying your own optimal level of stimulation is important for emotional well-being. First, it can help you to find roles with which you're most comfortable and most likely to succeed. And, second, it can help you understand how your comfort levels differ from others'—a factor that's significant when you bid for connection. If you've got a highly activated Explorer command system like Merrill, for example, you're likely to have some conflicts with Carlos, who has a highly activated Sentry system. And if you're like Christopher, with his highly charged Commander-in-Chief system, you may have conflicts trying to make decisions with somebody who's also got a dominant Commander-in-Chief system, simply because you both want to be in charge. As you'll see later in this chapter, acknowledging such emotional similarities and differences is an important part of bidding and responding to bids.

What exactly are these emotional command systems? Imagine your nervous system as a railroad and your emotions as its trains. The emotional command systems are the tracks on which your emotions run. They take your feelings in various directions, depending on the service you need to perform—exploring your surroundings, seeking sex, making friends, and so on.

In reality, emotional command systems are nerve-based circuits that coordinate electrochemical signals in the brain. Using a variety of experimental methods, scientists have proven the existence of at least seven separate systems. These pathways transmit messages from one nerve cell to the next until various body parts get the information they need to carry out the service desired.

How important are these systems? Consider the one we've labeled the Sensualist. It's the emotional command system believed to coordinate sexual response. When this system is activated, a person may feel a surge of excitement at the sight of a mate or potential mate. That feeling might be accompanied by an intense desire to kiss and hold that person. If everything goes according to nature's plan, the two people come together and become physically aroused, perhaps resulting in intercourse. Current research tells us that this particular circuit in the brain coordinates these complex functions to help ensure survival of the species through reproduction. Other circuits handle other important functions, such as sleep (the Energy Czar), bonding with others (the Nest-Builder), obtaining power (the Commander-in-Chief), and so on.

Each person has his or her own comfort zone within each emotional command system, a factor that may influence that individual's personality. Depending on what's happening in your life, you may feel that a particular system is being underactivated or overactivated. When you get out of your own comfort zone, you may feel sad, frustrated, anxious, or angry. But if you're at a level that's "just right," you're likely to feel happy, calm, or energized. So one part of examining your emotional command systems is to learn more about your relationship with yourself.

The second part is to learn about similarities and discrepancies between you and the people around you. Here's an example of how that might work with the Nest-Builder, the system that coordinates feelings of friendship and affiliation with other people. Two employees are invited to a weekend team-building retreat with the rest of their staff. One employee is quite social and feels very comfortable when her Nest-Building system is highly activated. She stays in a chipper mood through most of the event. But the other employee, who consistently prefers to spend time alone, is more comfortable when her Nest-Building system lies idle. Working in groups for long hours leaves her feeling tense and drained. By the end of the weekend, she's had it. Three weeks later, however, when the workers are back in their quiet, isolated office cubicles, the situation is reversed. The employee who has high Nest-Building needs feels tense and frustrated at spending so much time alone. And the employee who has low Nest-Building needs feels serene and energized from all her recent hours of solitude.

Your ability to regulate how much stimulation each of your emotional command systems receives can affect your life moment by moment as well as over the long term. In the short term, feeling out of sync with your current lifestyle or with those around you may put you in a bad mood. Over lengthy periods, it can influence your whole personality. People whose emotional command systems are chronically overactivated or underactivated may develop personality characteristics such as pessimism, irritability, fearfulness, belligerency, or melancholy.

Such negative characteristics can affect a person's style of bidding for connection, further exacerbating his or her emotional stress. Consider, for example, the person whose Nest-Builder system is persistently underactivated. It's a problem typically caused by chronic loneliness. If this person becomes pessimistic about making friends, she may lose confidence and develop a style of bidding that's so nonassertive she never connects with others. Or, she may develop a style of bidding that's so "needy" she scares potential friends away.

Or think about the person whose Commander-in-Chief system is chronically overactivated. An example might be a man with little talent or desire for leadership who gets thrust into a manager's job at work. Hour by hour, he's called upon to bid for other people's participation and support in the projects he initiates. But he's not comfortable taking charge, and the constant stress he feels from it leaves him irritable and depressed most of the time. Consequently, he often presents his bids in such harsh or pessimistic tones that his employees turn away from his requests. Their response only makes the manager feel worse about his performance, so he grows increasingly depressed and anxious.

As this example demonstrates, problems in relationships may be the result of living with one or more of your emotional command systems overactivated or underactivated. Such an imbalance can reduce your success at bidding and responding to others' bids. Problems in bidding can also result from misunderstandings that occur between people who have different levels of comfort within the emotional command systems. But you can avoid such problems by learning more about these systems and how they affect you and your family, friends, and coworkers.

## The Seven Systems and How They Affect Us

Panksepp, who first identified these emotional command systems, believes there are probably more than seven of them, but these are the systems he has found so far by scouring the scientific literature for the anatomical and physiological evidence that proves their existence in the brains of all mammals. Knowing these systems exist across all mammalian species tells us they are part of our evolutionary heritage. This means we're born pre-wired with these systems, which respond unconditionally to circumstances in our environment that may affect our species' ability to survive and prosper.

Below, you'll find a brief description of each system, what it's responsible for, and what typically happens when it's underactivated or overactivated. The chart on page 98 gives an abbreviated version of this information.

**The Commander-in-Chief.**   This is the emotional command system in everybody's brain that coordinates functions related to dominance, control, and power. You're most likely to activate this system when you need to break free from restrictions, take charge of a situation, or force action. You might call upon the Commander-in-Chief inside you when you feel physically threatened, when you think you're being treated unfairly, or whenever you feel blocked from achieving a goal. It can be a great help during a competitive soccer game or a cutthroat sales contest.

Consider the baby who's frustrated after being held too close for too long. The system that makes her fuss, struggle, thrash, and cry is the Commander-in-Chief. She wants out of her front-pack, and she wants out now!

Think of a cruel dictator whose authority and power is challenged. The system that makes him lash out and attack the people who rise up against him is the Commander-in-Chief.

Or imagine that you're walking down the street and somebody tries to snatch your shoulder bag. The Commander-in-Chief makes you hang on tight and fight to keep it.

When your Commander-in-Chief is at its optimum level, you feel confident about the challenges you face, because you're not afraid to assert yourself to get what you need.

When your Commander-in-Chief is overactivated, you can be driven to anger, rage, aggression—even violence—to get what you want. When it's underactivated, you may feel impotent, frustrated, and overly passive—especially in the face of obstacles, injustice, or personal attack.

**The Explorer.**   Searching, learning, and satisfying one's curiosity are the functions that this system organizes. Our distant ancestors probably relied on the Explorer to find food, water, and a dry cave, but we're more likely to use it on a shopping expedition or while surfing the Internet for cool Web sites.

The Explorer comes into play whether we're seeking information for a business paper, ingredients for that special sauce, or a date for Saturday night. It may involve behaviors such as questioning, hunting, foraging, sorting, processing, planning, learning, and goal-setting.

You're likely to give your Explorer a good workout when you travel to a foreign country, take a seminar on a subject you've never studied before, or learn to play bridge.

When your Explorer is optimally engaged, you typically feel a sense of high expectation, pleasurable excitement, or intense interest. You're full of anticipation, and you feel a sense of mastery as you move closer to your desired goal.

When your Explorer is overactivated, you may feel compelled to keep exploring, keep searching, keep pressing forward even in the face of exhaustion. In extreme situations, an overactivated Explorer might be diagnosed as manic or schizophrenic behavior.

When the Explorer is underactivated, you may feel bored and restless, leading to irritability, anxiety, or depression.

**The Sensualist.** Of all seven systems, the Sensualist—which coordinates functions related to sexual gratification and reproduction—may be the one that seems most familiar. After all, people often describe sexual feelings as automatic responses. We speak of "falling in love" as though rational thought had nothing to do with it. We use the word "chemistry" to describe intangible bonds between lovers. We accept that sex-related hormones drive adolescents (of all ages) to behave erratically.

The Sensualist system can account for all this mystery. It organizes a broad gamut of sexual functions, including erotic dreams and fantasies; feelings of sexual attraction and excitement; involuntary physiological responses such as vaginal lubrication and penile erection; and sexual behaviors like flirting, kissing, and copulation.

When activated to its best advantage, the Sensualist allows a person to feel highly energized and pleasurably gratified.

When the Sensualist is overactivated, people may feel a sense of sexual longing that leads to inappropriate behavior such as the coercion of an unwilling partner. They might take sexual risks that threaten their health, such as having unprotected sex with a stranger. Or they might violate the integrity of their relationships with others through illicit affairs.

When the Sensualist is underactivated, a person might feel an aversion toward sex that causes problems in their marriage or love relationship. They also may feel sexually "shut down," leading to sadness and depression.

**The Energy Czar.** This system is responsible for making sure that the body gets the rest and care it needs to stay healthy. When you work or play too long, the Energy Czar sends your body signals that it's time to stop and get rejuvenated. Mild signals may include feelings of fatigue or boredom. Ignore them for a while and you're likely to become drowsy or irritable. Ignore them for a long time and you may develop serious problems, such as a weakened immune system or chronic illness.

In addition, the Energy Czar tells us when the body is hungry, thirsty, hot, cold, tired, or otherwise physically uncomfortable. When people find themselves in situations where these needs aren't being met, the Energy Czar ensures that the brain and body do what's necessary for comfort and survival.

We activate it when we plan restful vacations, choose activities we find relaxing, or resolve to get a good night's sleep. The Energy Czar can be a source of great pleasure as we anticipate a soak in a hot tub or schedule a massage. It's part of the relief we feel when we finish a grueling project or lay our heads down at the end of a long day.

The Energy Czar is operating at an optimal level when we can remain physically and emotionally comfortable without a lot of extra stress and effort.

When the Energy Czar is overactivated, we may become obsessed with issues like fatigue, stress, diet, exercise, or weight control. In extreme cases, such obsessions become the center of people's lives, leading to problems such as insomnia or eating disorders.

When the Energy Czar is underactivated, we may pay too little attention to issues of rest, stress relief, and physical comfort. We may disregard signs of exhaustion and keep going even when our bodies say it's time to stop. We may ignore the body's need for good nutrition, hydration, and exercise. Ignoring such needs can lead to a broad range of health problems related to stress, poor nutrition, lack of fitness, immune deficiency, and more.

**The Jester.** This system coordinates a class of functions much appreciated but often undervalued by many: play, recreation, and diversion. Behaviors associated with the Jester include playing games, seeking entertainment, telling jokes, engaging in make-believe, and simply "fooling around."

Imagine having lunch with a friend who *always* makes you laugh. Afterward, you feel refreshed, lighter, and better prepared to face life's challenges. Or think about a brainstorming session where the group feels free to say whatever comes to mind. All kinds of wacky notions surface, but together you also hatch some great new ideas. This is the Jester at work, helping people to both relax and renew. As the term *recreation* suggests, playfulness renews our creative abilities. It can lead to the formation of new bonds, enhance cooperation, and bolster our skills at creative problem solving. And because play reduces stress, it may reduce all sorts of health risks as well.

The Jester plays an especially crucial role in childhood. Children learn a tremendous amount through play: how to negotiate complex social structures, for example, and how to regulate emotions during periods of intense excitement. The need for such lessons doesn't disappear with age—which is why the Jester continues to be an essential part of our journey as adults.

When the Jester is activated to an ideal degree, you're likely to feel a sense of relaxed stimulation, a combination of serenity and joy.

The Jester can become overactivated, however. Think of children who get so "wound up" roughhousing that you have to separate them physically in order to get them to settle down. Like the person whose Explorer system is highly overactive, somebody with an extremely overactivated Jester might be considered manic.

When your Jester is underactivated, you're likely to feel inhibited, lethargic, or emotionally "dull." In the extreme, you might become chronically depressed.

**The Sentry.** It's no mystery how this emotional command system relates to survival. The Sentry coordinates functions in the body and mind related to worry, fear, vigilance, and defense. This system can keep you awake at night, wondering when you last replaced the batteries in your smoke alarm. It's what stops you cold at the sound of footsteps in a dark parking garage. It makes you yank your child out of a busy street or run like hell at the sight of a mountain lion.

When optimally activated, the Sentry helps you to regulate your fear by avoiding danger. Most days, that simply means you're motivated to take the right precautions. You wear a helmet while bike riding. You lock your doors at night. You don't pick fights in bars. But the Sentry doesn't *really* get to shine until you face an immediate, life-threatening situation, such as an auto accident, an armed robbery, or an encounter with a rattlesnake. In such situations the Sentry rallies your nervous system to make you hyper-alert and super-responsive so that you can fight, flee, or take whatever action you must to survive. In fact, the Sentry may call upon the Commander-in-Chief system to engage the functions of rage and attack, all in the name of defending self and others.

Although the Sentry is extremely active in such threatening situations, we don't consider it overactive. That's because it's helping the body to respond appropriately to threatening circumstances. The Sentry is overactivated when a person experiences unnecessary fears that interfere with living a normal, productive life. One example might be the person who feels constantly anxious about cancer risks—even after having all the recommended screenings. Parents who can never let their children out of their sight—even in a safe environment—are another example.

In extreme cases, an overactivated Sentry may be expressed as paranoia, phobias, or obsessive-compulsive disorder. Post-traumatic stress disorder—a condition that causes people to reexperience feelings of panic and fear long after an initial traumatic episode—may also be the result of an overactive Sentry.

When the Sentry is underactive, a person may not practice enough vigilance to stay safe. An example might be the thrill-seeker who enjoys "cheating death" through dangerous or careless activity.

**The Nest-Builder.** This system calls to mind all the nurturing, affiliating, and bonding behaviors and feelings typically activated in a solid parent-child relationship. That's because the Nest-Builder coordinates functions related to affiliation, bonding, and attachment. But we engage this system when we form other types of relationships as well, including friendship and marriage. It may also come into play as we become attached to work teams, jobs, clubs, schools, and other communities of people.

The Nest-Builder organizes our activities when we nurture another's growth, care for another's needs, and express affection. The Nest-Builder is what drives you to make new friends in your freshman year, join a church or synagogue, and call your aunt Betty on her birthday. A toddler who cries when his mother leaves does so because of the signals he receives via the Nest-Builder system.

In an ideal situation, activating the Nest-Builder helps you feel loved and needed. It brings about relationships that serve as a source of comfort and support in your life. You get a sense of belonging. And because the Nest-Builder organizes functions related to bonding, it's also activated when affiliations are broken because of death, divorce, the breakup of an affair, or the deterioration of a friendship. When you feel emotionally hurt because of the way a loved one is treating you, that pain is probably brought to you by the Nest-Builder.

What happens when the Nest-Builder is chronically overactivated? People may have problems establishing personal boundaries in their relationships. A person who constantly subordinates his or her own needs to those of others is one example. A person who seems incapable of making decisions independently, or who constantly seeks others' approval, is another. Those with overactive Nest-Builder systems may feel panicky at the thought of separation. Sadly, such relationships often collapse under the weight of irritation, resentment, and martyrdom.

A chronically underactivated Nest-Builder may be a result of isolation and loneliness, which leads to feelings of sadness and anxiety. In the extreme, a person in this situation may experience chronic depression and despair.

## Command Systems Often Act Together

Although we have described the way emotional command systems act separately, the brain can also activate two or more of them in the service of a specific need. For instance, a mother who lashes out at a bully threatening her child is activating the Nest-Builder and Commander-in-Chief systems at the same time. The Nest-Builder mediates her loyalty to her child, while the Commander-in-Chief coordinates her energy to attack.

Here's another example: A couple might activate both their Sensualist and Jester systems to have a great time on a date. And if they take their Nest-Builder along, they might launch a romance to last a lifetime.

The Explorer system is often called upon to help other systems find elements necessary to complete their functions. The Sensualist system, for example, might need help from the Explorer to find a mate. And the Energy Czar might depend on the Explorer to forage for food.

## What Determines How You Use Your Command Systems?

Many factors can affect how comfortable you feel when your emotional command systems are active at various levels. Some of these factors are "pre-wired." In other words, we're born with them. Other factors are the result of our experiences.

The temperament you inherit is one of those pre-wired influences. If your mother was the ultimate trailblazer, for example, you may also have a natural tendency to prefer high activation in the Explorer system. On the other hand, if you inherited your father's more conservative, homebody nature, you may be naturally prone to seek less adventure. In this case, you'd feel driven to keep your Explorer system fairly inactive.

Gender is also important, according to the anthropologist Richard Leakey. While male and female groups seem to be equally comfortable activating the Sensualist, the Explorer, and the Energy Czar, Leakey points to differences that appear in the other systems. Males generally seem to have a much stronger tendency to activate the Commander-in-Chief system, with its functions of coordinating dominance, and the brain's Sentry, with its utility for protection and vigilance. Males also show more development in the Jester system, which coordinates diversionary activities, like playing games and seeking amusement. Females, on the other hand, tend to have a more highly developed Nest-Builder, the system that controls affiliation, bonding, and attachment.

In addition to the gender and temperament you're born with, your life experiences can also influence the development of your emotional command systems. It may seem obvious that a child raised in a family that displays a great deal of fear, for example, is more likely to grow up to be a hypervigilant person than a child reared in a more trusting environment. And a child who is raised with lots of humor, fun, and play appreciates a good laugh as well. What's more surprising, however, is the idea that our environment actually affects the way nervous pathways in the brain get

## Seven Emotional Command Systems

| Emotional command system | Functions the system coordinates | Behaviors linked to the system | Feelings linked to the system | When the system is overactivated | When the system is underactivated |
|---|---|---|---|---|---|
| Commander-in-Chief | Dominance, control | Seeking power, freedom; forcing action | Confidence, power | Anger, aggression, rage, violent attack | Impotence, passivity, frustration |
| Explorer | Exploration, discovery | Seeking, learning, questioning, planning, goal-setting | Curiosity, anticipation, excitement, interest, mastery | Intense sensation-seeking, overwork, manic behavior | Restlessness, boredom, irritation, anxiety |
| Sensualist | Sexual gratification, procreation | Sexual seeking, flirtation, arousal, sexual contact, intercourse | Excitement, pleasure | Sexual risk-taking, coercion, sexual harassment | Aversion, depression |
| Energy Czar | Regulates need for energy, rest, relaxation | Rest, relaxation, nourishment, exercise | Anticipation, satiety, pleasure, satisfaction | Obsession with stress relief, sleep, diet, body weight | Fatigue, exhaustion, depression, weakened immune system |
| Jester | Recreation, diversion | Play, amusement, joking, creative pursuits, sports, games, make-believe | Relaxation, joy, serenity, ecstasy | Extreme silliness, manic behavior | Lethargy, depression, inhibition |
| Sentry | Defense, vigilance | Worry, seeking safety, prevention, protection | Apprehension, tension, anxiety, fear | Unrealistic fears, phobia, paranoia; overprotectiveness; intense anxiety; obsessive-compulsive disorders; hyper-vigilance | Cavalier behavior, carelessness, unsafe risk-taking |
| Nest-Builder | Affiliation, bonding, attachment | Nurturing, caring, forming friendships, expressing affection, experiencing loss and grief | Love, belonging, self-worth, being needed, separation, distress, grief | Irritability, loss of personal boundaries, martyrdom, panic when faced with separation | Loneliness, depression, anxiety, trouble healing from loss or grief |

built. In other words, the brain is actually quite malleable in its construction, and appears to stay that way throughout life. Brain scientists believe, for example, that the amount of gentle, nurturing attention an infant receives influences the way the nerve cells in her brain are arranged within her Nest-Builder system. Consequently, people who have had lots of cuddling and affection as babies may seek more of this kind of stimulation than people who didn't get this type of care. By the same token, the amount of wrestling, tickling, and game-playing a child gets may affect the formation of the system that coordinates play—the Jester. In similar ways, the development of other emotional command systems may be influenced by a person's experiences.

Our emotional command systems may be modified through single experiences as well, although this is probably more rare. As an extreme example, consider what happens to people who survive extremely frightening, life-threatening events and then develop post-traumatic stress disorder. In such instances, the Sentry—the system that coordinates fear and vigilance—produces a bombardment of electrical and chemical signals that cause a strong fear response throughout the body, affecting respiration, heart rate, and other bodily functions. This strong response may be totally appropriate given what's happening to that person in the moment. But the extraordinary power of this one traumatic event can also change the way the Sentry responds in the future. When trauma survivors are exposed to stimuli that remind them of their initial traumatizing event, their Sentry systems may respond with those same fearful reactions, even if the current situation is not at all dangerous. A war veteran, for example, may always feel panicky at the sound of fireworks on the Fourth of July. A victim of childhood sexual abuse may always feel anxious around sights, smells, or sounds that remind her of her abuser.

Understanding emotional command systems helps us to see that emotional processes are part of our evolutionary heritage. Our feelings are an integral part of the body's nervous system. We don't fabricate emotions merely to amuse and torment ourselves, or to manipulate other people. Rather, emotions are part of nature's design to help the species survive. As human beings, we can make conscious choices about the way we interpret and express our feelings. But some of our emotional experience is involuntary—the result of an organic electrochemical process in our nervous system. Whether the systems we use to process emotional reactions are formed by the genetic material we've inherited, by our life experience, or by both, our emotions are partly the result of the way our brain and nervous system are physically wired.

By the same token, people may or may not have much control over the level of activation they need (or don't need) within a particular emotional command system. If you're born with a high need for activation in the Nest-

Builder arena, for example, you may crave affiliation with others all your life, and be unsatisfied unless you have it. And no matter what you or others do to try to change that in you, such change may not be possible. The same might be true for another person when it comes to the Sentry, the Sensualist, and so on.

But through better understanding of our emotional command systems and how they affect us, we can bring about positive changes in our lives and in our relationships. We may be better able to recognize, for example, that ongoing conflicts with others may stem from discrepancies in our command systems. By identifying such discrepancies, we can find ways to accept them and work around them.

## Evaluate Your Emotional Command Systems

On the following pages you'll find a set of self-tests to help you assess your own comfort level within each of seven emotional command systems. You'll also find questionnaires designed to test whether your current life experience is overstimulating you or understimulating you within each system.

Completing these tests may help you in three ways. It can:

1. **Build your awareness of your own emotional needs.** Your answers may shed light on why you're attracted to certain people, activities, or subject matter—why you sometimes feel certain irrepressible longings or feel compelled to behave in certain ways. Better knowledge of your own comfort zone within each emotional command system may help in planning your leisure time, guiding your career, choosing friends, or finding a mate.
2. **Improve your ability to make bids and respond to other people's bids for connection.** Instead of making bids in ways that are unconscious or ambiguous, you'll be able to say, "I know what I need and I understand why I need it."
3. **Help you to better understand the people you're close to.** The exercise gives you a structured way to consider how others in your life are affected by their own emotional command systems, and how these effects may color your relationships with them.

Like the other exercises in this book, you can complete these questionnaires alone or you can invite your spouse, a friend, or a family member to complete them with you. Keep in mind that this exercise is very detailed and revealing. So, if you're going to do it with another person, you'll need a good level of trust to start with. If you choose to do it with someone, I encourage you to share your results with one another in a spirit of fun and adventure.

After all, you'll be learning new things about each other that may enhance your relationship and your life.

If you choose to do the exercise alone, you can still use it to do a partial evaluation of your relationship, simply by filling out the questionnaire for the other person, imagining how he or she might answer the questions.

Obviously, the first approach is best because it fosters communication, which is essential to building deeper, richer relationships. But the second way may also help, because it encourages you to imagine the world as that person experiences it. Either way, you may gain a better understanding of this person—an understanding that can lead to deeper empathy, tolerance, and acceptance.

Whether you decide to complete the questionnaires on your own or with another person, try to set aside about an hour of uninterrupted time to do so. And remember, there are no right answers, no norms to aim for. In fact, you may find that your answers change quite a bit as your lifestyle changes. Getting married, having a child, getting divorced, growing older— all these events can greatly influence how you activate various emotional command systems. Imagine that you're studying a map to find your current location. Once you know where you are, you can choose the path you'd most like to pursue in the future. The journey includes discovering more about yourself and others so that you can improve your ability to bid and respond to bids for connection. At the end of this chapter you'll have a chance to see how this new knowledge can be integrated into your bidding process.

## The Commander-in-Chief System

### What's your comfort level?

For each item, circle the alternative that best fits you.

**SA** = strongly agree
**A** = agree
**N** = neutral
**D** = disagree
**SD** = strongly disagree

1. Sometimes I enjoy a good fight.  **SA   A   N   D   SD**
2. I will not let anyone take what is rightfully mine.
   **SA   A   N   D   SD**
3. I often feel righteously indignant.  **SA   A   N   D   SD**
4. I am relentless at accomplishing a goal.  **SA   A   N   D   SD**
5. If anything blocks my goal, I will become angry.
   **SA   A   N   D   SD**

**6.** I know what to do to deal with frustration and get what I want.
**SA  A  N  D  SD**

**7.** I enjoy being assertive.  **SA  A  N  D  SD**

**8.** I become angry quite easily.  **SA  A  N  D  SD**

**9.** I feel comfortable in a commanding role.  **SA  A  N  D  SD**

**10.** If crossed, I become hot under the collar.  **SA  A  N  D  SD**

**11.** I easily become angry in traffic.  **SA  A  N  D  SD**

**12.** I sometimes enjoy getting angry.  **SA  A  N  D  SD**

**13.** I hate to wait, and easily become impatient.  **SA  A  N  D  SD**

**14.** I enjoy being powerful in a work group.  **SA  A  N  D  SD**

**15.** In a group, I have trouble not being in control.
**SA  A  N  D  SD**

**16.** I demand my rights when I have to.  **SA  A  N  D  SD**

**17.** I don't usually back down when confronted with opposition.
**SA  A  N  D  SD**

**18.** I can imagine subduing someone who challenges my authority.
**SA  A  N  D  SD**

**19.** I enjoy a good debate for its own sake.  **SA  A  N  D  SD**

**20.** My goal in competition is to win.  **SA  A  N  D  SD**

**21.** I have trouble getting motivated for a task if I can't beat someone at it.  **SA  A  N  D  SD**

**22.** I am a competitive person.  **SA  A  N  D  SD**

**23.** My interest in a job position increases if I learn that someone else wants it, too.  **SA  A  N  D  SD**

**24.** I consider doing well at work something of a conquest.
**SA  A  N  D  SD**

**25.** I like being the one in charge.  **SA  A  N  D  SD**

**26.** I hate having my word challenged.  **SA  A  N  D  SD**

**27.** I can be authoritarian at times.  **SA  A  N  D  SD**

**28.** I will usually fight to get what I want.  **SA  A  N  D  SD**

**SCORING**

**SA** = 2 points
**A** = 1 point
**N** = 0 points
**D** = −1 point
**SD** = −2 points

**FOR THIS QUESTIONNAIRE**

A score of 25 or above is *high.*
A score of 12 to 24 is *medium.*
A score of 11 or below is *low.*
Add to get your total Commander-in-Chief Comfort Level score: _____.

### YOUR COMMANDER-IN-CHIEF COMFORT LEVEL SCORE

If you scored 12 or above, you're most comfortable when your Commander-in-Chief system is activated in the high to medium range. This means that you like a powerful role; you're comfortable with anger and assertiveness. You're most at ease when the Commander-in-Chief in you is activated a lot.

If you scored 11 or below, you're comfortable when your Commander-in-Chief system is fairly quiet. Most likely, you are comfortable being led. You don't need to compete much, or be in charge. You are slow to anger.

## Is your life in sync with your Commander-in-Chief system?

Next, evaluate your current experience with the Commander-in-Chief system by answering these questions. For each item, circle the alternative that best fits you.

### Part One

1. My current life does not provide me with enough opportunity to be in charge. **SA  A  N  D  SD**
2. I am too controlled by others. **SA  A  N  D  SD**
3. My authority is not really appreciated right now.
   **SA  A  N  D  SD**
4. I don't get much of a chance to be assertive right now.
   **SA  A  N  D  SD**
5. I miss being able to have a good argument or debate.
   **SA  A  N  D  SD**
6. Unfortunately, I keep suppressing my anger these days.
   **SA  A  N  D  SD**
7. I am stifling my instincts of leadership these days.
   **SA  A  N  D  SD**
8. I wish that I had a job with more power and responsibility.
   **SA  A  N  D  SD**
9. I would like to get a chance to show people that I can be in command.
   **SA  A  N  D  SD**
10. There is not enough of a chance for me to be effective and forceful in my life right now. **SA  A  N  D  SD**

### SCORING

**SA** = 2 points
**A** = 1 point
**N** = 0 points
**D** = −1 point
**SD** = −2 points

Add your score on Part One (items 1–10): _____.

*Part Two*

11. I don't enjoy being domineering. **SA A N D SD**
12. I don't get much pleasure from bossing people around.
    **SA A N D SD**
13. I wish I didn't have to be so commanding. **SA A N D SD**
14. I wish others would take more leadership than they do.
    **SA A N D SD**
15. I resent having to be the one who organizes everything.
    **SA A N D SD**
16. I am tired of being in charge all the time. **SA A N D SD**
17. I don't like having as much responsibility and control as I have to take.
    **SA A N D SD**

Now add your score on Part Two (items 11–17): _____.

**YOUR COMMANDER-IN-CHIEF CURRENT LIFE SCORE**

On Part One (items 1–10), if you scored 6 or more, you feel that your current life understimulates your Commander-in-Chief system. You need a life that provides more opportunities to be in charge than your current situation does.

On Part Two (items 11–17), if you scored 4 or more on these items, your current life pushes you to be more of a Commander-in-Chief than you want to be.

If you scored below 6 on Part One and below 4 on Part Two, your current life is just right for your Commander-in-Chief system.

## *The Explorer System*

### What's your comfort level?

For each item, circle the alternative that best fits you.

**SA** = strongly agree
**A** = agree
**N** = neutral
**D** = disagree
**SD** = strongly disagree

1. I become excited about the prospect of learning something new.
   **SA A N D SD**
2. I dislike the comfort of routines and usually welcome all changes.
   **SA A N D SD**
3. I enjoy change for its own sake. **SA A N D SD**

4. I become bored very easily. **SA A N D SD**
5. I am often thrilled about the possibility of exploration and adventure.
   **SA A N D SD**
6. I don't like things in my life to be very predictable.
   **SA A N D SD**
7. Life is a grand adventure for me. **SA A N D SD**
8. I am curious about what's just over that "next hill" in life.
   **SA A N D SD**
9. I like to seek new stimulation. **SA A N D SD**
10. I feel a thrill in mastering something new. **SA A N D SD**
11. After doing the same thing for a while, I am anxious to move on.
    **SA A N D SD**
12. I often want to visit new places and try new foods.
    **SA A N D SD**
13. Once I master something, I hate for conditions to stay the same. I'm
    looking for something new to master. **SA A N D SD**
14. At times, I find myself longing for new experiences.
    **SA A N D SD**
15. I love surprises. **SA A N D SD**
16. I love to travel. **SA A N D SD**
17. I am curious about many things I don't know about.
    **SA A N D SD**
18. I generally feel comfortable traveling. Travel for me is a pleasant expe-
    rience. **SA A N D SD**

**SCORING**

**SA** = 2 points
**A** = 1 point
**N** = 0 points
**D** = −1 point
**SD** = −2 points

**FOR THIS QUESTIONNAIRE**

A score of 20 or above is *high.*
A score of 12 to 19 is *medium.*
A score of 11 or below is *low.*
Add to get your total Explorer Comfort Level score: _____.

**YOUR EXPLORER COMFORT LEVEL SCORE**

If you scored 12 or above, your comfort level in the Explorer system is in the
medium to high range. This means that you like a lot of discovery, adventure,
and new experiences in your life. You're most at ease when the Explorer in
you is activated a lot.

If you scored 11 or below, you prefer predictability. You dislike change and don't require a great deal of adventure and new stimulation in your life. You are generally content with the way things are and enjoy routine. You are not much of an Explorer right now. You're most at ease when the Explorer in you is fairly quiet.

## Is your life in sync with your Explorer system?

Next, evaluate your current experience with the Explorer system by answering these questions.

1. My current life does not provide me with enough stimulation, newness, or adventure. **SA A N D SD**
2. My current life provides me with too much routine.
**SA A N D SD**
3. I find a lot in my life to be the same old thing and I am tired of it.
**SA A N D SD**
4. There is not enough stimulation in my life for me.
**SA A N D SD**
5. I think life moves at too slow a pace. **SA A N D SD**
6. I am bored a lot right now. **SA A N D SD**
7. I wish the pace of my life would speed up for a while and I could see more changes. **SA A N D SD**
8. I wish my life was less predictable. **SA A N D SD**
9. I yearn for more adventure. **SA A N D SD**
10. There are far too few surprises in my life. **SA A N D SD**

**SCORING**

**SA** = 2 points
**A** = 1 point
**N** = 0 points
**D** = −1 point
**SD** = −2 points

Add to get your total Explorer Current Life score: _____.

**YOUR EXPLORER CURRENT LIFE SCORE**

If you scored above 5, you feel that your current life understimulates your Explorer system. You need a life that gratifies the Explorer in you more than it does.

If you scored between −9 and 4, you feel that your current life is just right for stimulating your Explorer system.

If you scored below −10, you feel that your current life overstimulates your Explorer system. Your current life pushes you to be more of an Explorer than you want to be.

## *The Sentry System*

### What's your comfort level?

For each item, circle the alternative that best fits you.

**SA** = strongly agree
**A** = agree
**N** = neutral
**D** = disagree
**SD** = strongly disagree

1. It is easy to become a victim if you aren't vigilant.
   **SA   A   N   D   SD**
2. I treat the world as if it were a dangerous place.
   **SA   A   N   D   SD**
3. I see part of my role as making sure my loved ones are safe.
   **SA   A   N   D   SD**
4. I rarely feel totally safe myself.   **SA   A   N   D   SD**
5. I try hard to avoid unpleasant surprises and shocks.
   **SA   A   N   D   SD**
6. I believe that a little bit of forethought can avoid disasters.
   **SA   A   N   D   SD**
7. I tend to look for potential danger in ordinary situations.
   **SA   A   N   D   SD**
8. I have a hard time relaxing.   **SA   A   N   D   SD**
9. I tend to worry about the future.   **SA   A   N   D   SD**
10. I hate being startled.   **SA   A   N   D   SD**
11. Some seemingly normal situations can make me apprehensive, for good reason.   **SA   A   N   D   SD**
12. I think of myself as a protector of others.   **SA   A   N   D   SD**
13. Sometimes I can become a bit nervous or on edge.
    **SA   A   N   D   SD**
14. I am anxious in some social situations.   **SA   A   N   D   SD**
15. I can sense trouble brewing before other people can.
    **SA   A   N   D   SD**
16. I work hard to create a safe environment for myself and for people close to me.   **SA   A   N   D   SD**
17. It is important to me that my work environment creates very little anxiety.   **SA   A   N   D   SD**
18. I like to stay in control of things to avoid unpleasant surprises.
    **SA   A   N   D   SD**
19. I make myself stay vigilant so that I can be aware of potential trouble.
    **SA   A   N   D   SD**
20. I tend to be a worrier.   **SA   A   N   D   SD**

**21.** I dislike being alarmed.  **SA   A   N   D   SD**

**22.** I am easily frightened.  **SA   A   N   D   SD**

**23.** I can become panicky when things are not in order.
   **SA   A   N   D   SD**

**24.** I think of myself as a kind of guard or sentry for myself and the people close to me.  **SA   A   N   D   SD**

### SCORING

**SA** = 2 points

 **A** = 1 point

 **N** = 0 points

 **D** = −1 point

**SD** = −2 points

### FOR THIS QUESTIONNAIRE

A score of 20 or above is *high.*

A score of 12 to 19 is *medium.*

A score of 11 or below is *low.*

Add to get your total Sentry Comfort Level score: _____.

### YOUR SENTRY COMFORT LEVEL SCORE

If you scored 10 or above, your comfort level in the Sentry system is in the medium to high range. This means that you like the role of a Sentry; you are comfortable being vigilant for danger. You're most at ease when your Sentry is activated a lot.

If you scored below 10, you tend to stay carefree and relaxed. You're slow to become apprehensive. You are not into being much of a Sentry right now. You're most at ease when your Sentry is fairly quiet.

## Is your life in sync with your Sentry system?

Next, evaluate your current experience with the Sentry system by answering these questions.

**1.** My current life involves too much anxiety.  **SA   A   N   D   SD**

**2.** I need to be too wary in my everyday life.  **SA   A   N   D   SD**

**3.** I feel apprehensive about several aspects of my current life.
   **SA   A   N   D   SD**

**4.** I am worried a lot of the time.  **SA   A   N   D   SD**

**5.** Tensions often make it hard for me to get a good night's sleep.
   **SA   A   N   D   SD**

**6.** These days I have trouble letting down my guard.
   **SA   A   N   D   SD**

**7.** These days I find it very hard to relax.  **SA   A   N   D   SD**

**8.** I wish that I had more job security. **SA A N D SD**

**9.** I would like to feel more at ease with people important to me.
**SA A N D SD**

**10.** I could be a lot more creative if I felt safer. **SA A N D SD**

**11.** I have too much responsibility as a protector of the people I care about. **SA A N D SD**

**12.** I wish people looked to me less for their security.
**SA A N D SD**

**13.** I don't enjoy having to take care of other people's safety needs.
**SA A N D SD**

### SCORING

**SA** = 2 points
**A** = 1 point
**N** = 0 points
**D** = −1 point
**SD** = −2 points

Add to get your total Sentry Current Life score: _____.

### YOUR SENTRY CURRENT LIFE SCORE

If your score is above 7, you feel that your current life overstimulates your Sentry system. You need to feel safer in your life, less filled with apprehension. Your current life pushes you to be more of a Sentry than you want to be.

If you scored between 0 and 6, your Sentry system is being activated at just the right level for your comfort.

If you scored below 0, you feel that your current life understimulates your Sentry system.

## The Energy Czar System

### What's your comfort level?

For each item, circle the alternative that best fits you.

**SA** = strongly agree
**A** = agree
**N** = neutral
**D** = disagree
**SD** = strongly disagree

**1.** I usually have a lot of energy. **SA A N D SD**

**2.** I get little pleasure out of working so hard that I am burned out.
**SA A N D SD**

3. I can renew my energy when I am tired. **SA   A   N   D   SD**
4. I can monitor my life so that I don't usually become too exhausted. **SA   A   N   D   SD**
5. I have generally been able to create an environment that allows me enough rest and relaxation. **SA   A   N   D   SD**
6. I rarely long for vacations or time off from work. **SA   A   N   D   SD**
7. I am able to get enough sleep most nights. **SA   A   N   D   SD**
8. I don't need a nap most days. **SA   A   N   D   SD**
9. I usually wake feeling refreshed. **SA   A   N   D   SD**
10. It's easy for me to get away and reduce my stress level. **SA   A   N   D   SD**
11. In my life, things usually seem effortless. **SA   A   N   D   SD**
12. I rarely get exhausted and stressed out. **SA   A   N   D   SD**
13. I have lots of drive to get things done. **SA   A   N   D   SD**
14. I have little trouble finding the motivation to accomplish my goals. **SA   A   N   D   SD**
15. I find my life exciting. **SA   A   N   D   SD**
16. I generally have the will to accomplish anything I choose to do. **SA   A   N   D   SD**
17. I have little trouble finding the right balance between work and fun. **SA   A   N   D   SD**
18. I have quite a bit of drive. **SA   A   N   D   SD**
19. I always make sure that I eat the proper foods. **SA   A   N   D   SD**
20. I rarely ignore my basic daily physical needs (thirst, hunger, elimination). **SA   A   N   D   SD**

## SCORING

**SA** = 2 points
**A** = 1 point
**N** = 0 points
**D** = −1 point
**SD** = −2 points

## FOR THIS QUESTIONNAIRE

A score of 10 or above is *high.*
A score of 5 to 9 is *medium.*
A score of 4 or below is *low.*
Add to get your total Energy Czar Comfort Level score: _____.

## YOUR ENERGY CZAR COMFORT LEVEL SCORE

If you scored 7 or above, your comfort level in the Energy Czar system is in the medium to high range. This means that you feel you have a lot of energy to accomplish the things you set out to do in your life.

If you scored below 7, you have some trouble managing your energy level so that you can do the things in your life you value. You may feel tired a lot and you feel it's difficult for you to rejuvenate yourself.

## Is your life in sync with your Energy Czar system?

Next, evaluate your current experience with the Energy Czar system by answering these questions. For each item, circle the alternative that best fits you.

1. My life is currently too tiring. **SA   A   N   D   SD**
2. My job is exhausting. **SA   A   N   D   SD**
3. The demands on me are unreasonable, and I am burning out trying to meet them. **SA   A   N   D   SD**
4. There is so much stimulation in my life that it's ruining my sleep. **SA   A   N   D   SD**
5. Life is wearing me out. **SA   A   N   D   SD**
6. I am "wiped out" a lot. **SA   A   N   D   SD**
7. I haven't had a vacation in a long time. **SA   A   N   D   SD**
8. I don't have very much balance in my life right now. **SA   A   N   D   SD**
9. I yearn for more calm. **SA   A   N   D   SD**
10. There are too many stressful days in my everyday life. **SA   A   N   D   SD**

### SCORING

**SA** = 2 points
**A** = 1 point
**N** = 0 points
**D** = −1 point
**SD** = −2 points

Add to get your total Energy Czar Current Life score: _____.

### YOUR ENERGY CZAR CURRENT LIFE SCORE

If you scored 5 or above, you feel that your current life understimulates your Energy Czar system. You need more opportunities to restore your Energy Czar than your current life provides.

If you scored below 5, you are feeling "just right" related to your Energy Czar. You are managing the flow of energy in your life well right now.

## The Sensualist System

### What's your comfort level?

For each item, circle the alternative that best fits you.

**SA** = strongly agree
**A** = agree
**N** = neutral
**D** = disagree
**SD** = strongly disagree

1. I am a lusty person.  **SA  A  N  D  SD**
2. I enjoy flirting.  **SA  A  N  D  SD**
3. I seek out sexually provocative situations.  **SA  A  N  D  SD**
4. I love the initial phases of courtship.  **SA  A  N  D  SD**
5. I really enjoy sex.  **SA  A  N  D  SD**
6. I enjoy giving physical pleasure to someone I am attracted to.
   **SA  A  N  D  SD**
7. I am very sensual.  **SA  A  N  D  SD**
8. I enjoy having someone I am attracted to really excite me sexually.
   **SA  A  N  D  SD**
9. I see sexual possibilities in many situations.  **SA  A  N  D  SD**
10. I get horny easily.  **SA  A  N  D  SD**
11. I often lust after someone I have just met.  **SA  A  N  D  SD**
12. I love being in love.  **SA  A  N  D  SD**
13. I masturbate often.  **SA  A  N  D  SD**
14. I have sexual fantasies at the strangest times.  **SA  A  N  D  SD**
15. I get sexual cravings that I just can't stop.  **SA  A  N  D  SD**
16. I enjoy many forms of physical sensuality.  **SA  A  N  D  SD**
17. I enjoy fondling, caressing, kissing, and cuddling.
    **SA  A  N  D  SD**
18. Just being with someone attractive can really excite me.
    **SA  A  N  D  SD**
19. At heart I am very horny.  **SA  A  N  D  SD**
20. I strongly value the excitement of making love.  **SA  A  N  D  SD**
21. I think about sex often every day.  **SA  A  N  D  SD**

**SCORING**

**SA** = 2 points
**A** = 1 point
**N** = 0 points
**D** = −1 point
**SD** = −2 points

**FOR THIS QUESTIONNAIRE**

A score of 11 or above is *high.*
A score of 6 to 10 is *medium.*
A score of 5 or below is *low.*
Add to get your total Sensualist Comfort Level score: _____.

**YOUR SENSUALIST COMFORT LEVEL SCORE**

If you scored 6 or above, your comfort level in the Sensualist system is in the medium to high range. This means that you like a lot of sensual and sexual excitement in your life. You're most at ease when the Sensualist in you is activated a lot.

If you scored below 6, you prefer a limited amount of sexual and sensual stimulation in your life. You are not into being much of a Sensualist right now; you're most at ease when the Sensualist in you is fairly quiet.

## Is your life in sync with your Sensualist system?

Next, evaluate your current experience with the Sensualist system by answering these questions. For each item, circle the alternative that best fits you.

*Part One*

1. My current life does not provide me with enough sexual stimulation.
   **SA   A   N   D   SD**
2. In my current life, I don't get to have enough sensual experiences.
   **SA   A   N   D   SD**
3. My lusty side is not really appreciated right now.
   **SA   A   N   D   SD**
4. There is too much sexual distance in my life now.
   **SA   A   N   D   SD**
5. I am more of a lover than anyone gets to see these days.
   **SA   A   N   D   SD**
6. I need to find some more sensual experiences.
   **SA   A   N   D   SD**
7. I wish that I had a life with more sexual passion.
   **SA   A   N   D   SD**
8. I yearn for more romance in my life.
   **SA   A   N   D   SD**
9. I feel horny too much of the time.   **SA   A   N   D   SD**
10. There is not enough playful sex in my life right now.
    **SA   A   N   D   SD**

**SCORING**

**SA** = 2 points
**A** = 1 point
**N** = 0 points
**D** = −1 point
**SD** = −2 points

Add your score on Part One ＿＿＿.

## Part Two

**11.** I am overly involved in sexual thoughts.　**SA　A　N　D　SD**
**12.** My life demands more sex of me than I want.　**SA　A　N　D　SD**
**13.** I dislike how much I have to think about sex.　**SA　A　N　D　SD**
**14.** It's uncomfortable to be as sexually turned on as I usually am.
　　**SA　A　N　D　SD**

Add your score on Part Two ＿＿＿.

**YOUR SENSUALIST CURRENT LIFE SCORE**

For Part One (items 1–10), if your score is 4 or above, you feel that your current life understimulates your Sensualist system. You need more opportunities in your life to gratify the Sensualist in you than your current situation provides. If you scored below 4 on Part One, you feel that your current life is just right for stimulating your Sensualist system.

For Part Two (items 11–14), if your score is 3 or more, you feel that your current life overstimulates your Sensualist system. You need to be able to say no to situations that pressure you to be more sensual than is comfortable for you right now.

## The Jester System

### What's your comfort level?

For each item, circle the alternative that best fits you.

**SA** = strongly agree
**A** = agree
**N** = neutral
**D** = disagree
**SD** = strongly disagree

**1.** I enjoy seeing the absurd in life's situations.　**SA　A　N　D　SD**
**2.** I enjoy playful teasing.　**SA　A　N　D　SD**

**3.** Puns are delightful to me.   **SA   A   N   D   SD**
**4.** I love rough-and-tumble play.   **SA   A   N   D   SD**
**5.** I like poking fun at pompous people.   **SA   A   N   D   SD**
**6.** I sometimes like pretending I'm someone else.   **SA   A   N   D   SD**
**7.** I enjoy make-believe.   **SA   A   N   D   SD**
**8.** I have a well-developed silly side.   **SA   A   N   D   SD**
**9.** I can sometimes be carefree and rambunctious.
   **SA   A   N   D   SD**
**10.** I sometimes see the humor that others miss.   **SA   A   N   D   SD**
**11.** I like to clown around.   **SA   A   N   D   SD**
**12.** I enjoy a good snowball fight.   **SA   A   N   D   SD**
**13.** I like to tickle some people.   **SA   A   N   D   SD**
**14.** I have enjoyed rolling down a hill and laughing.
   **SA   A   N   D   SD**
**15.** I like being tickled.   **SA   A   N   D   SD**
**16.** I can imagine enjoying prancing around like a horse.
   **SA   A   N   D   SD**
**17.** I like to have pretend arguments with friends.   **SA   A   N   D   SD**
**18.** Mockery appeals to me.   **SA   A   N   D   SD**
**19.** I love to play with children.   **SA   A   N   D   SD**
**20.** I find slapstick comedy appealing.   **SA   A   N   D   SD**
**21.** I am a bit of a jester at heart.   **SA   A   N   D   SD**
**22.** I have chosen friends on the basis of our laughter together.
   **SA   A   N   D   SD**
**23.** I sometimes get into giggling fits.   **SA   A   N   D   SD**
**24.** Farting sounds are funny.   **SA   A   N   D   SD**

### SCORING

**SA** = 2 points
**A** = 1 point
**N** = 0 points
**D** = −1 point
**SD** = −2 points

### FOR THIS QUESTIONNAIRE

A score of 25 or above is *high.*
A score of 10 to 24 is *medium.*
A score of 9 or below is *low.*
Add to get your total Jester Comfort Level score: _____.

### YOUR JESTER COMFORT LEVEL SCORE

If you scored 10 or above, your comfort level in the Jester system is in the medium to high range. This means that you like a lot of play, humor, amusement, fun, hilarity, and make-believe in your life. You're most at ease when the Jester in you is activated a lot.

If you scored 9 or below, you prefer things in your life to be fairly serious, and you do not require a great deal of play in your life. You are not into being much of a Jester right now. You're most at ease when the Jester in you is fairly quiet.

### Is your life in sync with your Jester system?

Next, evaluate your current experience with the Jester system by answering these questions. For each item, circle the alternative that best fits you.

**1.** My current life does not provide me with enough fun.
**SA  A  N  D  SD**

**2.** My current life does not have enough playfulness in it.
**SA  A  N  D  SD**

**3.** My wit is not really appreciated right now.  **SA  A  N  D  SD**

**4.** There is too much seriousness in my life now.  **SA  A  N  D  SD**

**5.** I don't get enough of a chance to be carefree and cut up.
**SA  A  N  D  SD**

**6.** I am more of a clown than anyone gets to see these days.
**SA  A  N  D  SD**

**7.** I am stifling my playful instincts these days.  **SA  A  N  D  SD**

**8.** I wish that I had a life with more lightheartedness.
**SA  A  N  D  SD**

**9.** I yearn for more silliness in those around me.  **SA  A  N  D  SD**

**10.** There is not enough laughter in my life right now.
**SA  A  N  D  SD**

**SCORING**

**SA** = 2 points
**A** = 1 point
**N** = 0 points
**D** = −1 point
**SD** = −2 points

Add to get your total Jester Current Life score: _____.

**YOUR JESTER CURRENT LIFE SCORE**

If you scored above 6, you feel that your current life understimulates your Jester system. You need a life that gratifies the Jester in you more than your current situation does.

If you scored between −9 and 5, you feel that your current life is just right for stimulating your Jester system.

If you scored below −10, you feel that your current life overstimulates your Jester system. Your current life pushes you to be more of a Jester than you want to be.

## The Nest-Builder System

### What's your comfort level?

For each item, circle the alternative that best fits you.

**SA** = strongly agree
  **A** = agree
  **N** = neutral
  **D** = disagree
**SD** = strongly disagree

1. I enjoy nurturing others.  **SA   A   N   D   SD**
2. I enjoy taking care of other people.  **SA   A   N   D   SD**
3. I often like to see to people's needs.  **SA   A   N   D   SD**
4. I love to see children develop.  **SA   A   N   D   SD**
5. It gives me a sense of meaning to help other people.
   **SA   A   N   D   SD**
6. I like creating a cozy home.  **SA   A   N   D   SD**
7. I do (or would) enjoy teaching children.  **SA   A   N   D   SD**
8. I have a strongly developed parental side.  **SA   A   N   D   SD**
9. I often feel sad when I am alone.  **SA   A   N   D   SD**
10. I get lonely when I am not in a close relationship.
    **SA   A   N   D   SD**
11. I like making new friends.  **SA   A   N   D   SD**
12. I take the time needed to take care of my friends.
    **SA   A   N   D   SD**
13. I like to listen to my friends' problems.  **SA   A   N   D   SD**
14. I tend to think of other people's needs before my own.
    **SA   A   N   D   SD**
15. I think the greatest accomplishment in life is raising a good child.
    **SA   A   N   D   SD**
16. I make it a priority to spend time with friends.  **SA   A   N   D   SD**
17. I don't mind people depending on me.  **SA   A   N   D   SD**
18. I sometimes love to take care of children.  **SA   A   N   D   SD**
19. At heart, I am very parental.  **SA   A   N   D   SD**
20. I strongly value the cozy times of family closeness at home.
    **SA   A   N   D   SD**
21. I love cooking for the people I am closest to.  **SA   A   N   D   SD**

**SCORING**

> **SA** = 2 points
> **A** = 1 point
> **N** = 0 points
> **D** = −1 point
> **SD** = −2 points

**FOR THIS QUESTIONNAIRE**

A score of 20 or above is *high.*
A score of 12 to 19 is *medium.*
A score of 11 or below is *low.*
Add to get your total Nest-Builder Comfort Level score: \_\_\_\_.

**YOUR NEST-BUILDER COMFORT LEVEL SCORE**

If you scored 12 or above, your comfort level in the Nest-Builder system is in the medium to high range. This means that you like a lot of attachment and bonding, and you are a nurturing person. You're most at ease when the Nest-Builder in you is activated a lot.

If you scored below 12, you prefer independent relationships where people go their own separate ways much of the time. You don't require a great deal of bonding or caretaking in your life. You are not into being much of a Nest-Builder right now; you're most at ease when the Nest-Builder in you is fairly quiet.

## Is your life in sync with your Nest-Builder system?

Next, evaluate your current experience with the Nest-Builder system by answering these questions. For each item, circle the alternative that best fits you.

**1.** My current life does not provide me with enough intimacy.
**SA   A   N   D   SD**

**2.** In my current life, I don't get to take care of others enough.
**SA   A   N   D   SD**

**3.** My tender side is not really appreciated right now.
**SA   A   N   D   SD**

**4.** There is too much emotional distance in my life now.
**SA   A   N   D   SD**

**5.** I feel lonely too much of the time.   **SA   A   N   D   SD**

**6.** I am secretly more of a caretaker than anyone gets to see these days.   **SA   A   N   D   SD**

**7.** I need to make more close friends.   **SA   A   N   D   SD**

**8.** I wish that I had a life with more intimacy.   **SA   A   N   D   SD**

**9.** I yearn for more connection with those around me.
**SA   A   N   D   SD**

**10.** There is not enough affection in my life right now.
**SA   A   N   D   SD**

**SCORING**

> **SA** = 2 points
> **A** = 1 point
> **N** = 0 points
> **D** = −1 point
> **SD** = −2 points

Add to get your total Nest-Builder Current Life score: _____.

**YOUR NEST-BUILDER CURRENT LIFE SCORE**

If your score is above 6, you feel that your current life understimulates your Nest-Builder system. You need a life that gratifies the Nest-Builder in you more than your current situation does.

If you scored between −9 and 5, you feel that your current life is just right for stimulating your Nest-Builder system.

If you scored below −10, you feel that your current life overstimulates your Nest-Builder system. Your current life pushes you to be more of a Nest-Builder than you want to be.

## Exercise: Your Emotional Command System Score Card

After completing the Emotional Command System questionnaires, you may want to spend some time considering the implications this information holds for your life, your relationships, and the way you bid for connection. This exercise is designed to help you do that.

In the chart that follows, circle the word in the second column that describes your scores on the Comfort Level tests in each of the seven areas. This will help you to see at a glance how much (or little) you like to have each of the seven command systems activated in your life.

If you completed the questionnaires with another person (or if you imagined doing so), circle the word in the third column that describes how that person scored. In this way you can compare your comfort levels with those of your partner.

Finally, you can circle "yes" or "no" in the last column according to how you scored on the questionnaires that determined whether or not your current life is in sync with each of your emotional command systems. This may help you identify areas where you'd like to make changes in your life.

As you consider the information on this chart, you may also gain insights by answering the questions below. You may want to discuss your answers with someone close to you or write down your answers in your Emotion Log (see page 54).

| Emotional command systems | Comfort level | | Are you in sync with your system? |
| --- | --- | --- | --- |
| | Yours | Other's | |
| Commander-in-Chief | High | High | Yes |
| | Medium | Medium | No |
| | Low | Low | |
| Explorer | High | High | Yes |
| | Medium | Medium | No |
| | Low | Low | |
| Sentry | High | High | Yes |
| | Medium | Medium | No |
| | Low | Low | |
| Energy Czar | High | High | Yes |
| | Medium | Medium | No |
| | Low | Low | |
| Sensualist | High | High | Yes |
| | Medium | Medium | No |
| | Low | Low | |
| Jester | High | High | Yes |
| | Medium | Medium | No |
| | Low | Low | |
| Nest-Builder | High | High | Yes |
| | Medium | Medium | No |
| | Low | Low | |

**Questions to consider:**

- Which of your emotional command systems would you like to use more in your life?
- What changes would you need to make for this to happen?
- Which of your emotional command systems would you like to use less in your life?
- What changes would you need to make for this to happen?
- How are you different from others around you, in terms of the way you each use your emotional command systems? How are you the same?
- How might the recognition of these differences and similarities help your relationships?
- How do your differences or similarities affect the way you bid for connection with this person? How do they affect your responses? What changes could you make to improve this process?

## Putting Your Knowledge to Work

When I first learned about the concept of emotional command systems, I was excited for many reasons. Mostly, I was intrigued at how the concept might help people to use their emotional energy to achieve positive life goals.

Too often, people feel angry, sad, or fearful, and they're not sure why. But when you understand your own emotional command systems, you have a direction in which to take your negative emotions. For example, rather than simply saying, "I feel angry," you can say, "I feel angry because I can't seem to control my own work schedule. I need to activate my Commander-in-Chief to get more control and power in my life." Or, "I feel a sense of fear in life. Why is that? How can I activate my Sentry and make myself feel safer?" From this perspective you can plan to make changes that will help you feel more at ease within the various command systems. You can also take steps to bolster the emotional connections with people in a broad range of relationships. By doing so, you can enhance your feelings of well-being and improve your life.

Let me give you an example from my own life. In 1999, Neil Jacobson, a close friend and collaborator of mine, died suddenly of a heart attack. The months following his death were very difficult for many of us, and I found myself feeling depressed much of the time. Neil had been one of my oldest and dearest colleagues, and once he was gone, there were no other men in my life at the university with whom I felt so close.

When I thought about this sadness in terms of the Nest-Builder—the system that organizes our emotions around affiliation and friendship—I could see that my emotional life without Neil was clearly underactivated. No wonder I felt so sad for so long. And while I know there's no way that I can possibly replace what I had with Neil in my life, I could see that, to move through my sadness, I needed closer ties with other male friends in my community. With this insight, I knew what to do with my sadness. I was able to develop a plan of action to start working through my grief.

## Accepting Ourselves and Others

Knowing that our brains are wired in various and highly individualized ways allows us to be more compassionate and tolerant toward ourselves and others. It helps us to build better relationships through understanding and accepting our differences.

There's a scene in Woody Allen's classic comedy *Annie Hall* that illustrates this challenge beautifully. Annie and her boyfriend, Alvie, are each talking to their therapists in separate frames. The therapists simultaneously ask how often the couple has sex.

"Hardly ever," Alvie complains. "Three times a week."

"All the time," whines Annie. "Three times a week."

The scene draws big laughs because it speaks to one of the most universally difficult aspects of close relationships: how to reconcile our distinct preferences about matters such as sex, adventure, power, and friendship. All those issues are regulated by our emotional command systems. They are also the issues over which we must come together in order to connect emotionally. So, if we want to form solid, emotionally satisfying relationships with others, we must learn to manage these differences. We must learn to compromise. Understanding emotional command systems gives us a framework to do just that.

Let me give you another example from my own life. My wife, Julie, loves to travel to exotic places, to experience new challenges, to try new things. In the language of emotional command systems, I'd say that Julie has a highly activated Explorer. I, on the other hand, have an Explorer system that's more conservative. I like to travel, but I'd rather visit cultural exhibits or ancient ruins. I don't enjoy the kind of experiential adventure travel that my wife likes.

Last year Julie organized a group of women to climb to the top of Nepal's Kala Patar, which is the base camp for ascents of Mount Everest. The group took three weeks to hike about seventy-five miles, reaching an altitude of 18,500 feet. It was a rugged hike, for which Julie trained for over a year.

At first I didn't want her to go. In fact, you could say the whole event aroused my Sentry system to the extreme. I was afraid that she might be robbed or ambushed or killed. I feared that she would develop pulmonary edema and have to be taken down the mountain in a stretcher by helicopter. I knew better than to read *Into Thin Air*, Jon Krakauer's memoir of the 1996 Everest disaster, until after Julie's trip. It would just fuel all the catastrophic fantasies I was keeping to myself.

In the end, however, I knew that I had to set all my fears aside. Why? Because I know how active the Explorer is in Julie. In fact, it's one of the things I love best about her. And I know that for her to feel happy and fulfilled, she's got to experience that sense of discovery and adventure in her life. Without it, she grows restless and grumpy. With it, she is energized, excited, and exciting to be around.

At the same time, Julie knows how much quieter the Explorer is in me, so she doesn't expect me to go along on adventures like this. We joke about our differences. I say the IMAX film about Everest was about as much as I can take. I tell her I'd be willing to accompany her if she could just get me good room service during the trek. But she and I both know that the altitude alone would be too physically challenging for me. We both recognize that I'm better off at home, comfortably working with my highly activated Nest-Builder.

Still, it wasn't easy to say good-bye to Julie the day she left. Nor was it always easy to keep my worries and grumbling in check while she was gone. I figured it was a major accomplishment that I didn't whine even once during her satellite phone calls home every few days. No, I planned to save my whining until she got home.

But once she returned and shared with me the photos of her trek, I knew that my struggle to accept her wanderlust was worthwhile. There's one image in particular that I love. She's sitting at the top of Kala Patar, above Mount Everest base camp, with Everest in the background, and she's wearing the most blissful smile I've ever seen. That picture is absolutely priceless to me! It makes me feel proud that we have the kind of marriage that encourages Julie to have adventures like this. And I'm happy that our differences are a source of pride for us, rather than resentment.

## Expect Mismatches and Work with Them

Whether we like it or not, life is filled with opportunities either to celebrate or bemoan our differences with other people. Conflicts can arise from our contrasting comfort levels within any of the seven emotional command systems.

One brother has a highly activated Jester system, for example, and he's willing to go to just about any lengths to get a laugh. The other brother isn't so driven toward humor and playfulness. Imagine what might happen at a dinner party where the Jester brother keeps cracking jokes at the expense of the non-Jester brother's new girlfriend.

Conflicts can also come up between two people who are driven in the same direction within an operating system. Picture what transpires when the boss and her assistant both have a highly activated Commander-in-Chief. If there's no one in the partnership who's willing to follow, they've got problems.

In addition, clashes can arise when people are operating from totally different, highly activated systems that are at odds with one another. Think back to the reunion of friends that I described at the beginning of this chapter. Can you imagine the conflicts that are likely to arise as they pursue activities together during their great wilderness adventure? Just picture them gathered around that kerosene lamp on their first evening as they plan their activities together.

"Hey, look at the description I found of this great hike," says Merrill (the Explorer), as she hands the trail guide to Katie (the Energy Czar). "The view from the top is supposed to be magnificent. And tomorrow's weather is going to be crystal clear. What do you say?"

"Whoa!" says Katie. "This says the trail climbs five thousand feet in six miles! I don't know if we're up for that. Besides, I thought we were getting together this week to *relax*."

"Well, five thousand feet might be a challenge for some of you, but I think it's doable," says Christopher (the Commander-in-Chief). "There is a problem, however. I already booked a river-rafting trip for tomorrow. We're supposed to meet the outfitter at the landing at seven A.M."

"River rafting?" says Carlos (the Sentry), surprised. "Who said anything about river rafting?"

"I just assumed you'd want to do it," Christopher replies. "I mean, you don't come to this terrain in early July without spending some time on the river."

"Chris is right," says Peter (the Jester). "I hear it's a blast. I've always wanted to do it."

"Okay, but he should have checked with us first," says Merrill. "The weather's going to be perfect for this hike tomorrow. Can't we do the river trip later?"

"I already gave them a nonrefundable deposit," Chris responds.

"Well, thanks for the heads-up!" says Merrill, as Carlos shakes his head in disgust.

"Let's not argue about it, okay, you guys?" says Shelby (the Nest-Builder). "We're only going to be together for a few days. We should try to get along, don't you think?"

"I want to know about the wet suits," says Katie (the Energy Czar). "Do they have them, or are we just going to freeze to death?"

"They have wet suits," Christopher says, "and I ordered one for each of us."

"How did you know our sizes?" asks Katie.

"I just eyeballed it," says Christopher.

"I'll bet you did," says Darrin (the Sensualist). "I just want to know who gets to sit next to Merrill . . ."

And so it goes.

Do any of these conflicts sound familiar to you? If so, take heart. Once you begin to understand the source of your clashes with other people—that you're each using the brain's emotional command systems differently—you're in a better position to adjust your bidding processes accordingly.

## Bidding Across Emotional Command Systems

The following examples show how you can use your knowledge of emotional command systems to connect better with others. Below are several bids for connection between two people who are relying on differing emotional command systems. First you'll read a scenario where the connection fails because neither person acknowledges the differences that are causing a conflict. Then you'll read a second scenario that shows how the connection can succeed if the pair acknowledges their differences and makes room for compromise. As you'll see, sometimes it's the bidder who makes the difference; sometimes it's the respondent. Either way, the bid succeeds and the relationship is enhanced when people realize they're approaching the issue from different perspectives and they need to find some middle ground.

## Commander-in-Chief vs. Explorer

**Failed connection**

> STUDENT (Explorer): I know I'm supposed to write a report about what we learned on our field trip. But I'd like to try something different with this assignment.
>
> TEACHER (Commander-in-Chief): That's not a good idea. Just follow the instructions I gave you.
>
> (Student leaves. End of exchange.)

**Successful connection**

> STUDENT (Explorer): I know I'm supposed to write a report about what we learned on our field trip. But I'd like to try something different with this assignment.
>
> TEACHER (Commander-in-Chief): It sounds like you're the kind of person who likes to try creative new approaches. And I'm kind of a stickler for the tried and true. But I might give you extra credit for doing something different. Tell me what you have in mind.
>
> (Conversation continues.)

## Commander-in-Chief vs. Jester

**Failed connection**

> EMPLOYEE A (Jester): So this guy walks into a bar—
>
> EMPLOYEE B (Commander-in-Chief): Can we get back to the agenda?
>
> (Staff proceeds to discuss the budget.)

**Successful connection**

> EMPLOYEE A (Jester): So this guy walks into a bar—
>
> EMPLOYEE B (Commander-in-Chief, smiling and pointing to her watch): This better be good—and it better be quick, because we've got to get back to the agenda.
>
> (Employee A tells the joke quickly. Staff laughs, then proceeds to talk about the budget.)

## Commander-in-Chief vs. Energy Czar

**Failed connection**

> MOM (Energy Czar): Aren't you going to have breakfast?

DAUGHTER (Commander-in-Chief): No, I'm not. And why is everybody always trying to make me look fat?

(Mom frowns and daughter leaves.)

### Successful connection

MOM (Energy Czar): Aren't you going to have breakfast?

DAUGHTER (Commander-in-Chief): No, I'm not. And why is everybody always trying to make me look fat?

MOM: I'm just concerned that you'll be hungry, and you want to be in charge of what you eat. Here's a dollar in case you want to buy a snack at the break.

(Daughter accepts the dollar and leaves.)

## Commander-in-Chief vs. Sentry

### Failed connection

WIFE (Sentry): I'm worried about your gun. What if one of the grandkids gets hold of it? I think you should just get rid of it.

HUSBAND (Commander-in-Chief): I can't believe you're caving in to that government propaganda. We can't let them tell us what to do.

(End of exchange.)

### Successful connection

WIFE (Sentry): I'm worried about your gun. What if one of the grandkids gets hold of it? I think you should just get rid of it.

HUSBAND (Commander-in-Chief): I can't believe you're caving in to that government propaganda. We can't let them tell us what to do.

WIFE: I understand that you're worried about government control. And I'm worried about the kids. Let's go down to the gun shop and see what kind of trigger locks or lockboxes they recommend.

(Husband agrees.)

## Commander-in-Chief vs. Nest-Builder

### Failed connection

EMPLOYEE (Nest-Builder): I'd like to do some team-building exercises at our staff retreat.

BOSS (Commander-in-Chief): Those things can get out of control. Let's just focus on the training material.

(End of exchange.)

**Successful connection**

> EMPLOYEE (Nest-Builder): I'd like to do some team-building exercises at our staff retreat.
>
> BOSS (Commander-in-Chief): Those things can get out of control. Let's just focus on the training material.
>
> EMPLOYEE: It sounds like you have some pretty defined ideas about the retreat agenda. But maybe we could do some team building in other ways—like having some regular, after-hours social event so people can relax and get to know one another better.
>
> BOSS: That's a great idea.
>
> (Employee and boss plan some social events.)

## Commander-in-Chief vs. Sensualist

**Failed connection**

> LOVER A (Sensualist): Why can't you just relax? My philosophy is "If it feels good, do it."
>
> LOVER B (Commander-in-Chief): It's not that easy. I just can't let go like that.
>
> (Exchange ends.)

**Successful connection**

> LOVER A (Sensualist): Why can't you just relax? My philosophy is "If it feels good, do it."
>
> LOVER B (Commander-in-Chief): It's not that easy. I just can't let go like that.
>
> LOVER A: Sounds like you want to take things at your own pace and I've been rushing it. That's okay. You don't need to let go. In fact, you take the lead. You tell me what you want and I'll follow.
>
> (Exchange continues.)

## Explorer vs. Jester

**Failed connection**

> SPOUSE A (Explorer): I found some stuff on the Web for our trip to Hawaii. There are some really great places to backpack on Kauai. It's really remote!
>
> SPOUSE B (Jester): Backpacking! No way! When I agreed to go to Hawaii, I was thinking fancy hotels, luaus, the nightlife in Waikiki!
>
> SPOUSE A: That does it! We're taking separate vacations.
>
> (End of exchange.)

**Successful connection**

> SPOUSE A (Explorer): I found some stuff on the Web for our trip to
> Hawaii. There are some really great places to backpack on Kauai.
> It's so remote!
>
> SPOUSE B (Jester): Well, this is a familiar story. You're looking for the
> great outdoor adventure, and I just want to kick back. Let's see
> what kind of resorts they've got on Kauai. Then maybe we can do
> a little of both.
>
> (Collaborative Web search continues.)

## Explorer vs. Sensualist

**Failed connection**

> FRIEND A (Explorer, studying a class catalog): Let's sign up for the
> women's kayaking workshop during spring break. I've heard it's
> really challenging.
>
> FRIEND B (Sensualist): Women's kayaking? How are we going to meet
> guys that way? Now, here's one . . . salsa dancing.
>
> FRIEND A: I'm not interested in salsa dancing. Forget it.
>
> (Exchange ends.)

**Successful connection**

> FRIEND A (Explorer): Let's sign up for the women's kayaking workshop
> during spring break. I've heard it's really challenging.
>
> FRIEND B (Sensualist): Women's kayaking? How are we going to meet
> guys that way? Now here's one . . . salsa dancing.
>
> FRIEND A: Look, I'm interested in outdoor adventure and you're inter-
> ested in men. Wow . . . here's one. Coed rock-climbing . . .
>
> (The two friends register for the workshop.)

## Explorer vs. Energy Czar

**Failed connection**

> CHILD (Energy Czar): Look! There's McDonald's! Can we eat?
>
> DAD (Explorer): Eat? We'll never get to the Grand Canyon if we stop at
> every McDonald's!
>
> (Exchange ends, and then picks up again in five minutes.)

**Successful connection**

> CHILD (Energy Czar): Look! There's McDonald's! Can we eat?

DAD (Explorer): Okay. You're hungry, and I want to get to the Grand Canyon. So let's get gas, stock up on food, and use the bathroom now. Then maybe we won't have to stop again until we get to Arizona.

(Dad steers toward freeway exit.)

## Explorer vs. Sentry

**Failed connection**

FRIEND A (Explorer): Wow! Look at those waves! Let's go rent some boogie boards!

FRIEND B (Sentry): I don't think so. I've heard the current on this beach is really treacherous.

FRIEND A: Don't be such a chicken.

FRIEND B: I'm not a chicken. I'd just rather sunbathe.

(Friends go their separate ways.)

**Successful connection**

FRIEND A (Explorer): Wow! Look at those waves! Let's go rent some boogie boards!

FRIEND B (Sentry): You're so gung-ho. But I'm a little more cautious. I've also heard the current on this beach is really treacherous. How about if we go down to that other beach where's there's a lifeguard on duty?

(Friend A agrees and they're off together.)

## Explorer vs. Nest-Builder

**Failed connection**

HUSBAND (Explorer): This is fantastic! The bureau chief called. They're sending me to get footage of the hostage crisis.

WIFE (Nest-Builder): Oh, great. What if you're not back in time for your son's graduation?

HUSBAND: I can't believe you don't understand.

WIFE: And I can't believe that you don't.

(Exchange ends.)

**Successful connection**

HUSBAND (Explorer): This is fantastic! The bureau chief called. They're sending me to get footage of the hostage crisis.

WIFE (Nest-Builder): Oh, great. What if you're not back in time for your son's graduation?

HUSBAND: I know that we don't see eye-to-eye on this. I need to do this because this chance might not come again. You think it's more important for me to be here with Justin. But I think Justin will be able to see it from my point of view, and I think he'll be proud of me. I'll talk to him. I'll make sure he knows why I feel I have to go.

WIFE: Well, maybe you're right. You talk to him.

(The exchange continues.)

## Sensualist vs. Energy Czar

### Failed connection

LOVER A (Sensualist): Why not?

LOVER B (Energy Czar): Because it's almost midnight, I've got to get up at five A.M., and I'm exhausted! Besides, I think Tyler is still awake.

(Lover A rolls over, angry. Lover B is hurt.)

### Successful connection

LOVER A (Sensualist): Why not?

LOVER B (Energy Czar): Because it's almost midnight, I've got to get up at five A.M., and I'm exhausted! Besides, I think Tyler is still awake.

LOVER A: You're tired. I want you. But it's okay. I'll just think of Saturday afternoon when Tyler's away at soccer practice. It'll be so good.

LOVER B: That's sweet. I'll think of it, too.

(Lovers fall asleep . . . or maybe not.)

## Sensualist vs. Jester

### Failed connection

LOVER A (Jester): Why are you mad?

LOVER B (Sensualist): I wanted you to think it was sexy. I didn't want you to laugh.

(Lover B, embarrassed and angry, leaves.)

### Successful connection

LOVER A (Jester): Why are you mad?

LOVER B (Sensualist): I wanted you to think it was sexy. I didn't want you to laugh.

LOVER A: Wait. I'm sorry. I didn't mean to laugh. I'm just a clown and we see things differently sometimes. But I really do think you're sexy. Will you forgive me? Come here. Let me hold you.
(Exchange continues.)

## Sensualist vs. Sentry

**Failed connection**

LOVER A (Sentry): Wait! Stop! I've got to get the condom!
LOVER B (Sensualist): Oh, jeez, do we have to?
LOVER A: Look, if it's too much trouble for you, I'm not interested.
(Exchange ends.)

**Successful connection**

LOVER A (Sentry): Wait! Stop! I've got to get the condom!
LOVER B (Sensualist): Oh, jeez, do we have to?
LOVER A: Yep. I'm more careful than you, but don't worry. I've got lots of ways to keep it interesting.

## Sensualist vs. Nest-Builder

**Failed connection**

SPOUSE A (Sensualist): We need to get away for the weekend—just you and me.
SPOUSE B (Nest-Builder): That would be great. But I don't think the baby's old enough to stay with a sitter that long.
(Exchange ends.)

**Successful connection**

SPOUSE A (Sensualist): We need to get away for the weekend—just you and me.
SPOUSE B (Nest-Builder): That would be great. But I don't think the baby's old enough to stay with a sitter that long.
SPOUSE A: I know you're worried about the baby. But I need some time alone with you. Let's see if your mom would fly up for the weekend. We could spring for the ticket.
(Spouse B agrees.)

## Energy Czar vs. Jester

**Failed connection**

FRIEND A (Jester): I know! Let's stay up all night watching *Star Wars* videos.

FRIEND B (Energy Czar): You're nuts! We'd be too tired to work on our Darth Vader costumes for the party tomorrow.

(Exchange ends, with Friend A hurt, and Friend B feeling kind of bad.)

### Successful connection

FRIEND A (Jester): I know! Let's stay up all night watching *Star Wars* videos.

FRIEND B (Energy Czar): Wow! You're the most extreme *Star Wars* fan I know. That's what I like about you. But I'm afraid we'd be too tired to work on our Darth Vader costumes for the party tomorrow. And I know you want to do that, too.

FRIEND A: You're right. Let's just watch *The Empire Strikes Back* tonight and the rest on Monday, Tuesday, and Wednesday. It will be a *Star Wars* festival!"

(Friends head for the VCR.)

## Energy Czar vs. Sentry

### Failed connection

ROOMMATE A (Energy Czar): I'll never get enough sleep if you leave that night-light on!

ROOMMATE B (Sentry): But I've always had a night-light. I don't like the dark.

(Exchange ends in a stalemate.)

### Successful connection

ROOMMATE A (Energy Czar): I know you feel safer with the light on, but I can't fall asleep with light in my eyes. And I really need my sleep. How about if I get you my flashlight? You can keep it under your pillow. Then if you hear something or get scared, you can turn it on.

ROOMMATE B (Sentry): Okay. I'll try it.

## Energy Czar vs. Nest-Builder

### Failed connection

CHILD (Nest-Builder): I'm the only kid in the class who brings milk. Why can't I have pop like everybody else?

MOTHER (Energy Czar): Because you can't get by on sugar water, that's why.

(Exchange ends.)

**Successful connection**

>CHILD (Nest-Builder): I'm the only kid in the class who brings milk. Why can't I have pop like everybody else?
>
>MOTHER (Energy Czar): I know it's hard to be the only one who does something different. But I really care about your nutrition, and pop is nothing but sugar water. We could try a compromise, though. Something like orange juice?
>
>CHILD: Okay.
>
>(Exchange ends happily.)

## *Jester vs. Sentry*

**Failed connection**

>FRIEND A (Jester): When we go to the Pearl Jam concert, we're heading straight for the mosh pit.
>
>FRIEND B (Sentry): Are you crazy? People have gotten trampled to death in there!
>
>FRIEND A: You're such a wimp.
>
>(Exchange ends on a sour note.)

**Successful connection**

>FRIEND A (Jester): When we go to the Pearl Jam concert, we're heading straight for the mosh pit.
>
>FRIEND B (Sentry): Are you crazy? People have gotten trampled to death in there!
>
>FRIEND A: Well, we're kind of different, you and me. I'm willing to take that risk because I love the experience. And you're not.
>
>FRIEND B: That's right. Tell you what—I'll meet you at the bar after the concert and you can tell me all about it.
>
>FRIEND A: Cool.
>
>(Exchange ends on a friendly note.)

## *Jester vs. Nest-Builder*

**Failed connection**

>EMPLOYEE A (Nest-Builder): I can't believe you told that joke in front of the board members. What if you offended somebody?
>
>EMPLOYEE B (Jester): Oh, relax! People laughed, didn't they? That's what matters.
>
>(Exchange ends on an uncomfortable note.)

**Successful connection**

>EMPLOYEE A (Nest-Builder): I can't believe you told that joke in front of the board members. What if you offended somebody?

EMPLOYEE B (Jester): Oh, relax! People laughed, didn't they? That's what matters.

EMPLOYEE A: Of course they laughed. You've got such a wild sense of humor! But I guess it's just the way I'm wired—I'm always worried about whether something might hurt somebody's feelings. Do you think it would be all right if I checked in with a few key people to see if any apologies are needed?

EMPLOYEE B: Sure, if that will make you feel better, go ahead.

(Exchange ends on a peaceful note.)

## Nest-Builder vs. Sentry

**Failed connection**

SIBLING A (Nest-Builder): I think we should invite Marvin for Christmas dinner. He's made some mistakes, but he's family. And he says he quit drinking. We ought to give him another chance.

SIBLING B (Sentry): No way. I've already given him plenty of chances. I'm not going to take the risk again.

(Exchange ends.)

**Successful connection**

SIBLING A (Nest-Builder): I think we should invite Marvin for Christmas dinner. He's made some mistakes, but he's family. And he says he quit drinking. We ought to give him another chance.

SIBLING B (Sentry): No way. I've already given him plenty of chances. I'm not going to take the risk again.

SIBLING A: Well, after all that's happened, I can understand why you feel that way. Still, I feel the need to reach out to him. Let me try this. I'll go visit Marvin a few times between now and Christmas. We've got a few weeks. I'll see how he's doing and I'll let you know. I just want you to keep an open mind.

SIBLING B: Well, you can try it if you want to. But I'm not making any promises.

SIBLING A: Okay.

(Exchange ends on a hopeful note.)

# Still More Connections

As the preceding examples show, bidding and making connections despite our differences isn't always easy. Emotional command systems are, after all, hardwired into the anatomy of the brain. That means we do indeed get our hearts and minds "set" on having things a certain way.

Still, connection is possible—especially when we acknowledge those differences, accept them, and build them into the bidding process. This results in more stable relationships based on common respect for one another's emotional needs.

Acknowledging differences in emotional command systems isn't the whole story, however. How you bid and respond to bids also depends, in large part, on past emotional experience. That's the focus of the next chapter.

# 5

# Step Three: Examine Your Emotional Heritage

*P*art of my research on relationships involves asking people about their past experiences with emotions. How, for example, did your parents let you know that you were loved?

"My father always kept his distance," one woman told me. "Even on his deathbed. When he was dying, I said, 'Dad, you never told me that you loved me. And now that it's almost over, that's the one thing I wish that I could hear.' But do you know what he said? 'If you don't know by now, you never will.'

"And then he died. I walked out of that hospital room and I was so angry. He was gone forever, and all I could feel toward him was anger."

When I asked her how this event had influenced her life from that moment forward, she was clear: "I tell my kids every day that I love them," she said. "And I tell my husband that, too. No matter what's going on, I always find a way to do it."

I tell this story because it illustrates the power that our emotional heritage has on our current relationships. By "emotional heritage," I mean the way we were treated in the past, and the way such treatment made us feel. It includes the way the people close to us acted when they were angry, sad, happy, or fearful—what they said, what they didn't say.

In this chapter you'll read about several aspects of your emotional heritage, evaluating how they affect your current relationships. These elements include emotional history—that is, the lessons you learned about feelings as a child. You'll also look into your family's emotional philosophy, or what your family felt and believed about the expression of emotion. And, finally, you'll explore your enduring vulnerabilities—events or relationships so painful that they continue to be a strong influence on you for the rest of your life.

Your emotional heritage has a strong impact on your ability to connect emotionally. It affects your awareness of your own emotions, how you express them, and how you bid for connection. It also colors your ability to see, interpret, and respond to other people's bids.

Just imagine being close friends with the woman in the story above. How important do you think it would be to let her know that you appreciate her? Obviously, her past experience with her father makes the explicit expression of affection very valuable to her. And the better that people around her understand this, the stronger their emotional connection to her will be.

As we learned in previous chapters, individual people often feel and react differently in similar situations. Their emotional heritage is one factor that contributes to those differences. And unless we're aware of those differences, they can interfere with our ability to connect.

We can begin by imagining arriving at work one morning to find this message from your boss: "Please see me at nine A.M. Something has come up that we need to discuss."

What would be your first reaction? Fear? Excitement? Anger? Amusement? Your answer probably depends on many things—your job performance, for example. Or the ways you've seen your boss handle crises in the past. But it's also likely to be affected by your emotional heritage—that is, by the way your personal history influences your current way of dealing with emotional situations.

If you're like Jim, for example, you might feel stunned and anxious. Jim was raised by a harsh father whose behavior was hard to predict. One day the man would be totally supportive, heaping praise on him for all the chores he had done around the house. But the next day he'd berate and punish Jim for the smallest infraction—the muddy shoes he'd left by the back door, or the pile of leaves he'd raked but forgotten to bag. Consequently, Jim spent much of his childhood feeling as if something bad could happen at any minute and there was nothing he could do about it. Those feelings carried over into adulthood, and whenever something unexpected happened at work, Jim's first response was fear and defensiveness. What had he done wrong this time? How was he going to be made to pay?

Lisa, on the other hand, would respond to the boss's message as the jolt of energy she'd been craving. The oldest of five kids in a family with a high sense of adventure, Lisa loved an emergency. "You're always so responsible," she'd been told throughout childhood. Whether she was rescuing a sibling from some mishap, or organizing the gang for a camping trip, she heard the same message over and over: "We know we can depend on you." So whenever a crisis arose at work, she intrinsically believed it could be one more chance to feel good about herself. If the boss needed to meet with her right away, she guessed it was for good reason: He probably needed to brief her about a problem only she could handle.

Then there's Denise, who'd react to the boss's invitation with resentment. "How am I supposed to be prepared for a meeting on such short notice?" she'd think. "What if I'd had an appointment scheduled?" She'd even think of missing the meeting—"on principle"—but in the end she'd make herself go. Skipping out would just get her into more hot water, because people in power always make ridiculous demands. At least that's the way Denise's mother had treated her. The woman suffered from severe mood swings, which meant her children got lots of mixed signals about how to behave and what was expected from them. In all the chaos, however, one thing was sure: Denise's mother could and would control her children with an iron hand. Consequently, Denise learned two lessons: First, life was unfair; second, it was better to keep your mouth shut than to complain.

So now, as an adult, it didn't matter how mad Denise got; she'd never complain to her boss. It wouldn't do any good, she believed. In fact, she thought that showing her feelings was a sign of weakness, that it would lead people to take advantage of her. "I'd better keep my guard up," she told herself. "There's less chance of getting hurt that way."

Like most people, these characters' emotional heritage was formed largely by what happened in their families of origin. Many other factors—such as peer relationships, job-related incidents, and influences from the community and culture at large—combine in complex ways to make other important contributions as well. They all come together to form a foundation upon which current emotional connections are made. And the better we understand the strengths and weaknesses of that foundation, the more insight we'll have into our current relationships.

## What Our Experience Tells Us

Although exploring your emotional heritage may be helpful, it's not always easy. In fact, most people find it at least a bit uncomfortable; some find it downright excruciating. Many try to avoid thinking about the past altogether, because they fail to see the payoff. Why stir up a lot of memories you'd just as soon forget? Why expose yourself to all those unresolved problems—especially when they involve parents, siblings, old friends—the very same people you're going to have to share every major holiday with for the rest of your life?

There are many good reasons to look back. In fact, as scientists learn more about the way the brain processes emotions and stores emotional memory, it becomes increasingly clear that yesterday's feelings influence our ability to make and keep emotional connections today. If we want to have relationships that are more meaningful in the future, it helps to have some insight about the past. In fact, looking back thoughtfully may eventually help you to build better connections with the very folks gathered around that holiday table.

To see how your past affects your current relationships, it helps to understand the relationship between issues of emotional heritage and the brain's emotional command systems, which we discussed in chapter 4. Simply put, each influences the other. For example, a woman who was raped as a youngster might develop a much more active Sentry system as a result of that experience. And another woman, who's been cautious all her life because she inherited a strong Sentry system, might learn to let down her guard after living in a community where she feels extremely safe and secure.

While emotional command systems are partially determined by genetic inheritance, they're not completely "hardwired." In fact, the neural pathways of the brain that carry emotional messages are quite malleable and can be changed by our experiences—particularly those in early childhood, because that's when the brain is growing rapidly and these systems are under construction. Just as a young tree grows at a certain angle as its branches bend in the wind or reach toward the sun, so we are formed emotionally by interpersonal events in our environment.

Just imagine the immature nervous system as a field of newly fallen snow, and the tracks through that snow as the various ways that your body can express emotion through thought and behavior. The first time you experience an emotional stimulus, it follows a new track through that snow field. But with each subsequent stimulus that reminds you of that initial experience, you're increasingly more likely to follow that established path. In this way the patterns of feeling that we've experienced in the past determine the way we're likely to feel in the future.

When you say that your brother "really pushes your buttons," it's because you feel that he knows how to elicit an automatic response from you. Your brother utters some familiar remark "guaranteed" to make you angry, and—*whoosh!*—your feelings take off down that old familiar path. Hard as you might try to change it, you end up feeling the same way you've always felt when those buttons get pushed. This explains why it's often so hard for people who've had difficult relationships with parents or siblings to improve those relationships. Family members get caught in patterns of emotional thought and behavior that were set early on and practiced over and over again through childhood.

These patterns can also be detrimental to new relationships, particularly if you see and react to the behavior of new people in your life as if they were "just like my mother," "just like my stepdad," "just like my ex-wife," and so on.

Although you may have fixed patterns of reacting emotionally to a particular kind of comment or situation, many scientists and therapists believe people can change their responses, particularly if they can reexperience the same kind of stimulus under new and different life circumstances. That's why the goal of so many forms of therapy is to help the patient revisit painful events from the past. Such therapy gives you a chance to reexperience your feelings in a safer or more neutral setting. You can use memory and imagination to visualize moments in your past when you felt hurt, angry, or devastatingly sad. You can actually feel the emotion you were feeling at that time. You can't necessarily erase the pain—at least not initially—but you may gain new insights. ("The way I was treated really hurt. But I'm older now and I know it wasn't right." "That was a harmful place to be. But I'm in a safe environment now. I don't have to be afraid anymore." "I was dependent on people who sometimes hurt me. But now I know how to take care of myself." "What they told me about myself was wrong. I don't have to believe everything they said.") Such insights can help you to feel differently about similar situations and relationships in the future. You don't have to keep reacting to new events and new interactions with the same automatic, painful responses.

Understanding how yesterday's feelings color today's experience can make a difference in your ability to form strong, healthy bonds with others. You can gain new insights into the configuration of your own emotional life, as well as the emotional lives of others. This will make you more conscious of the filters of past experience through which you view your current existence. And when you're fully aware of your own filter, you'll be able to read and interpret other people's bids for connection more accurately. You'll also be able to respond to bids based on who you are today.

## *Exercise: What's Your Emotional History?*

On the next few pages you'll find a self-test designed to help you explore your emotional history. In it you'll see lots of questions about your childhood, your family, and the home in which you were raised. Some of the questions are rather general, encouraging you to think about the overall tenor of your childhood years. Did you, for example, feel loved, valued, and accepted as a child? You'll also find questions about the emotional behavior of the people closest to you. That's because kids take so many emotional cues from the words and actions of the people around them. Specific questions about the way your family expressed pride, love, anger, sadness, and fear may help you to uncover memories that provide insight into your current attitudes about emotional expression.

To take the self-test:

**1.** Complete each item, indicating the extent to which you agree or disagree with each statement about yourself. For each item, circle the alternative that best fits:

**SA** = strongly agree

 **A** = agree

 **N** = neutral

 **D** = disagree

**SD** = strongly disagree

**2.** Complete each item again, this time pretending to be somebody who is close to you, such as your spouse or a close friend or relative. (Or, if possible, ask that person to fill out the items. Then share your results and talk about them.)

1. My parents often showed me that they were proud of me.
   **SA A N D SD**
2. When I was growing up, my family always attended the important events in which I participated (e.g., plays, concerts, sports events).
   **SA A N D SD**
3. My parents helped me to feel proud of myself.  **SA A N D SD**
4. My family taught me to believe in my talents.  **SA A N D SD**
5. I learned from my past to feel good about what I have accomplished.
   **SA A N D SD**
6. I learned from my parents that mastery is all about believing in yourself.  **SA A N D SD**
7. My family taught that if I am failing at something, it usually has very little to do with bad luck.  **SA A N D SD**
8. My past history makes it easy for me to feel proud of the achievements of those close to me.  **SA A N D SD**
9. I easily express my pleasure in the achievements of others.
   **SA A N D SD**
10. When I was growing up, there was lots of affection shown in my home.  **SA A N D SD**
11. My parents often showed me that they loved me.
    **SA A N D SD**
12. As a child, I felt really accepted by most of my peers.
    **SA A N D SD**
13. My family touched, hugged, and kissed one another a lot.
    **SA A N D SD**
14. I came from a very emotionally expressive family.
    **SA A N D SD**
15. My parents often said "I love you" to me when I was a child.
    **SA A N D SD**
16. I feel comfortable expressing affection to those I care about.
    **SA A N D SD**
17. From their actions I always knew I was important to my parents.
    **SA A N D SD**

18. As a child, my preferences and interests really mattered to my parents. **SA A N D SD**
19. My parents responded to my emotions when I was growing up.
    **SA A N D SD**
20. I feel comfortable receiving affection from those I care about.
    **SA A N D SD**
21. It's easy for me to say "I love you" when I feel it.
    **SA A N D SD**
22. I was afraid of my father's anger. **SA A N D SD**
23. It was hard for me to show my own anger to my parents.
    **SA A N D SD**
24. I feel highly uncomfortable when people are angry with me.
    **SA A N D SD**
25. I was taught as a child that anger is very similar to aggression.
    **SA A N D SD**
26. I was afraid of my mother's anger. **SA A N D SD**
27. I can't talk about my own anger with comfort. **SA A N D SD**
28. My family generally believed that anger was a destructive emotion.
    **SA A N D SD**
29. I try to avoid becoming angry. **SA A N D SD**
30. Not too many people can tell when I am angry.
    **SA A N D SD**
31. I will keep my anger controlled until I eventually blow up.
    **SA A N D SD**
32. I often feel that my anger is out of control. **SA A N D SD**
33. I've learned from my past that expressing anger is like throwing gasoline on an open flame. **SA A N D SD**
34. I keep my sadness to myself. **SA A N D SD**
35. Past experience has taught me that letting myself be sad is a waste of time. **SA A N D SD**
36. I'm rarely sad. **SA A N D SD**
37. My family taught me that feeling sadness was cowardly.
    **SA A N D SD**
38. I learned as a child that expressing sadness just brought everyone else down. **SA A N D SD**
39. I try to quickly get over being sad. **SA A N D SD**
40. I am impatient with other people's sad moods.
    **SA A N D SD**
41. When I was a child, my loneliness wasn't noticed by my parents.
    **SA A N D SD**
42. No one can tell when I am sad. **SA A N D SD**
43. I've learned through experience that there's very little point in talking to others when I'm downhearted. **SA A N D SD**

**44.** I hate being around sad people.  **SA   A   N   D   SD**

**45.** I could never openly express my worries and fears to my parents.
**SA   A   N   D   SD**

**46.** My parents believed that I should just get over my fears and not dwell on them.  **SA   A   N   D   SD**

**47.** As a child, I just wasn't allowed to be afraid.  **SA   A   N   D   SD**

**48.** I was taught as a child to avoid thinking too much about my fears, because doing so could paralyze me into inaction.
**SA   A   N   D   SD**

**49.** I learned when I was young to keep going even when I was afraid.
**SA   A   N   D   SD**

**50.** My family taught me that exploring my fears would make me a wimp.
**SA   A   N   D   SD**

### SCORING

**SA** = 2 points
**A** = 1 point
**N** = 0 points
**D** = −1 point
**SD** = −2 points

## Pride and Accomplishment

Items 1–9 score: _____

If you scored 5 or above, your emotional history allows you to feel comfortable expressing emotions such as pride in your own accomplishments and the accomplishments of others.

If your score was below 5, then you have doubts about your own mastery, strivings, and accomplishments. You probably feel uncomfortable expressing pride in yourself and others.

## Love and Affection

Items 10–21 score: _____

If you scored 10 or above, your emotional history allows you to feel comfortable in expressing love and affection, and in receiving expressions of those feelings from others.

If your score was below 10, then you sometimes have doubts about feeling loved. Also, you may feel uncomfortable in giving and receiving expressions of love and affection.

## *Anger*

Items 22–33 score: _____

If you scored 6 or above, you're probably not comfortable with the expression and experience of anger, and you have some difficulty in becoming angry, and in experiencing other people's expressions of anger.

If you scored below 6, then anger is a comfortable emotion for you.

## *Sadness*

Items 34–44 score: _____

If you scored 5 or above, you're probably not comfortable with the experience of sadness, and you may have some difficulty in being sad, and in experiencing other people's expressions of sadness.

If you scored below 5, then sadness is a comfortable emotion for you.

## *Fear*

Items 45–50 score: _____

If you scored 3 or above, you're probably not comfortable with the experience of fear, and you may have some difficulty in being afraid or worried, and in experiencing other people's expressions of fear.

If you scored below 3, then fear is a comfortable emotion for you.

As you look at your emotional history scores for each of these five feelings (pride and accomplishment, love and affection, anger, sadness, and fear), identify the ones that are most difficult for you. Consider what typically happens when you'd like to make a bid for connection around one of these emotions that's hard for you. Say, for example, that you find it hard to experience pride and a sense of accomplishment, but you've just won an award and you'd like others to know about it. Does your inability to feel proud of yourself prevent you from making that bid for connection? Do you make your bids in such a subtle way that people hardly even notice? If so, does your reluctance to bid leave you lonely, dissatisfied, or disappointed? What would happen if you just acknowledged your discomfort with pride, and made the bid for connection anyway?

Now think about what happens when somebody close to you makes a bid for connection that involves one of the emotions you've identified as difficult for you. If you have difficulty with the expression of sadness, for example, what happens when a friend comes to you in tears over a loss or disappointment? Do you have trouble acknowledging the emotion you see? Do you turn away from or turn against that person as a result? What would happen if you just acknowledged your difficulty with sadness and then proceeded to turn toward that person's bid for connection anyway?

Looking into your emotional history, identifying these areas of difficulty, and imagining how things might be different for you is an important part of improving your bidding process.

## Your Family's Philosophy of Emotion Matters, Too

Often, when we have trouble with emotional connection, the problem goes deeper than an inability to express emotion clearly. Sometimes it has more to do with our beliefs and feelings that underlie the emotions themselves. For example, we may believe that it's inappropriate to express sadness. Or we may feel that it's wrong to let others know we're angry. I refer to our collective beliefs and feelings about feelings as our "philosophy of emotion."

Every family has its own culture and its own philosophy of emotion. Thinking back, can you describe the philosophy of emotion in the home where you grew up? Did your family generally believe it was important for people to understand their own feelings and express them to others? Or did they believe it was better for family members to keep their feelings to themselves? When people in your household were extremely happy about something, were they allowed to express their joy? Or were they supposed to keep it under control? When family members got angry, was it okay to say so, or was the expression of anger treated as a punishable offense? Was it permissible to be sad sometimes, or were you often reprimanded for being gloomy?

Answers to questions like these can help you understand and refine your own personal philosophy of emotion. You may discover that your philosophy is quite similar to your family's, or you may realize that you've moved as far from it as possible. Either way, becoming more aware of the beliefs and feelings that underlie your behavior is an important step toward making positive changes and improving your bidding process.

Our research shows that families generally fall into four broad categories of emotional philosophy: (1) coaching, (2) dismissing, (3) laissez-faire, and (4) disapproving.

Those with a coaching philosophy accept the expression of all feelings—including anger, sadness, and fear. In emotional situations, these family members often help one another solve problems and cope with difficult feelings.

Dismissing families, on the other hand, tend to keep their feelings hidden, especially negative feelings. And since they don't acknowledge feelings, their members don't give one another much guidance on how to handle them.

Families with a laissez-faire philosophy are similar to coaching families in that they think the expression of emotion is okay. But members of laissez-faire families don't do much to help one another cope with anger, sadness, or fear. They're more likely to just wait for such feelings to pass.

Families with a disapproving philosophy are like dismissing families in their belief that people should keep their feelings hidden. But members of disapproving families take it a step further; they're likely to be hostile or critical toward those who express negative emotions.

These are broad generalizations, of course, and many families may switch from one philosophy to another depending on circumstances. For example, when family members' lives are going relatively smoothly, parents may be solid emotion coaches. But when their lives get hectic, they may have a tendency to switch into a more dismissing mode. Families may also be divided, with one parent subscribing to one philosophy while the other subscribes to a different one. Usually, however, one parent has a stronger influence on any particular child, and that parent's emotional philosophy has the greater impact.

You'll find detailed descriptions of these philosophies on pages 150–156. But first take a look at the following self-test. It's designed to help you determine which philosophies of emotion may have been most prevalent in the home where you grew up.

After you do the self-test, read the descriptions of each type of philosophy to see how your family's view may affect your relationships today.

## Exercise: What Was Your Family's Philosophy of Emotion?

Below are a series of scenarios in which a child is expressing an emotion to his or her parents. After each scenario, there's a list of four different responses parents might have to these situations. Thinking back to your childhood, choose the response that best represents the one you might have heard from your parents under similar circumstances. If your family was divided in its philosophy—that is, if each parent would have responded differently—choose the response from the parent who influenced you the most, the one whom you felt most inclined to follow.

1. You tell your parents you're angry because your younger sibling always gets to sit in the front seat of the car.
   A. "It's okay. It's just a short ride to the store anyway."
   B. "I know you get tired of sitting in back by yourself all the time. Can you think of a pretend game you could play back there to make it more interesting?"

    **C.** "It sounds like you're kind of jealous. I was jealous of my little brother when I was your age."

    **D.** "I don't want to hear you complain. Your brother is little, and you should understand why he needs to sit next to Mom."

2. Your uncle has just had a car accident and is in the hospital. Now you're unable to attend the championship football game with all of your friends. You're so angry you want to break something.

    **A.** "It's just a football game, you know. Sometimes other things come up."

    **B.** "I don't blame you for being upset. Maybe you could call one of your friends after the game and get some play-by-play."

    **C.** "That's a real shame. I know you'd really been looking forward to this game."

    **D.** "Honestly! You should listen to yourself. What would your uncle think if he knew you thought a football game was more important than him?"

3. Your younger cousins are visiting again, and they're messing up your toys. It's really making you angry, and you complain to your parents.

    **A.** "They're just little kids. You can put it all back the way it was after they leave."

    **B.** "That makes you mad, doesn't it? You put a lot of effort into keeping your room neat. I'll help you clean up later. In the meantime, maybe it would be fun to just play with them."

    **C.** "Yeah! Those little guys can really trash out a room in a hurry, can't they?"

    **D.** "I think you could be a little more generous. You know, you have some things they don't have. Go find something else to do if you can't play with them."

4. Your classmates keep borrowing your new color markers during art projects. When they return them, almost all the ink is gone!

    **A.** "Aren't there twenty-four colors in that set? Just use another color."

    **B.** "That must be frustrating. Maybe you could suggest they bring some new colors to share for the next week's art class."

    **C.** "Unbelievable! Why don't they get their own markers?"

    **D.** "I don't understand why you're letting them use your new markers in the first place. Those things are expensive."

5. Your best friend has moved to a distant suburb and a new school. You talk on the phone and see one another every now and then, but it's just not the same. It's been weeks now, and you're still sad about it.

    **A.** "People come and go. You just have to get used to these things."

    **B.** "I can remember going through the same thing when I was about your age. My friend's name was Angela. It's really, really hard. Let's sit down and try to think through some ways to deal with this."

    **C.** "Yeah, people come and go in this life. It can be tough. Really tough."

    **D.** "What's wrong with the friends you've got right here in your own neighborhood? Are they not good enough for you?"

6. You hear that an acquaintance had a party and invited most of your friends, but not you. You don't understand why you've been left out, and it makes you very sad.

    **A.** "Oh, people are fickle. You know that."

    **B.** "I'm sure that hurts your feelings. Maybe it was an oversight. Why don't we plan to have some of your friends over here soon? We can work on the invitations after dinner."

    **C.** "Ouch, that can sting! Better luck next time, huh?"

    **D.** "Really, I don't want to hear it. You have a more than adequate social life. I seem to spend half my time carting you and your friends all over town. I should own a taxicab!"

7. Your dog Shortstop died. You're sad.

    **A.** "We'll get a new dog."

    **B.** "I'm really sad, too. I've been thinking all day about the funny things Shortstop would do. Maybe it would be nice to gather some of our photos that he's in, and make a Shortstop scrapbook."

    **C.** "I'm really sad, too. Shortstop was a good dog."

    **D.** "I hate to break it to you, kid, but he was just a dog. And walking around like a sad sack all day isn't going to bring him back."

8. You've put heart and soul into applying for the yearbook staff. You wrote an essay, you were interviewed, and you thought you did a good job. But you're passed over for this plum after-school assignment. Worse, several of your friends were selected.

    **A.** "It's not like there aren't any other clubs for you to join."

    **B.** "What a shame. You worked really hard for this. Tell me all about what happened."

    **C.** "What was that sponsor thinking? Your essay seemed really good to me."

    **D.** "Are you going to mope around every time something doesn't go your way?"

9. You're afraid of the dark. Very afraid.

    **A.** "Believe me, there's nothing to be frightened of."

    **B.** "I can remember being afraid of the dark. It can seem strange when you can't see what's around you. You stay with us tonight, and tomorrow we'll get a new night-light for your room."

    **C.** "I can remember being afraid of the dark."

    **D.** "Don't be such a baby!"

10. You have an ear infection, and you're going to the doctor—the same doctor who gave you all your vaccinations. Afraid you'll get another shot, you start to cry.

    **A.** "Crying isn't going to help. I'm the parent, and you're going to the doctor."

    **B.** "I know you're afraid of the doctor. But he's going to help you feel better. Can we talk about what you're afraid of?"

    **C.** "I still hate getting shots."

    **D.** "Oh, grow up!"

11. Your family is flying to California for vacation. You saw a news story about a bad plane crash the previous month, and you've been scared to get on the plane ever since.

    **A.** "There's no reason to be nervous."

    **B.** "The thought of a plane crash is frightening. But it's really, really unusual for something like that to happen. And I wouldn't take you on this trip if I didn't think it was safe. Do you think it would help if we tried to think of some games to play during the ride?"

    **C.** "Yeah, I know what you mean. What goes up must come down, and all that."

    **D.** "Really, you're such a worrywart! It's safer than crossing the street. You always get carried away by the worst-case scenario!"

12. Your mother is having surgery. You're afraid she might die in the hospital.

    **A.** "It's not a big deal. She'll be home in a couple of days, as good as new."

    **B.** "It's scary to think of her being operated on, huh? It's a safe procedure, though, and she has a good doctor. Let's make some cards for her. You can tell her how you feel."

    **C.** "It's scary to think of her being operated on, huh?"

    **D.** "You've got to be braver than this. She expects you to be a big kid while she's gone."

13. You're ten years old and you have your first crush on a classmate.

    **A.** "When I was growing up, they called this puppy love. Don't worry about it."

    **B.** "Oh, yeah . . . I know who you're talking about. So tell me all about it."

    **C.** "Oh, yeah . . . I can see how you'd feel that way."

    **D.** "Oh, give me a break. You're only ten years old!"

### SCORING

Count the number of times you answered "A": _____. These answers represent an emotion-dismissing philosophy.

Count the number of times you answered "B": _____. These answers represent an emotion-coaching philosophy.

Count the number of times you answered "C": _____. These answers represent a laissez-faire philosophy.

Count the number of times you answered "D": _____. These answers represent an emotion-disapproving philosophy.

Compare your score in each category to see which of these philosophies best describes your family. Then read on to learn more about these philosophies and how they can affect your skill at emotional connection.

## The Emotion-Coaching Philosophy

If you came from a family with a coaching philosophy of emotion, you may have a high regard for emotional expression. That's because you were part of a culture where family members recognized and acknowledged one another's feelings of sadness, anger, or fear. Coaching families typically turn toward one another's bids for emotional connection. They help one another identify their feelings and they empathize.

Unlike the laissez-faire families, coaching families teach children how to express their feelings in ways that are appropriate and effective. They set limits on behavior. ("You can stomp your feet when you're mad, but you can't kick the wall.") Also, they help children develop problem-solving skills.

Coaching families believe in the value of all emotions—even the negative ones. They recognize anger as a creative, motivating force in people's lives. ("It sounds like you're mad because you think Davie was cheating. Why don't you tell him how you feel about it?") They see sadness as a signal that a person may need to make some positive changes in his or her life. ("You seem kind of depressed since you retired, Mom. Maybe you need to be more active. Have you thought about taking a class or getting more involved at church?")

Because they value the expression of emotion, they're more patient and tolerant with family members who are trying to cope with difficult feelings. They're less likely to turn away from or turn against those who display anger, sadness, or fear. At the same time, these families often have fewer tantrums, conflicts, and bouts of depression with which to deal. That's because they're used to responding to one another's bids for connection as soon as they notice them. People don't have to crank up the volume on their emotions in order to be heard. Also, people raised in such environments learn early how to soothe themselves when they're upset, so they're less likely to act out in harmful ways.

Because people raised in emotion-coaching homes are accustomed to loved ones being responsive to one another's feelings, they might have some difficulty understanding people who come from families where emotional expression is dismissed or subject to disapproval.

## The Emotion-Dismissing Philosophy

If you were raised in a family with an emotion-dismissing philosophy, you were subtly—or not so subtly—discouraged from showing your feelings. Still, tears, frustration, and worries inevitably come to the surface in all families. And when this happens in an emotion-dismissing family, members are likely to turn away. They may greet the emotional person with silence, or with some disregarding remark:

*"There's no need to get angry about it."*
*"Look on the bright side."*
*"There's nothing to be afraid of."*
*"Cheer up. You'll do better next time."*
*"Don't be so gloomy. Think positive!"*
*"You're a big boy! Big boys aren't afraid of the dark!"*

Tears go unnoticed, complaints are ignored, and fears are minimized or treated as a joke.

People may adopt an emotion-dismissing philosophy for a variety of reasons. In many families it happens because influential family members fear what might happen if they focus on negative feelings—their own or others'. They worry that anger, fear, or sadness could overwhelm the people involved and they would lose control, leading to catastrophic results. They believe that anger can turn to aggression and somebody might get hurt. They believe that sadness can become so deep and unrelenting that you'd never find your way out of a terrible depression. They believe that fear can turn to terror and there would be no escape. Because of these fears, whenever somebody makes a bid that includes even a glimmer of negative emotion, other family members turn away.

Some people dismiss negative emotions because they feel overly responsible for fixing all the problems that might be causing those feelings. Here's an example:

Carol notices that a friend at work looks quite sad one day. Maybe she's got some financial trouble or marital problems, Carol figures. Or maybe she just had a big fight with her boss. But Carol believes that she can't do anything to help her friend with these kinds of problems. So instead of asking her friend, "What's wrong?" she pretends she doesn't notice the woman's sad expression and listlessness. This is hard for Carol because she considers herself a compassionate person. She even feels guilty for ignoring her friend's bid. But it never occurs to her that just listening and being with her friend in her sadness might be enough. She wouldn't necessarily have to provide a solution.

Still others dismiss negative emotions because they believe that such feelings are like a poison that becomes more harmful the longer you dwell on it. Here's an instance: Louis's five-year-old son, Tom, is angry because his favorite toy just broke. Louis takes a look at it, but it can't be repaired. A compassionate father, he feels sorry for the boy. But instead of expressing this, he prods Tom to expel his anger as quickly as possible and replace it with positive feelings and an optimistic attitude. "You gotta roll with the punches, kid," he says. "It's no big deal. It's just a toy. Get over it."

Louis doesn't recognize Tom's sadness as a bid for connection. He doesn't realize that turning toward the boy with empathy would be one way to *help* his son get over it. Imagine how satisfying it might be for Tom to hear his dad say, "Gee, Tom. You must feel really sad. That was your favorite toy. What a bummer."

But Tom gets a more dismissive response instead. If this keeps happening over time, he'll learn to stop looking to his dad for emotional support; he'll become increasingly disconnected from his father.

Unfortunately, once you're in the habit of dismissing other people's emotions, you miss many chances for connection and intimacy. By turning away, you send a message that says "I'm unavailable" just when your friends, family members, or coworkers need you most.

This dismissing response is bad for all types of relationships, but it's particularly bad for children. It tells them that when they feel anything negative, the people closest to them don't want to know about it. But the kids aren't going to stop having negative feelings. Anger, sadness, and fear are part of life. A parent's dismissing attitude simply tells kids that it's a bad idea to bid for connection through the expression of emotion, that doing so will just make others withdraw their attention and turn away. Therefore, it's better not to be authentic. It's better not to let people know how you really feel. In fact, it may teach them that it's best not to feel at all.

Parents who turn away also miss the thousands of opportunities for guidance around handling difficult feelings. If a mother's main message is "Don't be sad," or "Don't be angry," she may never get around to telling her child, "Here are some ways to take good care of yourself when you're feeling down," or "Let's look at the problem that's making you so mad and see if we can solve it."

## The Emotion-Disapproving Philosophy

If you were raised in a family with an emotion-disapproving philosophy, you may have a lot in common with those from emotion-dismissing families. Both groups encourage their members to keep their negative feelings under wraps. The difference is that emotion-disapproving family members actually feel hostile toward those who express emotions like sadness, anger, or fear. In fact, they're likely to criticize, reprimand, or even punish members just for expressing negative emotions. If somebody makes a bid that's expressed with negative feeling ("I'm so damned frustrated! I wish I had some help!"), the emotion-disapproving person is likely to turn against that bid. ("I can't help anybody who talks to me like that!")

Below are some expressions commonly heard when a disapproving adult addresses a fussy or misbehaving child. Perhaps they'll remind you of reprimands you may have heard as a child.

*"Stop that crying or I'll give you something to cry about."*

*"Oh, don't be such a baby! Grow up!"*

*"Don't use that tone of voice with me!"*

*"Say something nice or don't say anything at all."*

Many people who disapprove of emotional expression tend to frame their relationships as power struggles. In this context, they see expressions of anger, sadness, or fear as an unfair strategy that people use to manipulate others. An emotion-disapproving person is likely to describe an upset family member as "spoiled." He or she might say, "If you don't get your way, you're going to cry about it—is that it?" Or, "He's just throwing a fit so we'll do what he wants to do."

This perspective fails to recognize an important choice we have in relationships: We can accept people's feelings, and even empathize with them, without having to agree with their position. For instance, you might say to a child, "You're very angry that you can't go outside right now because it's getting dark. I know how you feel. Sometimes I get angry, too, when I can't do what I want. That's when I take a deep breath and try to think what to do instead." Or you might say to your spouse, "I know you're not happy that I've decided to take this trip right now. I might feel the same way if I were in your shoes. But I feel that it's something I just have to do." To respond this way, you must first recognize the other person's anger as a bid for connection. This recognition allows you to turn toward another's feelings with empathy and support, and without having to disapprove of the way they feel.

One key factor to this approach is the ability to focus on the feelings underneath a person's behavior rather than on the behavior itself. Here's an example:

Craig's wife, Angela, comes home from work one night as angry as he's ever seen her. She barges into the house, slams the door, and heads straight for the bedroom, where she slams that door, too. Craig has talked to her about her temper before, and she knows he doesn't like it when she acts like this. He disapproves of her "tantrum," so he decides he'll try to nip the problem in the bud.

"What the hell's the matter with you?" he calls up the stairs. "Is that any way to shut the damned door?"

But because his response to her anger is so unsympathetic, Angela slams another door—the door to connection and intimacy.

"Screw you, Craig!" she yells back down the stairs.

Now imagine what might have happened if Craig had recognized Angela's anger as a bid for connection first and saved his concern about the door-slamming until later on. Upon her stormy arrival, he might have called up the stairs, "Angela, are you okay?"

To which she might have replied, "No! I'm so mad I could spit!"

Then he could have followed her upstairs and said through the door, "Well, that's kind of obvious. What happened?"

At that point she might have opened the door and blurted, "Everything went wrong! Jessie blew the presentation and then blamed me. We get back to the office and she runs to Mel. Then I get called on the carpet and he says he's putting me on probation! And it's all *her* fault! He wouldn't even listen to me!"

To which Craig might have responded, "That sounds awful. No wonder you're so upset. Come here and sit down. Take off your coat and I'll get you a drink. You look exhausted."

At this, Angela's rage melts into tears. She leans into Craig's arms and they spend the next hour talking it over. Although Angela feels the whole world is against her, she knows she's got Craig on her side.

Of course, this happy ending presumes that Craig can tolerate Angela's initially intense expression of anger and see it as a bid. If he can, he's got an opportunity for intimacy and connection by turning toward her in the midst of a crisis—the very time when she needs him most. If he can't tolerate her rage, he may turn against her and they could spend the rest of the evening in stony silence or arguing about the value of slamming doors.

Our research reveals that people who disapprove of emotional expression often have the same beliefs as those who dismiss it. They fear that negative feelings are toxic, uncontrollable, that they can overwhelm your life and leave you incapacitated. In addition, many in both groups talk about feelings as if they were a limited commodity. You don't want to "waste your tears" on problems that don't merit such strong emotion.

While some think it's okay to express anger, sadness, or fear for short periods, they believe that expression ought to be time-limited—that is, it's all right to be angry immediately following some betrayal or loss, for example, but you ought to get over it quickly. You've got to "get on with your life."

People raised in emotion-disapproving families eventually learn that emotional intimacy leads to trouble. Express your feelings and you're likely to get scolded, humiliated, and even abused.

And, finally, our studies show that kids who grow up in emotion-disapproving families have many of the same problems as children from emotion-dismissing families. They're not as capable as other kids of soothing themselves when they get upset, so they have more trouble concentrating and picking up on social cues. This leads to more behavior problems, academic failure, trouble with peers, and chronic health problems later on. In adulthood, it leads to greater loneliness.

## The Laissez-Faire Philosophy

If you were raised in a home with a laissez-faire philosophy of emotion, your family culture probably had a high tolerance for openly expressing negative feelings like fear, sadness, and anger. In fact, families with a laissez-faire philosophy seem to believe that expressing emotion is like "letting off steam." You convey your feelings freely, no matter what that expression entails— tears, temper tantrums, rants, rages—you name it. And once the storm is over, it's over. All your work is done.

Parents with this style usually turn toward their children's emotional bids with empathy, even if the bids involve the expression of anger, fear, or sadness. They might try to comfort a child who is crying, frustrated, or piping mad by saying something validating:

*"You must be feeling so sad."*

*"I can see that you're mad right now."*

*"I know you're frightened. That used to scare me when I was little, too."*

While such acknowledgments are validating, they're also lacking in an essential element—they give kids no guidance on how to soothe themselves or how to solve the problems that cause bad feelings in the first place.

Laissez-faire parents also have trouble setting limits on kids' angry behavior. A raging five-year-old might knock all his older brother's toys off the table, breaking a few along the way. A parent with a laissez-faire philosophy of emotion might see this behavior, turn toward the child's anger with empathy, and then let it go, without ever addressing the child's destructive act.

It's not that laissez-faire families intend to be negligent; most of them simply lack the knowledge and skills they need to help their children to cope. Many have been raised in chaotic, oppressive, or abusive homes, where they missed out on lessons about calming down and solving problems. Because of their difficult upbringing, these parents often vow to raise their own kids differently, but they don't know where to start. They don't know what to teach children about emotions, other than to accept emotional behavior unconditionally. Such lessons have their limitations, however—especially when children behave in ways that are detrimental to themselves and others. When this happens, parents with a laissez-faire philosophy may feel helpless to remedy the situation. Consequently they withdraw from the scene, failing to give the kids what they truly need in terms of limits and guidance.

Not all laissez-faire parents lack the knowledge and support they need, however. Some are simply distracted by problems or other life priorities. Many are like Amy, the single mother and law student described in chapter

2, in that they let their work take over their lives, stripping away the time and attention they need to guide their children.

What happens to people raised in a laissez-faire family? Because they've had little guidance on how to handle difficult feelings, they don't learn to regulate their emotions very well. When they're angry, for example, their anger is indeed more likely to turn to aggression. When they're sad, they may not have the ability to regulate that sadness, so they're more likely to become depressed.

## How Emotional Philosophy Influences Connections

| Emotional philosophy | What this philosophy sounds like | How it affects bidding | How those with this philosophy respond to bids |
| --- | --- | --- | --- |
| Emotion-dismissing | "You'll get over it." "Cheer up." | Leads to less bidding. | Turning away. |
| Emotion-disapproving | "You shouldn't feel that way." "You'd better change your attitude." | Leads to less bidding. | Turning against. |
| Laissez-faire | "I understand how you feel." | May or may not lead to more bidding. | Turning toward, but without offering guidance for coping. |
| Emotion-coaching | "I understand how you feel. Let me help you." | Leads to more bidding. | Turning toward, with guidance for coping. |

## Exercise: Emotional Philosophy and Today's Relationships

Here's a list of questions designed to help you explore how your family's emotional philosophy may be affecting your relationships today. (The exercise on pages 146–150—What Was Your Family's Philosophy of Emotion?—can help you determine whether your family was primarily emotion-coaching, emotion-dismissing, emotion-disapproving, or laissez-faire.)

Again, you can do this exercise either alone or with someone you trust, and then share your answers. If you do it on your own, you can try to imagine how somebody close to you might answer the questions about his or her own family's emotional philosophy. Doing so may provide insights into how the two of you connect.

Write your answers to the questions below in your Emotion Log.

- How does your family's philosophy of emotion affect your ability to express difficult emotions such as sadness, anger, or fear?
- Are there certain emotions that you have a difficult time acknowledging in others? In yourself?
- Do you often feel unjustified or guilty when expressing negative emotions? How does this relate to your family's philosophy of emotion?
- Think of a particular relationship that's important to you. When you have a choice to turn toward, turn away from, or turn against this person's bids for connection, what do you do? Are you likely to make the same choice, whether this person's bid is expressed in a negative or positive way? How do your choices differ from how your parents might have reacted in a similar situation?
- When somebody you're close to gets sad, angry, or fearful, do you focus more on their behavior or on the feelings underneath the behavior?
- Over the next two weeks or so, jot down the times you recognize people's expression of sadness, anger, or fear as a bid for connection.
- Do you usually respond to these expressions by turning toward, turning against, or turning away?
- Do you see a correlation between your response and the emotional philosophy with which you were raised?
- What happens if you turn toward other people's expressions of negative feelings with validation?
- What happens if you turn toward other people's expressions of negative feelings with more than validation? What if you offer support or guidance?

## Which Philosophy Works Best?

In our two ten-year studies of more than one hundred families, the answer is clear. Families that create emotion-coaching environments fare much better than families that are dismissing, disapproving, or have a laissez-faire attitude toward emotions. Couples who accept, respect, and honor each other's feelings are less likely to divorce. Their children tend to do better over the years as well. Because these emotion-coaching families create environments that help children to regulate their feelings, their children can concentrate better than can the kids in the other groups. They get better grades in school. They have fewer behavior problems, and they get along better with peers. Lab results show that they have fewer stress-related hormones in their bloodstreams and that, over time, they suffer from fewer minor health problems like coughs and colds.

## Emotional Intelligence Versus Detachment and Denial

My findings about families' emotional expression, along with concurring evidence from others in my field, attracted lots of media attention in the mid-1990s. Despite this growing evidence of the value of accepting and respecting one another's feelings, however, many experts still get it wrong. In fact, many promote the idea that "emotional intelligence" is simply a matter of *controlling* our emotions and substituting positive feelings for negative ones.

I disagree with this perspective. I think that people operate best when they can experience the whole breadth of their emotional palette, and then use those feelings in the service of the goals they most desire.

One example of the way experts have mischaracterized the nature of emotional intelligence involves a Stanford University study of four-year-olds and delayed gratification. In the study, each child was taken individually by an experimenter to a study room and given one marshmallow. Then they were told that the experimenter had to leave for fifteen minutes. If they wanted to eat the marshmallow while the experimenter was gone, that was fine. But if they waited until the experimenter returned, they would get another marshmallow as well.

The Stanford researchers found some remarkable differences between the kids who devoured the first marshmallow immediately and those who waited patiently for the second. By high school, for instance, the kids who couldn't wait for marshmallow number two were seen as more shy, stubborn, and indecisive. They were more likely to think of themselves as "bad" or unworthy. And their SAT scores were dramatically lower than those of kids in the other group.

These are interesting results, but here's the $64,000 question that the Stanford researchers didn't answer: What motivated the kids who delayed gratification to wait? In his book *Emotional Intelligence: Why It Can Matter More Than IQ* (Bantam Books, 1995), Daniel Goleman writes, "They were able . . . to distract themselves while maintaining the necessary perseverance toward their goal—the two marshmallows." In other words, he attributes their success to their ability to squelch their feelings of desire.

But I think there's more to the story than Goleman suggests. I think the children demonstrated an equally important strength: an ability to get in touch with their desire for marshmallows and allow that desire to motivate them to wait. Rather than simply denying themselves the object of their passion, they were able to project themselves into the future and imagine how happy they would be when they finally achieved their ultimate goal—two marshmallows. In this way the successful management of emotions is not a matter of denying "inappropriate" feelings. Instead, it's a matter of accepting all of our emotions—including our passion for goals that may or may not be within our reach—and then using the energy of that desire to propel us toward what we want most from life. This interpretation is most consistent with my own data, which show that people who accept emotion lead more successful, fulfilling lives.

There are many incentives in our culture to stay emotionally detached, to dismiss and deny uncomfortable feelings. For one thing, it takes time and effort to be with your emotions. While emotional awareness at work pays off in the long run, in the short term, grief, anger, and fear can be tremendously distracting from the workaday world. In other words, dealing with difficult emotions interferes with productivity.

Our culture also discourages people from paying attention to difficult feelings, because getting to the root of what makes you angry or sad can bring about change in your life. It can take you away from the role into which you've been cast—whether that role fits or not.

I'm reminded of the Nike ad that so pervaded our culture in recent years: "Just Do It." To me, the subtext read, "Don't think of how you *feel* about doing it, because then you may not do it at all. You may never set records, you may never achieve success. You'll wind up a failure."

But I suggest that if you look into your heart and find that you really *don't* want to do it—whether "it" is to pursue a certain career goal, commit to a new relationship, or go for some other brass ring that others define as ultimate success—then perhaps you shouldn't.

As a college professor, I see many students set aside their dreams to follow the job market, believing they'll have more satisfaction in a higher-paying field. I remember one woman in particular who had a passion for mathematics. She might have become a stellar mathematical theorist, but she discovered she could make more money in accounting. So, even though accounting bored her, she switched her major, became an accountant, and ended up quite successful financially. When I met her years later, she said she had been very depressed. Although she was proud of her success, she felt she couldn't enjoy it. Why? Her work lacked "spirit," she said. She regretted that she had silenced that small but uncomfortable voice inside that was telling her she was headed in the wrong direction.

Fear of changing paths is certainly a major reason that people try to detach from their feelings. But perhaps the strongest and most basic reason is to avoid experiencing the very real pain that emotions can bring. Self-help psychology sections in bookstores are bulging with titles from dozens of authors who offer simplistic "just be happy" formulas for modern life. Such prescriptions for detachment work, to some degree. But in the long run you pay a very high price for detachment—namely, depression and isolation.

It's hard to be authentic and feel close to people if you feel you must always "cheer up" and put a smiling face forward. Life is filled with opportunities to feel serene, content, happy—even joyful. But it's also filled with irritation, anger, terror, and despair. As our exploration of the brain's emotional command systems shows us, such feelings are written into our genetic code; they're part of what it means to be human. To deny the existence of difficult feelings is to live a half life. But here's the worst of it: If you always try to stay emotionally detached, you erect an obstacle between yourself and others who are in the same boat. Unless you know and understand your own feelings, you can't know and understand what others are feeling. And unless you can show evidence that you do indeed understand, you won't bond emotionally to others.

This lesson recently became quite clear to me after my friend Neil Jacobson died so suddenly. I went through a period of grieving, during which I did not feel productive or cheerful or optimistic or whole. In fact, I felt terribly sad and terribly angry. I was angry that Neil was gone from my life, and I was angry that doctors had not diagnosed his illness in time to save his life.

I didn't like feeling as bad as I did at the time. I would rather have been happy and carefree. But when I talked to Neil's wife, also a good friend of mine, I realized why it was important for me to be with my grief and anger and to understand it. Had I remained detached, I would not have been able to be with her in her pain. I would not have been able to say, "My heart is broken about his death, too. I know how horrible this feels."

Because others understand through their own experience what she is feeling, they can be a comfort to her as she adjusts to this new life without him. And in so doing, they can help her overcome her grief and keep on living.

## Understanding Enduring Vulnerabilities

When we're open to feeling and expressing our emotions, we can better understand the "enduring vulnerabilities" each of us carry as a result of surviving painful events and relationships. UCLA psychologist Tom Bradbury coined the term to describe the elements in our past that have had such a powerful negative impact on our lives that it's impossible to shake their influence. Often these elements are incidents of loss, betrayal, abuse, or trauma.

Examples include:

- Death of a loved one
- Being assaulted or physically abused, including being severely spanked as a child
- Rape or other forms of sexual assault and molestation
- Witnessing violence
- Being the victim of robbery or other crimes

- Divorce, or the end of a significant love relationship
- Marital problems, such as constant fighting or infidelity
- Being raised in a home with serious marital problems and conflict
- Getting fired
- Failing at school
- Loss of belongings in a fire or natural disaster
- Abandonment
- Emotional abuse, including threats and humiliation
- Cruel hazing, bullying, or teasing by peers in childhood
- Life-threatening or serious illness
- Depression
- Feeling suicidal
- Living with alcoholism or drug addiction
- Surviving war, terrorism, civil strife

Whether or not you've experienced events as dramatic as these, your emotional heritage probably includes some enduring vulnerabilities. Indeed, I believe that each of us has endured some psychological pain, and that we do our best to survive, to heal, and to protect ourselves against being hurt again. All of this injury and healing affects how we relate to other people. We may even become somewhat irrational at times—especially when others' actions inadvertently trample on these highly sensitive areas of our psyches. And even when we feel we have triumphed over past injuries, these painful events and our attempts to heal and protect ourselves have partially formed us.

Because such painful experiences may undermine our ability to trust ourselves and one another, they result in enduring vulnerabilities that typically show up as we try to form healthy new relationships. Most often, these vulnerabilities surface around issues of inclusion, affection, and control. Unless, therefore, we understand how painful events from the past have helped to form us, and unless we can talk about this formation with people we're close to, we may continually face problems that seem impossible to solve.

A man who suffered a lot of cruel teasing by peers in childhood, for example, might have persistent worries about exclusion many years later. This enduring vulnerability shows up as a feeling of being unfairly excluded from meetings at work. When he tells his coworkers about his concerns, they scratch their heads; they don't believe they're purposely excluding him from anything significant. "Why is he so oversensitive," they wonder. "Why do I always feel like the outsider," he asks himself.

A young woman was raised by a mother who went through a severe depression when the daughter was small. Usually tired and irritable, the mother often ignored the child's bids for attention. Consequently, the grown daughter now has an enduring vulnerability that makes her crave affection from people with the same kind of cold, snappish temperament. She often becomes too quickly involved with men who are emotionally distant and treat her badly. After a series of painfully long but failed affairs, the daughter asks herself, "Why do I keep making such a poor choice in partners?" It's a question that will confound her for many years to come.

With introspection and self-understanding, however, people do find answers. They come to see how past incidents create enduring vulnerabilities that become their "crazy buttons"—the issues most likely to cause problems in the course of current relationships.

One thing I always do in therapy with married couples is to help partners explore one another's enduring vulnerabilities. This allows each to become more aware of the other's crazy buttons. They develop greater sensitivity and can be more respectful when they talk about these issues. It helps them to avoid the worst arguments while building trust and intimacy.

Such an approach is exemplified by Suzanne and Dale, a couple who came to the Gottman Institute for therapy. In our sessions we discovered that Suzanne felt an intense need for control that sprang from two devastating betrayals she had suffered. The first was in childhood, when she was sexually molested by her grandfather. The second was in adulthood, when she lost custody of her preschool-aged son to her ex-husband's surprise legal maneuvers.

Since that time, Suzanne has remarried and the boy has grown to be a teen. Now he comes to spend summers with her, her new husband, and their child. When conflicts arise—as they often do between any teen boy and his stepfather—Suzanne flies into a rage. To her husband's eye, she becomes the mother tigress, desperately defending her young. She wants to control the environment around her son totally, protecting him from anyone who might harm him. It's as if she's saying, "I was hurt by my grandfather, my ex-husband hurt me and my son, and now nobody is going to hurt us again!" The problem is, she takes a stand that's so emotionally charged and rigid that the three of them can't find a way to compromise and work through their conflicts.

But once Suzanne and her new husband saw the enduring vulnerability—her sense of betrayal—underneath her strong feelings, they had a breakthrough. Now, when this conflict occurs, Dale is able to remind Suzanne gently that he's not trying to do anything that would hurt her or her son in any way. He's not going to betray her. He's just trying to get the boy to turn down his CD player a notch, treat his baby brother kindly, or share the television with the rest of the family. Realizing this, Suzanne is starting to feel less controlling. And although she'll probably always be vigilant—especially when it comes to her firstborn—she's able to approach family conflicts in a more constructive way.

When we share our enduring vulnerabilities with the people we trust, we put all the cards on the table. And we can use this shared knowledge to make bids for emotional connections that strengthen relationships.

It takes courage to share your emotional vulnerabilities in any relationship, and for many people it's especially hard in the workplace. At the same time, work is where issues of control, affection, and inclusion can be the most challenging. So it makes sense that this might also be the place where measured risk could result in a welcome gain.

That's how it was for an executive I know, who also had problems with control. His "emotional vulnerability" was easy to spot. He was a Vietnam veteran who had served in the infantry. For years he had vivid memories, flashbacks, and nightmares of sniper attacks. And although the intense images faded with time, at age fifty he still lived with an inordinate amount of tension. Combat was over long ago, but the anxiety remained and he felt constantly vigilant, as though he had to guard against trouble he could only imagine. Because he was rigid and high-strung, he had a lot of problems getting along with his colleagues. If somebody left him an incomplete message about a problem in the company, for example, he'd automatically jump to conclusions and imagine the worst. He often felt paranoid, as if people were just waiting for him to make a mistake and fail. If another executive brought a tough issue before the board without consulting him first, he would get extremely angry, accusing the man of trying to "blindside" him, trying to sabotage his career.

Eventually the man sought therapy. Only then did he begin to understand that his experience in the war was at the root of his problems. The trauma he had suffered would probably affect him for the rest of his life, the psychiatrist told him. He might never fully escape that sense of emotional tension he lived with because of the fear he had experienced in combat. But just because he often felt tense didn't mean he had to create crises in his current life to justify that tension. There were other ways that he could cope with his feelings, including getting more exercise and practicing meditation. In addition, he could talk with some of the coworkers he trusted, and explain his situation to them. He could tell them that because of this enduring vulnerability, he could use a little help. As it turned out, he did talk to two of his assistants and another manager, who were quite understanding. After listening to him, they began to see just why this man hated what he considered surprises. They said they'd try to be more careful to keep him apprised of sensitive matters as they came up in the company. And they'd try to be more complete in their communication so that he wouldn't spend so much time guessing, imagining the worst. The executive found these accommodations helpful, and he's getting along better with the rest of his colleagues. But it couldn't have happened unless he'd been willing to examine the past and how his war experiences had affected him.

## *Exercise: What Are Your Enduring Vulnerabilities?*

The following exercise is designed to help you remember specific events and relationships from your past that may have resulted in enduring vulnerabilities. Take your time answering these questions, realizing they may bring a number of painful memories to the surface. Once you've completed these questions, it may help to share your answers with somebody you trust.

You may also want to invite a spouse, relative, or friend with whom you want to build better emotional connections to do the exercise with you. If that's not possible, you might want to imagine how that person would answer the questions if he or she did the exercise. Doing so may give you insight about ways to improve your relationship.

Below is a chart with a list of emotional injuries that commonly happen in a variety of relationships and often result in emotional vulnerabilities. Put a check mark in the columns to indicate the injuries you've experienced in the past.

| | Parents | Siblings | Lovers | Peers | Close friends | Coworkers |
|---|---|---|---|---|---|---|
| Not having enough control | | | | | | |
| Being excluded | | | | | | |
| Being controlled or coerced | | | | | | |
| Being unfairly treated | | | | | | |
| Being abused or humiliated | | | | | | |
| Not receiving affection or signs of affection | | | | | | |
| Not being accepted | | | | | | |
| Being betrayed | | | | | | |
| Being rejected | | | | | | |

*(continued)*

| | Parents | Siblings | Lovers | Peers | Close friends | Coworkers |
|---|---|---|---|---|---|---|
| Being ignored or neglected | | | | | | |
| Being disrespected | | | | | | |
| Other injuries (describe) | | | | | | |

Now, on a separate piece of paper, in a journal, or in your Emotion Log, write about these topics related to each injury you've checked.

- Describe what happened.
- How did this injury affect you?
- What did you do to try to heal from this injury?
- What have you done to ensure that this doesn't happen again?
- What are the implications of this injury on your current life?
- What are the implications for your current life of your attempts to heal?
- Did this injury change the way you make bids for emotional connection? In what way?
- Did this injury change the way you respond to bids for emotional connection? In what way?

## What Awareness Offers

Unfortunately, being more aware of an enduring vulnerability doesn't make it go away. But having more insight about it means that the next time you're aware of it, you can say, "Oh, there it is again. What does this have to do with the current situation?" Often the answer is "not much," and you're able to move on without being compelled to act on that feeling of vulnerability. This freedom to act can be extremely important in relationships when you want to improve your ability to bid and to respond to another's bids for emotional connection.

Perhaps you recall Rick and Sarah, the couple I described in chapter 2, who learned to see Sarah's righteous indignation and stockpiled complaints as a bid for connection. As it turns out, they learned a few things about the way an enduring vulnerability from Rick's past was contributing to their problems as well. Rick's mother left his family when he was a small boy, so he was cared for by his paternal grandmother, who very much resented the responsibility. Because the grandmother resented him, she carped at him constantly, telling him he was a dirty, worthless boy who would never amount to anything. Rick's father felt bad about the way his son was treated in his mother's home, but felt he could do nothing about it, since he relied on her for childcare. Rick's dad would do his best to smooth things over, often saying things to the family like, "Ricky's just fine. He's going to do great, as long as he gets good grades and goes to college—as long as he achieves."

Is it any wonder, then, that Rick grew up to work such long hours? In fact, much of Sarah's anger at him had to do with the loneliness she felt when he stayed late at the office. But because of Rick's enduring vulnerability—his feelings of worthlessness—he couldn't hear the longing in Sarah's bids for attention. He had a hard time accepting any kind of affection from his wife because all he heard in Sarah's voice was his grandmother saying, "You're no good. You're such a failure. You're such a disappointment."

When we talked about these messages in therapy, we learned that Sarah didn't feel that way at all. "I've never seen you that way," she said. "I think you're clever and creative. You're sexy. You're a great lover. You're a great dancer. It's just that you ignore me sometimes when I need you."

Rick was surprised and very happy to hear these words from Sarah. How odd, it seemed in retrospect, that his grandmother had taken such a prominent place in his marriage. But now that Rick and Sarah could identify his grandmother's influence, it was easier to keep the older woman's recriminations in the past.

It didn't make Rick's feelings of self-doubt go away. But now when they come up, he's able to say to himself, "I'm having that feeling again. I know where it's coming from. It's my grandmother talking. But Grandmother's words have nothing to do with what's going on here and now. I can have this feeling without having to act upon it."

With this realization, Rick puts his grandmother's influence in its proper place. It's a fading memory. It's yesterday's news. Now he can be more aware of his current life and current relationships. Now he can be more open to Sarah's expressions of longing and affection.

Most of the stories of enduring vulnerability I've told thus far involve insights people discover about themselves or others in the course of therapy. But a good friendship can also serve as a powerful vehicle for such self-discovery. That's because friendship often involves telling one another your life stories. And within those stories we often reveal a great deal to one another about our history of loss and betrayal, if not trauma and abuse.

Such revelations typically happen over time. Your friend may reveal some detail of a loss or betrayal he or she suffered as a child, and the two of you find you have common ground. ("So your parents divorced when you were in high school? Mine did, too." "Your dad died of cancer? I know what it's like to lose somebody that way.") Then, together, you explore the meaning that these powerful episodes had in your lives and how they continue to affect you today.

I once invited a friend from work out for coffee at a time when our relationship was new and our mutual trust was just beginning. In the course of our conversation, the man began to tell me a long and powerful story about how he had been betrayed by friends in a previous job. His story was filled with messages about how much he valued trust and loyalty in his relationships. The story also told me how important he felt it was to stand up for yourself, to fight for what you believe in, and to seek justice when you feel you've been treated unfairly.

By listening carefully to this one story, I learned that the betrayal he had suffered was a deep and enduring vulnerability for him. I learned that the issue of loyalty was no small matter to him. And although he did not come right out and say it, I learned that if I was going to be this man's friend, I needed to take this matter seriously as well.

When you understand your own enduring vulnerabilities and are willing to talk about them with people you trust, you're in a good spot to form deep and solid relationships. Another essential element is your willingness to listen openly when a friend or loved one tells you stories of the hard times they have endured, the events that are the most unforgettable parts of their emotional heritage. Honored respectfully, such conversations are the foundations of profound emotional connection.

## Back to the Future

It takes a brave heart to look back thoughtfully at past injuries, your family's emotional philosophy, and your emotional history. But doing so with a clear intention of improving your current and future relationships is well worth the effort. Getting clear about the past allows you to separate yesterday's issues from today's reality. It allows you to be more present in your current relationships. And, as we'll learn in the next chapters on emotional communication skills, being fully present and aware is vital to improving your bidding process.

# 6

# Step Four:
# Sharpen Your Emotional
# Communication Skills

*A* friend recently told me about a visit with her brother, whom she hadn't seen for several weeks.

"I'm worried about Tim," Marie said. "He just broke up with his girlfriend. He says he's fine, but when I saw him last night, I wasn't so sure."

"Did you talk to him about it?" I asked, concerned.

"Sure, but he never tells you much. He just said he was glad it's over—that he and Pam should have split years ago."

"If he says he's doing okay, then why are you worried?" I asked.

"I don't know. There was just something about him," Marie explained. "We had a nice evening. But I could sense this feeling in him—in his eyes and the tone of his voice. Sort of a heaviness. And he was moving more slowly. He just seemed . . . sad."

"That would make sense—especially if he and Pam were close," I said.

"Maybe I'll call him later and see if he wants to go to a movie with us this weekend. I think he may need a little extra company for a while."

"That's probably a good idea," I said. "And maybe you could remind him that if he wants to talk about how he's feeling, you'll listen. Because it sounds like he might not bring it up on his own."

"Yeah, you're right," Marie replied. "I think I'll do that."

After Marie left, I thought about how fortunate Tim is to have a sister like her—someone who is so perceptive, so caring. He may have some rough times ahead. But with his link to Marie, he'll know he's not alone in his sadness.

I've learned from my clinical practice that there are a lot of Tims in the world—people who have trouble talking about their feelings. And unfortunately there are not enough Maries—people who can detect another person's unspoken pain as bids for connection, and turn toward it compassionately. But if Marie follows through, and Tim opens up to her—even slightly—it will strengthen their sense of connection, which may enhance the quality of their lives for many years to come.

As we've discussed in previous chapters, people typically start building skills for such emotional connections early in infancy. From first smile to first date, childhood is a tremendous training ground for learning to detect, convey, and respond to feelings. But that learning process doesn't have to stop after we grow up. Many people continue to develop their skills at emotional communication well into adulthood, allowing them to create richer, more satisfying relationships with others.

In this chapter we'll take a look at forms of emotional communication that people use to express, read, and turn toward one another's feelings. These include a variety of verbal and nonverbal cues, including:

- facial expressions
- movement
- gesture
- touch
- tone of voice
- descriptive words
- metaphors

In addition, we'll explore some basic listening skills that foster better emotional communication. The goal of all this examination is twofold: first, to become more aware of the way you may use these channels to express your own feelings, and, second, to become more aware of the way those around you use them, so that you can recognize and respond to others' emotions through the bidding process.

The more you understand these elements of emotional communication, the better you'll be at bidding and responding to others' bids in a meaningful way. You may learn to recognize simple communication problems that are interfering with your ability to make your bids as clear as you'd like them to be. You may also learn to detect and respond to bids for connection that are hidden or obscured by people's anger or sadness. You'll develop the skills to start new relationships on a stable course, and you'll learn how to repair problems in continuing relationships and make them stronger.

Communicating with one another on a heart-to-heart level is not as mysterious as it might seem. Nor is it necessarily intuitive or automatic. Whether we're aware of it or not, people constantly send one another signals that can reveal how they're feeling in the moment.

As Alan Garner writes in his primer on interpersonal communication, *Conversationally Speaking* (McGraw-Hill, 1981): "You can't *not* communicate. Whether you smile or maintain a blank face, look straight ahead or down at the ground, reach out and touch or hold back, you are communicating and others will attach meaning to that communication."

Through facial expression, tone of voice, gesture, word choice, and more, we're constantly revealing our true emotional experience to one another. The key is to become more observant and more aware of these signals in your own behavior and in the behavior of others. Once you do, you can use your awareness in a conscious way to improve your bidding process and form better emotional connections.

## Pardon Me, but Your Feelings Are Leaking

There are many reasons why people refrain from expressing feelings—especially such negative emotions as sadness, anger, and fear. Many people want to avoid or deny negative experiences, to keep their distance from things that are upsetting. By putting a positive spin on events, they believe they won't have to think about things that sadden, anger, or scare them. Some people believe that their feelings are too frightening or disturbing to put into words. Or they may feel ashamed or embarrassed by what they're feeling, so they don't want to share their experience with others. Lots of people would like to avoid burdening their friends and relatives with emotional matters. They may believe that their feelings don't matter and don't deserve the attention of others, or they may feel that their problems would be too "upsetting" for others to bear. In addition, some people are so unused to expressing emotion that they can't find the words to say what's happening. And some, of course, simply value their privacy and so they're unwilling to reveal how they're feeling.

But as Tim's experience shows, just because people try to conceal their feelings doesn't mean that their emotions don't show. A videotaped study of unhappily married couples, conducted several years ago at the University of Oregon, graphically demonstrated this point. The experimenters told the stressed couples that their task was to "fool the cameras" and pretend that they were happily married. Then they asked the couples to make believe they had just been given a large sum of money and they had to decide together how to spend it. Looking at the printed transcripts of the couples' conversations, you'd think that most of them faked being happy quite well. The words show them to be loving, respectful, and conflict-free. But when you watch and listen to the videotapes of the couples' conversations, you get a much different impression. Their tones of voice and facial expressions betray their performances at every turn. Lines like "Whatever you say, dear" and "It's up to you" are punctuated with sarcasm and contempt. Their interactions are like sieves, leaking hostility everywhere. In fact, that's the verb psychologists use to describe the way we involuntarily show our emotions: Our feelings "leak" through. This and other studies demonstrate that no matter how much most people try to conceal their emotions, their true feelings usually become evident.

Studies also show that most people trust nonverbal cues more than they trust one another's words. Researchers have conducted experiments in which they deliberately combined facial, verbal, and vocal signals in inconsistent ways to see how people react. A speaker might say "Have a nice evening," while wearing a frown and speaking in a loud, abrasive tone of voice. Or a speaker might say "Go to hell," while offering a friendly wave and a warm, charming smile. In one study, when the research participants were asked to state which part of the message they relied on to discern the speakers' true attitudes, they said they relied only 7 percent on the spoken word. But they relied 38 percent on elements such as tone of voice and pace of speech. And they relied 55 percent on facial expressions and other body language.

That's how it works in real life as well. In cases where a person is saying one thing with words, but delivering an opposite message with tone of voice, posture, and facial expression, people almost always disbelieve the spoken words and trust instead the manner in which they were said. When it comes to sharing emotional information, we tend to look most closely at facial expressions and patterns of eye contact. We also watch body gestures, as well as how we position ourselves in relation to one another.

This is not to say that verbal channels are always ignored. In one study of parents and children in a waiting-room situation, some anxious mothers tended to smile while they sharply cautioned their children to behave. The smile was a positive mask on the negative threat from Mom. The researchers found that the children were not at all confused by this inconsistency. They concluded that most children will believe any source of genuine negative emotion, whether it's expressed verbally or nonverbally.

For some people, "reading" emotional information doesn't seem to require a lot of conscious thought. A woman may see a friend, for example, and know that he's angry without actually thinking, "Tom's furrowed brow and compressed lips tell me that he's mad." On the other hand, some people find it quite hard to read others' emotions intuitively; these people need to make a more concerted effort to look for signals.

Either way, it can be extremely helpful to consciously study how people express emotions through words, facial expressions, tone of voice, and so on. Doing so leads you to see all the subtle cues people pass back and forth as they bid and respond to one another's bids for emotional connection. With this heightened awareness, you can ensure that the messages you send via body language match the messages you send with your spoken language. You can avoid sending mixed messages or unwittingly discouraging interaction. You can also improve your ability to recognize, interpret, and respond to emotional cues others convey.

Learning better emotional communication skills can be helpful in many different arenas. Consider, for example, the supervisor who needs to assess whether a new employee is catching on to his job. Afraid of criticism, the worker may be reluctant to disclose any problems. But if the boss can read the employee's facial expressions for signs of tension, he can take steps to ensure that the worker has the training and resources he needs.

The trainee may find it useful to pay attention to his own nonverbal signals, as well. Say, for example, that he's in the middle of a training session and he realizes that he's been sitting in the same tense position for a very long time. What does the tension tell him about the learning experience? Is the trainer addressing all the issues he's concerned about? Is there some question he needs to have answered before he can feel assured, and therefore more physically relaxed?

Consider the parent who's worried about her teenager's grades. The mom knows her son is overbooked, and she wants to help him do a better job of setting priorities. But she also knows that if her son becomes defensive in a conversation about the issue, they'll never agree on a plan. If the mom can listen to her son's body language as well as his words, however, she may be able to steer the conversation in a more productive direction. She'll be able to see when she's having a calming effect on her son, and when he's becoming agitated. It will be easier for her to determine when he feels the same way she does about some issue, and when they disagree. She will also know when her son truly understands what she's saying, and when he's just pretending to understand so they can get the conversation over with. The mother will know when he's telling the truth and when he's holding back information, fearful of his mom's reaction.

Recognizing feelings, identifying them, and demonstrating your understanding—all of these are important steps to building better emotional connections. And all of them can be enhanced through the emotional communication skills described in the next several pages.

## Understanding the Face

Think about the pictures of friends and family that we keep in our wallets, on our desks, or hanging in the family den. Are these images of our loved ones' hands? Are they portraits of their feet? Probably not. People are much more likely to keep pictures of their friends' and relatives' faces nearby. It's their faces that you love to gaze upon. It's their faces that tell us so much of what a person is feeling—about us, about themselves, about the world around them.

Because faces are such a significant tool for making and responding to bids for connection, it's important to have a clear sense of how your facial expressions come across to other people. It's also important to learn all we can about the way others use their faces to convey feelings.

Among all the parts of the body, the face is the most uniquely suited for the function of expressing emotion. With the exception of muscles that are attached to the jaw for chewing, there are approximately thirty-three muscle groups in the face that are not attached to moving bones. Instead, their primary purposes include the transmission of emotional signals from one person to another. Information is exchanged via rapid changes in the shape of the forehead, the brows, the eyelids, the cheeks, the nose, the lips, and the chin.

Research conducted in the nineteenth century by the British naturalist Charles Darwin shows that people worldwide use the same facial expressions to communicate certain emotions. Darwin first explored the evolution of facial expressions by circulating questionnaires to missionaries and others in remote parts of the world. He asked how the native peoples showed when they were happy, sad, angry, and so on. If their answers differed, he could assume that expressions such as smiles were culturally based and not part of our genetic inheritance. But that's not what he found. Instead, his research showed people around the globe used the same expressions to show the same emotions. And from this he could assume that certain facial expressions were innate and biologically universal. In other words, our tendencies to smile when we're happy and grimace when we're angry are built into the "wiring" of our nervous systems and our facial musculature. Such manifestations of emotion are part of what it means to be human.

Many facial expressions evolved as a way for the human species to survive. Think about the way people grit their teeth and even bare them when they're extremely angry or threatened. We share this common and highly intimidating expression of rage with our evolutionary cousins—gorillas, chimpanzees, and orangutans. Or think about the way most people raise their upper eyelids when they feel surprised. Such a wide-eyed look allows you to take in as much visual information as possible—an expression that's been useful since our prehistoric ancestors first responded to unexpected bumps in the night. And finally, think about the way the nose crinkles in an expression of disgust. With raised nostrils and squinting eyes, our nasal passages and eyes are less exposed to noxious fumes.

Over the eons, emotional expressions have become more ritualized and less related to survival. Under most normal circumstances, for example, we settle our disputes without biting each other, so teeth-baring expressions aren't a literal threat. But we've come to interpret this facial expression as rage, and we're wise to respond to it in that spirit. And what about nose-wrinkling? It's still an expression of disgust today, even though we use it to respond to many things other than unpleasant or poisonous vapors.

Knowing that certain facial expressions are part of our genetic heritage helps us to understand that they're universal and instinctive. These notions were reexamined in the 1970s by Paul Ekman and Wallace Friesen, research psychologists at the University of California at San Francisco, and Carroll Izard at the University of Maryland. As part of their early research, they showed photos of faces displaying basic emotional expressions to people from around the world. Their findings supported Darwin's theory: People across many cultures use and recognize the same facial expressions for happiness, fear, anger, sadness, surprise, and contempt or disgust.*

That's not to say that some cultural differences don't exist. Friesen and Ekman found such differences with an experiment where they videotaped the facial expressions of American and Japanese people as they watched a horrific film of an industrial accident. Because the Japanese culture places a higher value on masking one's emotions, they expected to see less emotional reaction from the Japanese participants. And, in fact, when an official-looking, white-coated experimenter stayed in the room with each participant as he or she watched the film, that's exactly what the researchers found. The American participants showed a wide range of distressed facial expressions, while the Japanese participants responded with polite smiles, if at all. Things changed, however, when study participants were left completely alone to watch the film. When they thought nobody was watching them, the people of both cultures showed similarly distressed facial expressions. This led Friesen and Ekman to conclude that even when a culture has strict rules about public displays of emotion, its people still use the same basic facial expressions in private.

Although there's still lively debate on this issue, most social scientists now agree that the seven emotional expressions shown in the illustrations on the next two pages are basic to nearly every culture, and the ways they are facially expressed worldwide are stunningly similar. Of course, there are many different variations of these basic emotions. And we often feel more than one of them at a time. But we can consider these seven expressions to be primary colors on a palette. Just as colors can be mixed to create an endless variety of hues, facial expressions can be blended to express a wide range of emotion.

*Ekman and Friesen did find one exception: The Fore people, a fairly isolated tribe in New Guinea, did not distinguish between fear and surprise.

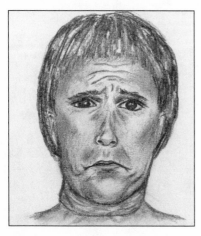

### Sadness

*The inner corners of the eyebrows come* up *and together* when a person is sad. This *creates a set of wrinkles in the form of an upside-down U at the middle of the brow. There's also a slight vertical furrow between the eyes. Taken together, this brow effect is called "Darwin's grief muscle." The outside corners of the lips point down.*

### Anger

*When people are angry, the inner corners of their eyebrows are drawn down and together in a prominent vertical wrinkle called a "knit brow" or "furrowed brow." They may open their upper eyelids more widely, displaying the whites of their eyes. They may also create an intense expression by contracting the lower eyelids. Lips may be tightly pressed together, and the pink part of the upper lip may disappear.*

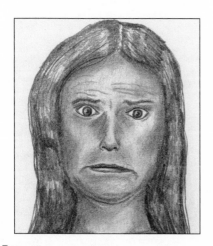

Illustrations by Julie Schwartz Gottman

### Fear

*A frightened person's eyebrows may appear nearly horizontal, with wrinkles stretched across the entire brow. As with anger, scared people show more of the whites of their eyes as the upper eyelid is raised. The corners of their lips may be pulled to the sides of the face in a tight horizontal line.*

### Happiness

*Happiness causes muscles in the cheeks to rise, and muscles around the eyes to contract. This creates wrinkles in the corners of the eyes. The corners of the mouth also curve upward, in a symmetrical smile. Eye wrinkles are the main way to tell authentic smiles from phony ones.*

**Surprise**
*When people are surprised, they typically raise their upper eyelids, exposing the whites of their eyes. Also, the mouth or jaw may drop open.*

**Contempt**
*When people feel contempt, the left corner of the lip is pulled out to the side, creating a dimple. An eye roll often accompanies contempt as well.*

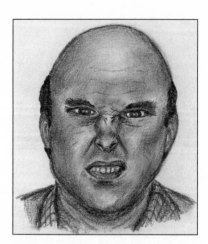

**Disgust**
*When people are disgusted, they often wrinkle their noses as if smelling something bad. As a result, horizontal wrinkles may appear at the top of the nose between the eyes, and the upper lip may be raised.*

While the information about facial expressions presented here is based on careful observational research, it can only give you clues to the way individual people are feeling. Each person expresses emotions in his or her unique way, so the only way to find out how a person is really feeling is to engage with that person in a sensitive way and discuss his or her experience. Still, learning to recognize these basic components of emotional expression in faces can be helpful on many levels. Visual cues provide objective evidence of something we often believe is picked up through intuition. So even if you consider yourself an emotionally intuitive person, you can check your subjective perceptions against objective evidence, validating and enhancing your skills. And if you don't have a great intuitive skill for reading emotions, conscious study of facial expressions can be a real boon. Visual cues also give you a factual, evidence-based foundation from which to explore other people's feelings.

Here are four points to keep in mind as you improve your ability to read emotions through facial expressions.

**1. Get familiar with a person's face in its most neutral state.** In other words, how does this person's face appear when she's not smiling, frowning, or stressed? Then compare that to how her face changes when she's responding to various emotional stimuli. How do her facial muscles react when you think she's happy, sad, scared, or surprised? How do your impressions compare with the information you're learning about emotional expression? As you consider these questions, don't be afraid to check out your impressions with the person you're observing. That's where real emotional communication happens. It's enriched by questions like "How are you feeling right now?" or statements like "It looks like you're angry [sad, disgusted, happy, scared, etc.]. Am I right?"

**2. Keep in mind that people often feel more than one emotion at once.** When this happens, you may see a confusing mixture of feelings on a person's face. Their mouth may be smiling, but their eyes look sad. Or you may see a split-second expression of rage in the midst of a much longer expression of sadness—a blend that's quite common among people who feel depressed.

People may also present a mixture of expressions when they are trying to conceal their feelings. Imagine, for example, the stressed-out "courtesy clerk" whose job requires a constant smile. She may keep her lips and cheeks turned up for eight hours a day, but her eyes defy any emotional involvement. And if she's having a particularly bad day, you're likely to read her anger and tension in her brow as well.

Here are three clues to whether a person's smile actually reflects happiness:

- Raised cheeks and compression or wrinkles around the sides of the eyes, where "crow's-feet" typically appear.
- A symmetrical smile. Manufactured smiles tend to be lopsided, with left-handed people smiling more strongly on the right side and right-handed people smiling more strongly on the left side.
- Right timing. Real smiles usually come on fast, are held for a longer period of time, and then fade in an irregular way.

If these clues are absent, the smile you see is probably a posed or "unfelt" smile—the type that photographers get when they tell people to "say cheese."

**3. Don't misinterpret permanent physical features as fleeting emotional expressions.** A person whose mouth continually turns down at the corners, for example, may have inherited this physical feature from his mom and his grandfather before that. At first glance, the feature may seem to indicate that he's always sad. But as you get to know him better, you realize that's just the natural shape of his mouth. He can be feeling perfectly chipper and still look a bit despondent to those who don't know him well.

There was a time in the late nineteenth century when people believed in the pseudoscience of physiognomy, which held that certain facial features revealed truths about a person's character. A high forehead, for example, was supposed to be a sign of natural intelligence, or thin lips meant a person was innately anxious. Such ideas have no scientific merit and were disproved long ago. Rather than focusing on permanent features, it's more important to watch how a person's face changes when he's responding to various emotional stimuli. Does the left corner of his mouth move slightly to the side in an expression of contempt? Do his eyes suddenly widen because he's surprised?

**4. Take time to look.** Skilled observation takes vigilance, especially considering that most meaningful facial expressions happen fast. In fact, valuable information is often gleaned through actions that psychologists call "micro-expressions"—flashes of feeling that may last just a fraction of a second, but may contain emotional data that the person would rather hide. Even the more common and purposely shared facial expressions only last up to ten seconds. So you've got to be watching closely or you'll miss these displays.

At the same time, people have lots of reasons not to look too closely at one another's faces. In many cultures, including those of the United States and Britain, people consider a constant gaze, or staring, to be an invasion of another person's privacy. So unless you're feeling particularly bold or aggressive, you don't do it.

In some societies, it's considered impolite to look directly at a person of higher status. When I worked with Pima Indians in Arizona, for example, I learned that a young person would not look directly at an older person; it's considered disrespectful. Also, when two men in that culture stare at each other, it's thought of as a challenge and can lead to a fistfight.

Many people avoid looking at one another too closely because they don't want to bear the burden of what they might find out. They may ascertain, for example, that the other person is depressed or lonely, needy or afraid, and they don't want to take the trouble to help.

People raised in abusive environments may avoid looking at others' faces because they associate such intimacy with getting hurt.

Some people don't look at one another because they want to maintain power and control. During conversation, the speaker typically looks into another's eyes as a sign that he or she is willing to give up the floor. But if the speaker doesn't want to stop talking, she simply avoids eye contact. As long as the speaker's eyes are averted, she can't be expected to know that another person wants some air time. She's able to control the floor and the conversation.

The problem with not looking, of course, is that it limits the exchange. It's hard to connect with the people you're speaking to unless you look into their faces. Eye contact with the listener reveals how that person is reacting emotionally to what you're saying. Is he interested? Entertained? Angry? Surprised? Scared? Does she agree with you? Do his facial expressions and other body language tell you that he respects what you're saying, that he understands? In a face-to-face conversation, we can't be sure of any of this unless we look at one another.

Through careful observation, we can tell whether two people are aligned in their feelings or just pretending to be. For example, a couple I recently saw in therapy was having considerable conflict over disciplining their teenage son. The husband felt his wife was too permissive and forgiving, while the wife felt her spouse was much too harsh and restrictive. The problem came to a head when they caught the boy and his girlfriend secretly smoking pot in their home, breaking a rule the boy had agreed to. The husband said they both felt the same way about the episode: "He violated our trust and we're mad." His wife nodded in agreement. But as the pair continued to talk about the episode, I noticed a subtle difference in their facial expressions. The husband was pressing his lips together in a way that said he was indeed primarily angry. And although the wife's nod said she was angry, too, the emotional expression she wore on her brow revealed something else. In fact, the inside corners of each eyebrow were lifted up in a classic and intense expression of grief, using what's called "Darwin's grief muscle."

When I told them that I observed this difference in their feelings through their expressions, they were surprised. But soon the wife started to acknowledge, for the first time, her sense of loss. She had held this image of her son as an innocent, carefree boy, and now all of that was changing. She expressed this to her husband and he said he understood, but he added that this wasn't the way he felt at all. In his heart, all he could feel was duped, put upon. He felt that his son had taken advantage of all the privileges they had afforded him and he was returning their favor with nothing but disrespect.

Being able to see and acknowledge the differences in their feelings didn't solve the conflict for the couple, but it was a start. And the evidence that brought their differences to the surface was the expressions they wore on their faces. In this way, an objective examination of facial expressions can reveal emotional truths that people won't or can't admit, even to themselves.

Paying closer attention to facial expressions may feel a bit awkward or contrived at first. That's because it requires you to do many things at once. You must remind yourself to keep looking at the mechanics of facial expression at the same time you're trying to carry on a "normal" conversation—one in which you feel more comfortable focusing on what's being said rather than on *how* it's being expressed physically.

When I was in graduate school and first learning Ekman and Friesen's rather complex system for observing and codifying facial expressions, I used to practice my observation skills everywhere I went. I would walk around campus, noticing more angry expressions than I wanted to see. And conversations with my girlfriend at the time were particularly hard.

"Stop staring at my brow!" she would say. Or, "Stop looking at my mouth."

"But that's where most of the emotional information is," I'd reply.

"No, that's not true," she'd argue. "Everything you need to know is in my eyes. Look into my eyes!"

Well, that was the myth. In truth, I was learning to find subtle clues to her emotional world all over her face—in her eyes, her brows, her cheeks, her lips, her chin. It was all so exciting to discover—and so distracting! Eventually, however, my skills improved and I began reading emotions in a less obvious way. It became automatic.

Your skills can improve over time, as well. And once they do, looking for emotion-revealing cues will become second nature to you, requiring less and less effort. You see a certain contour on your brother's mouth, or a compression of your sister's brow, and you won't have to stop and think, "What does that mean?" Instead you'll automatically identify the emotion, and you'll do so with less hesitation or self-doubt. You'll see it as a signal to tune in to their perspective, to find out what's up. You may even catch a glimpse of yourself in the mirror one morning and notice an expression of fear, anger, or sadness "leaking" through your composure. "What is this about?" you can ask yourself. "What can I do right now to get more centered, more prepared for the day ahead?"

## Exercise: Log Your Observation of Facial Expressions

You can use your Emotion Log to document your observations about the way emotions appear in facial expressions. Over time, these observations will help you to grow in awareness of the way people use their faces to bid for emotional connection and respond to other people's bids.

Below are several questions to consider as you write in your log. For this exercise you may want to think about a particularly powerful or difficult interaction you've had with an important person in your life over the past several days. Write down your impressions of that person's facial expressions, or your own, during that incident.

- What interesting facial expressions have you noticed recently?
- Who wore the expressions?
- What did they look like? (Make simple sketches, if you'd like. Or clip pictures from newspapers or magazines that show various emotions.)
- What did these expressions tell you about the way this person was feeling?
- Were you aware of people responding to your facial expressions? What did you notice?

## Reading Movement and Gestures

Although facial expressions are usually the first place we look for emotional information, feelings can be detected as well in the way people use other parts of their bodies. A swift, downward hand-chop can indicate a speaker's passion, for example. A shrug of the shoulders shows when somebody is feeling confused or helpless. Some social scientists have suggested that while the face can tell you what people are feeling, it's the body that reveals just how strong those feelings are.

Researchers have observed, for instance, that people who feel extremely tense tend to fidget, shifting positions often and touching themselves on the nose, chin, or mouth. Some psychologists have suggested that such self-touching subconsciously imitates the calming action of being stroked by a parent or lover. But for the observer it's also a sign that this person is anxious. It may even be a sign that he or she is trying to deceive others.

People sometimes communicate their lack of interest in one another through gestures. The sociologist Erving Goffman identified a series of behaviors that indicate when people are "away"—that is, not engaged with those around them. They touch their own faces with their hands, for example, usually covering the mouth. They bite their lips or the insides of their cheeks. They start manipulating "props," such as their own hair, beard, glasses, or a pen. Such distracted behavior sends the message that whatever others are saying or doing, it's not very stimulating.

Posture can also reveal emotions. In fact, when I furnished one part of my observational research lab, I purposely chose chairs that were slightly uncomfortable so that my study participants felt compelled to readjust their positions every few minutes. With each shift, I got a new opportunity to observe people using their spines, shoulders, legs, and arms in positions that expressed how they were feeling in the moment. When a wife gets irritated with her husband, for example, she might turn her back to him slightly. And even though she keeps her face pointing politely ahead, her hips, knees, and feet may turn away—as though she's subconsciously getting ready for her escape.

Crossing your arms across your chest during a conversation is another common emotional cue. It may tell observers that you're dissatisfied or opposed to what's going on. Cross your legs or draw your knees tightly together, and you intensify the message that you're closed to participation or influence.

An open posture—in which you sit with your arms relaxed, your legs slightly apart, and your body tilted a little forward toward your conversation partner—gives just the opposite message: You respect this person and you want to offer your full attention. Adopt this position and you communicate that you're open to influence, you're available for interaction.

You can also express affiliation by copying the posture of the person with whom you're speaking. You may be sitting with a good friend at opposite ends of a sofa, for example, when you notice that you've adopted exactly the same position. Your back is turned in the same way. You're holding your shoulders, arms, legs, and hands at exactly the same angle. While this kind of mirroring often happens subconsciously, you can also do it intentionally, quietly mimicking another person's posture as a way to build rapport.

Even small babies are sensitive to posture cues. Studying interactions between parents and their three-month-old infants, the psychologist Elizabeth Fivaz Depeursinge found that body position made an important difference in how long babies would stay engaged with their moms or dads. Babies whose parents sat with their hips aligned toward them would play happily for longer bouts than babies whose parents sat with hips swiveled away.

How closely we stand or sit next to one another also sends an emotional message. When you feel affectionate or sexually attracted to another person, getting physically close is typically a pleasant experience. But if somebody steps into another person's personal space without acceptance or permission, reactions may range from slight irritation to rage. Videotaped studies have been conducted of people at parties, for example, where an experimenter purposely crowds an unwitting guest. By consistently standing just a few inches too close (according to American standards), the experimenter can back the other guest across an entire room. When guests are interviewed about their impressions after such interactions, they typically describe the experimenter as interesting, but much too aggressive.

How close is too close among people who aren't on intimate terms? This sense of personal space differs considerably from one culture to the next. People from the Middle East represent one end of the spectrum. It's not unusual, for example, to see public vendors in Arab countries standing nose to nose as they transact business. But people from North America and Great Britain prefer a lot more room—three to five feet between strangers, and one and a half to three feet among friends. I've sometimes heard this U.S./British preference described as "cocktail party distance" because it's approximately equal to the space created by two people standing face to face with forearms stretched out from the waist, as if they were holding drinks.

In general, the distance people keep between them differs based on the type of relationship, the setting, and the person's mood. You don't want to get so close that your conversation partner feels uncomfortable. Nor should you be so far away that you seem aloof or defensive. Keep in mind that people can generally tolerate more closeness when they're feeling relaxed. When angry or stressed, they need more space. Also, try to get on eye level with the other person. This may mean crouching or kneeling when you're speaking to small children. And if you talk to someone who's seated, pull up a chair for yourself, if that's appropriate.

## Exercise: Log Your Observation of Movement and Gestures

Use your Emotion Log to document your observations about the way emotions appear in people's movement and gestures. As you make entries in your log, you may want to think about a particularly emotional incident you've had recently with a loved one, or with somebody else important in your life.

- What interesting movements or gestures did you notice others sharing recently?
- Who used them?
- What did they look like? (Make simple sketches or clip pictures, if you'd like.)
- What did these expressions tell you about the way that person was feeling?
- Were you aware of people responding to your movement or gestures? What did you notice?

## The Language of Touch

Just as the space between us is important, so too are the bridges that we build across that space via touch. Touch can be an important tool in bidding and responding to others' bids for connection. It can convey underlying channels of feelings in so many situations. Maybe you've experienced a few of these emotion-filled examples:

- Shaking hands with the person who offered you your first "real" job
- Holding hands with your first girlfriend or boyfriend
- Sharing a "high five" with teammates after the big win
- Slipping your hands into your lover's back pockets
- Bathing your newborn
- Patting your best friend's back on his wedding day
- Hugging your child as he returns from summer camp
- Holding hands with a dying parent as she slips in and out of consciousness
- Cuddling front to back with a lover in the middle of the night

Studies prove that touching and being touched can have a tremendous impact on people's feelings of health and well-being. Research by University of Miami psychologist Tiffany Field, for example, reveals the benefits that touch can provide in the emotional development of infants—even when the babies' mothers are depressed. It's an important finding, because Field's previous work showed that having a depressed mother can potentially harm the way a baby's brain learns to process feelings. In one of Field's experiments, for instance, babies of depressed moms were uncharacteristically wary of stimuli as harmless and entertaining as watching soap bubbles rise. But when the researchers taught the mothers to touch and massage their babies, this effect was reversed. The study further revealed that the mother's touch had a lasting positive effect on the baby and might even compensate for the negative effects of being cared for by a depressed mom. So powerful are such findings that Field has set up several Touch Research Institutes in university settings to further study the healing power of touch.

Because people often use touch to communicate their attachment to one another, it plays a strong role in both courtship and committed romantic relationships. By studying unattached men and women at singles bars, restaurants, and parties, one researcher observed that a woman's touch can be extremely influential in attracting men. The study showed what power women wielded by touching men with their hands, knees, thighs, or breasts. In fact, such courtship signals were a better predictor of a man's interest in her than the woman's physical appearance.

Touching is an important way for two people to signal to others that they're attached. Erving Goffman called behaviors such as holding hands in public "tie signs." In one of his studies, an interviewer approached couples in line at a movie theater and started to ask either impersonal or intimate questions. If the interviewer was a man asking a woman intimate questions, the man she was with showed more tie signs than he did if the questions were impersonal. Studies have also shown that the amount of touching couples do in public varies according to the stage of a relationship. Early in heterosexual dating relationships, men touch more than women. Later, when relationships become more serious, the amount of touching is equal. And in early marriage, women touch more than men.

In addition to communicating affection or comfort, touch can be used as a demonstration of power and control. Observational studies in work situations have shown that people feel much freer to touch their subordinates than their superiors. With this finding in mind, think about the various ways an assistant might interpret the boss's pat on the back. Regardless of the boss's intention, the assistant's reaction may range from feeling acknowledged to patronized to intimidated to sexually harassed. If the assistant feels offended by the touch, the imbalance of power in the relationship may make it hard for the assistant to complain. The same dynamic is common in abusive family situations. It's the abuser who decides when and where it's okay to touch. The victim typically has no power over the situation.

Because touch can evoke strong emotions, it's important to pay close attention to cultural norms. In many European countries, for example, people greet one another socially with a kiss on each cheek. In the United States, however, a handshake or a light hug will suffice. And in Japan, no touch is expected; a slight bow of the head is considered most appropriate.

Norms can also differ according to age, gender, religion, profession, or other characteristics. If you're aware of the norms, you can follow them to fit in more easily, to mix and socialize without drawing undue attention to yourself. You can also choose to make a statement by *not* following the norms. When you sense a mutual sexual attraction to someone new, for example, a tender touch may create just the kind of attention you're after.

But if you're *not* aware of the norms, you may make statements you never intended to make. I know of a retired Air Force officer, for instance, who was hired as sales director for a health-related business. Although he was competent in his new position, he had a habit of greeting clients with a handshake so strong that they found it painful. His super-firm greeting was probably an asset in the military, but among hospital and clinic administrators, it was considered oddly aggressive, and it got in the way of building rapport.

Rules can also change depending on the setting. American male football players, for example, often pat one another on the butt during the game, and it's not considered a sexual overture. But if that player tried the same behavior during a quiet dinner with another player, it might be perceived quite differently.

The key lesson to remember is that touch is powerful. It can have a big impact on other people, negative or positive. When you touch someone, it's important to be aware of the message that your touch may convey. Is it likely to strengthen the relationship or to weaken it? And if someone else touches you in a way that you find unclear or confusing, ask yourself about the source of your confusion. Such questions might include the following:

- Does this person feel warmly toward me?
- Is this touch affectionate? Comforting? Friendly? Sexual? Pleasant? Aggressive? Threatening?
- Is this touch meant to control me?
- Do I like being touched in this way?
- Does this touch make me feel uneasy?
- Would I want to be touched by this person in this way again?

Trust your feelings, and talk to the other person about feelings that surface, if possible.

Remember that touching and being touched is important to our sense of well-being and to feeling connected with others. Used wisely, it can communicate your affection, concern, and affiliation with others, and foster the development of warm, open, trusting relationships.

## Exercise: Log Your Observation of Touch

Use your Emotion Log to document your observations about the way people express their feelings through touch. Below are some questions to consider as you make entries in your log. As you do this exercise, it may help to think about a particularly difficult, comforting, or pleasurable interaction you've recently had with another person.

- What observations have you recently made about the way people use touch to express their feelings?
- Who was involved?
- What did these gestures look like? (Make simple sketches or clip pictures, if you'd like.)
- What did these gestures tell you about the way that person was feeling?
- Were you aware of people responding to your touch? What did you notice?

## What the Voice Reveals

In addition to the words we speak, our voices provide listeners with a wealth of emotional information. Knowing more about the voice can help you to more effectively express what you're feeling, and to hold a listener's interest. You'll also learn to listen for emotional cues in others' voices. Common emotional signals include changes in the pitch, rate, and volume at which people talk.

According to research by Geneva psychologist Klaus Scherer, voice pitch goes up for a majority of people when they're feeling angry or fearful. The voice moves from what Scherer calls "the chest register," which is low, relaxed, and resonant, to the "head register," which is higher and more tense. Their speech may also become louder and faster. But if a person is naturally a fast speaker, his or her speech may slow down when mad or scared.

Sadness is harder to detect in the voice than anger and fear, says Scherer. Still, there's some evidence that pitch goes down and the rate of speech becomes slower when people feel sad.

Pitch may also vary depending on whether the information shared is negative or positive. If a speaker says, "I've got a meeting in Chicago next week," and he's looking forward to that meeting with optimism, the pitch of his voice is likely to rise at the end of his statement. But if he's worried about that meeting, and he's approaching it with a sense of dread, the pitch of his voice will deepen as he gravely tells you, "I've got a meeting in Chicago next week."

Linda Camras, a psychologist, observed that this optimistic rise in pitch usually is accompanied by eyebrow raising, whereas the pitch-lowering worry is likely to be accompanied by drawing the brows down and together. If you want to see for yourself, try saying, "My mother-in-law is coming to visit," in a worried tone, and simultaneously try raising your brows. Then try saying it in a happy, optimistic tone while lowering your brows. It's hard to do.

It's also difficult for people to monitor the way their own voices sound to others, which is one more reason the voice can provide so much emotional information. Think about how strange it sounds to hear your own voice on a tape recorder. Unless you regularly work with audio equipment, you're probably surprised by how you sound on tape compared with the way you sound to your own ear while you're speaking. If you don't know what your voice sounds like in the first place, it's hard to change your voice to mask your feelings.

Still, social scientists—especially those involved in the study of law enforcement—have put a lot of effort into trying to read fear and tension in the voice. Common signs of such emotions include the following:

- Changes in mid-sentence ("I have a book that . . . the book I need for finals is . . .")
- Repetition of words or phrases in mid-sentence ("I often . . . often I work at night . . .")
- Stuttering ("Y-y-you wouldn't be thinking of l-l-leaving . . .")
- Omitting words or leaving words unfinished ("I went to the lib . . .")
- Incomplete sentences ("He said the reason was . . . anyway, he couldn't go.")
- Slips of the tongue ("I went to the grocery stair for milk and eggs.")
- Intruding incoherent sounds ("I don't really know why . . . dh . . . I went . . .")

If you want to use your voice to communicate your feelings more clearly, pay attention to the pitch, rate, and volume at which you speak. Remember that a slow, quiet monotone does not foster interest. But if you vary your pitch, rate, and volume in ways that emphasize the points you want to make, you'll be a more interesting speaker. You'll have a better shot at connecting with others on an emotional level.

To read emotion in others' voices, pay attention to changes in their pitch, rate, and volume. As with facial expressions, such changes can't tell you the absolute truth about the way another person is feeling, but they are an indication that a significant level of emotion is being expressed. Don't be afraid to follow your hunches and ask the speaker questions about your perceptions: "Your voice gets so low when you talk about going to Chicago. I have the feeling you don't want to go." Or, "You're talking so fast. Are you kind of anxious about this meeting in Chicago?" Such queries may lead to conversations that foster emotional connection.

## Exercise: Log What You Hear in People's Voices

You can use your Emotion Log to document the emotional information you hear in people's voices. Below are some questions to consider as you make your entries. You may want to think about a recent incident or two in which you and another used your voices to express your feelings.

- What interesting vocal expressions have you noticed recently? (Consider changes in pitch or rate of speech, speech patterns, or tone of voice.)
- Who used these vocal expressions?
- What did these expressions tell you about the way this person was feeling?
- Were you aware of people reacting to emotional expressions in your voice? What did you notice?

## Putting Feelings into Words

There are many good reasons to focus on your emotions, give them a name, and then talk about them.

First, naming your feelings engages the part of the brain that controls the functions of logic and language. So when you identify your feelings and put them into words, you get a better sense of control over them. This can help you to cope with negative emotions like fear, anger, or sadness.

Second, naming your feelings and talking about them is essential for connecting with others; people around you can't know for certain what you're feeling unless you tell them.

Relationships grow when one person helps the other to name his or her emotions. Here's a simple example: Your friend tells you that his favorite aunt just died. If you say, "That must be very sad for you," you show that you understand your friend's experience, which helps you to connect emotionally.

What's even more helpful, however, are those instances when a friend is not sure what he's feeling and you help him figure it out:

"Jenny left last night without even saying good-bye."

"That must have been upsetting."

"It was. I didn't know what to think."

"Were you angry?"

"Sort of. But it was more than that. We've always been so close."

"So it sounds like you're kind of disappointed and sad."

"Yes, I'm really sad. And kind of scared, too. I don't know what I'd do if she left for good."

The ability to identify feelings and express them in words comes easily for some. These people are often quite aware of what they're feeling moment by moment, and have a rich vocabulary with which to describe their emotions.

But other people struggle all their lives to understand their feelings, name them, and converse about them. They may know they're feeling *something,* but they're just not sure what the feeling is. For those who have this kind of challenge, it may be helpful to take an intellectually based, or "cognitive," approach to exploring emotion. This involves remembering recent experiences in your life and thinking about the way such experiences typically lead people to feel.

Here's an example: Carl comes home from work and finds a note from his wife. It says she's gone to a PTA meeting, his son has gone to a movie, and his daughter is off with her girlfriends. He rummages through the refrigerator, finds some leftover pizza, heats it in the microwave, and settles in front of the television to watch a news program, the topic of which is the unstable economy.

Later that night, as Carl is lying in bed, he's aware that he feels vaguely uncomfortable, but he's not sure why. In fact, he's not sure that he *wants* to know why. But he's tired of this undefined angst that seems to be haunting him, and he'd like to get to the bottom of it. So he begins to think about this negative energy he's experiencing.

At this point he can only describe his feelings as "unsettled." Then he starts to reflect back on the evening's events—how unpleasant it was to come home to a dark, empty house when he was expecting to see his wife, his kids, and dinner on the stove. There was definitely something missing for him in this situation. And he knows that when things are missing from people's lives, they often feel sad. So he concludes, "I wanted to be with my family and they weren't here. This made me feel lonely. Lonely and disappointed."

Still, Carl feels there's more to the evening's negative energy. He thinks about the TV program. The economy has been strong for quite a while, and he and his wife have enjoyed a nice sense of economic security. But the program talked about how volatile the markets have become—how investors could lose a great deal very quickly. The program made him realize that his investments might not be that secure after all. And he knows what happens when people question their safety. They begin to feel anxious and fearful. "So this energy I'm feeling is more than loneliness and disappointment about not seeing my family," he tells himself. "It's also anxiety. I'm anxious about our investments."

Now that his feelings of loneliness, disappointment, and anxiety are defined, Carl decides he can do something about the discomfort he's feeling. He can talk with his wife about how he missed seeing her and the kids that night; perhaps they can plan to do something enjoyable together in the next few days. He can talk to his financial adviser and his wife about their investments and make some adjustments if they decide that's a prudent course.

Exploring emotions in such an analytical way may seem strange to people who have a more intuitive sense of what they're feeling moment by moment. But this cognitive approach can be a real benefit to people like Carl, who lack easy access to words and concepts that can help them cope with their feelings. Rather than expressing a vague sense of irritation at his family over who-knows-what, Carl can now talk specifically about what he's feeling. This puts him in a better position to express his needs and to connect with others emotionally. Identifying his emotions in an analytical way gives him the structure he needs to take steps toward feeling more settled and peaceful.

## Exercise: What Am I Feeling?

This exercise is designed to help you to define what you're feeling and to put your emotions into words. It may also help you to be a better listener—somebody who helps others to name their feelings and talk about them.

To start, think about a recent experience that left you feeling uncomfortable or unsettled in a way that was hard for you to define. Write down a short description of the incident in your Emotion Log.

Then look at the following series of questions, which are intended to help you determine in a general way what you might have been feeling at the time. After you've answered these questions, scan the Emotional Vocabulary List on the following page to find more specific ways to describe your feelings.

Once you've identified the emotions you were feeling, do you feel as if you have a better idea of how to express those feelings to people that matter? Can you think of steps you can take to soothe uncomfortable feelings, or to solve problems that are causing the discomfort? Write about these insights in your Emotion Log as well.

First ask yourself if the emotion you're experiencing is pleasant (positive) or unpleasant (negative).

### If the feeling is pleasant:

- Do you think you'd like to explore some topic or get to know some person better? If so, you're probably feeling *interested.*
- Did something good happen? If so, you're probably feeling *happy.*

### If the feeling is unpleasant:

- Do you think that something is lost, absent, or missing from your life that ought to be there? If so, then you're probably feeling *sad.*
- Do you think there's an obstacle to what you're trying to accomplish? If your goal is blocked, then you're probably feeling *angry.*
- Are you thinking that things are unsafe in your world? If so, then you're probably feeling *fearful.*
- Are you thinking that someone or something should be judged as beneath you or against your values and morals? If so, then you're probably feeling *contemptuous.*
- Are you thinking that you just can't tolerate things as they are anymore, or that you just can't "swallow" a current situation? If so, then you're probably feeling *disgusted.*

## *Emotional Vocabulary List*

Describing your feelings can help you to connect emotionally. It can also help you to cope with difficult feelings. This list, divided into general categories of emotion, may help you to name your feelings and to talk about them.

## Interested

Stimulated
Fascinated
Engrossed
Engaged
Involved
Attentive
Eager
Excited
Anticipatory
Looking forward to
In awe
Entertained
Amused

## Happy

Pleasantly
  surprised
Pleased
Contented
Satisfied
Cheerful
Glad
Appreciative
Grateful
Feeling good
Gratified
Proud
Jovial
Delighted
Loving
Liking
Attached to
Affectionate toward
Adoring
Blissful
Joyful
Ecstatic
Elated
Euphoric
Jubilant

## Sad

Unhappy
Sorry
Sorry for
Regretful
Depressed
Discouraged
Disappointed
Dejected
Glum
Despondent
Dismayed
Down in the dumps
Blue
Heartbroken
Heartsick
Miserable
Disheartened
Despairing
Grieving

## Angry

Displeased
Dissatisfied
Envious
Jealous
Resentful
Offended
Frustrated
Annoyed
Irritated
Mad
Fuming
Irate
Heated
Cross
Crabby
Bitchy
Exasperated
Furious
Incensed

Livid
Enraged
Outraged

## Fearful

Timid
Nervous
Uncomfortable
Scared
Afraid
Disturbed
Uneasy
Concerned
Apprehensive
Anxious
Worried
Dread
Petrified
Terrified
Horrified

## Contemptuous

Offended
Appalled
Indignant
Judgmental
Disdaining
Disrespecting
Despising
Bitter

## Disgusted

Dislike
Hate
Loathe
Repelled by
Repulsed by
Aversion to
Revulsion
Sickened
Aghast

## Metaphorically Speaking

Just as the voice provides clues to what's happening in the hearts of people talking, so do the metaphors they choose.

Many of us learned about metaphors in a high school literature class, and often during a poetry lesson. Reading Alfred Noyes's words "The road was a ribbon of darkness over the purple moor," we understood that the road wasn't *really* a ribbon. It was made of soil and rocks, after all. But the metaphor helped us to *see* the road as a ribbon. And as we did, we could imagine the whole moonlit landscape just as the highwayman of the poem's title saw it. We could be there with him, hearing his horse's hoofbeats, feeling the night wind, experiencing his fateful ride.

The metaphors we use when we talk about our feelings do the same thing. We can use metaphors to convey our emotional perspectives more clearly. We can listen for metaphors when people talk about their feelings in order to experience matters from their points of view.

When people use metaphors as simple figures of speech, the imagery they choose can provide little windows into their emotional reality. And when people use metaphors to draw parallels between their current lives and what happened in the past, their metaphors can open entire doors into the kinds of emotional-heritage issues we explored in chapter 5.

Either way, metaphors become one more tool as we bid and respond to others' bids for emotional connection.

**Common metaphorical figures of speech can be revealing.** Here are just a few examples of familiar metaphors you might hear in conversation, as well as the emotional meaning you can guess from their usage. Keep in mind that the meanings you draw from metaphors are just that— guesses. But they often provide a great springboard for conversation as you seek to learn more about another person's feelings. And once you understand that person's metaphors, you can then use them yourself in making bids for emotional connection. Here are some examples:

*"Our marriage was a train wreck."* The speaker feels that his marriage was broken and irreparable in a very chaotic and destructive way. It's likely that people got hurt. And because he characterizes it as an accident, he probably didn't expect this outcome. It wasn't supposed to happen this way.

*"I want to stay afloat financially."* The speaker believes that her finances could reach a crisis state where she'd be "over her head" in debt and "drowning." She fears that her financial survival may be in doubt.

*"My father likes to play God."* The speaker feels that her father is autocratic and controlling, like a benevolent dictator. She also feels that his attempts at benevolence lack integrity and commitment. He's not *being* God, he's only *playing* at it. Therefore, she not only resents his interference, she mistrusts it.

As the psychologist Richard Kopp writes in *Metaphor Therapy* (Brunner/ Mazel, 1995), such figures of speech do more than provide us with colorful language; they help us create a framework upon which to consider significant matters. They influence how we perceive issues and think and feel about them, and what actions we take.

Kopp uses the example "Time is money." Once you accept this metaphor as true, you start acting it out. You become more conscious of how you "spend" your time. You stop "giving" your time to others without expecting something in return. Instead, you try to "save" time so that you can "invest" it in worthwhile activity.

Imagine how you might act differently, however, if you accepted the metaphor that "time is a river." It "flows" continually, so you don't have to worry about giving it away; there's always more time coming down the channel. Time "carries" you along whether you want to go or not, so you might as well relax and enjoy the ride.

Now imagine the conflicts that might arise in a partnership between two people, each of whom constructs his or her reality around these contradictory metaphors. Working together on a project, one person might constantly be struggling to "save time" as the other attempts to "let go" of time constraints. But by listening to each other's metaphors, the pair may be able to come to a better understanding of their differences.

Kopp speculates that one reason metaphors are so powerful is that they activate the same mechanisms in the brain that we used in infancy to think about the world. As babies, we could not think of abstract concepts such as "security," "nourishment," or "nurturing." But we did think about the concrete objects associated with such concepts. There was the blanket, the bottle of milk, the mother, and so on. Even though we didn't have words for these things, we had the images of how they looked in reality, and how they looked in our minds. The blanket *was* security. The milk *was* nourishment. The mother *was* nurturing.

Because concrete images were so important as our brains formed and our thinking processes developed, we continue throughout our lives to find such images useful for learning and communicating abstract concepts. Now, if we want to think about an abstract concept in a new way, comparing it to something tangible can help. (Time is a runaway train; there's no stopping it. Time is a furnace; it's burning our resources. Time is a carousel; we'll get another chance the next time around.) And from that new image we build a new conceptual framework, a new way to think about the concept, a new way to communicate with one another about it.

**Memories can be metaphorically revealing as well.** Metaphors involving significant events or relationships from your past—particularly early childhood—can also help you understand your emotions. They can help you examine matters of emotional heritage, such as the long-lasting effects of your parents' emotional philosophy or your enduring vulnerabilities, issues we explored in depth in chapter 5.

If you're struggling with a problem, and a certain memory keeps cropping up, you might explore whether this memory has some kind of metaphorical significance in your life. Could that past event, or past relationship, hold a current insight?

Let me give you an example. Anthony and Teresa, a couple I was seeing for marital therapy, had a conflict over a career move Teresa was about to make. To Teresa, the move seemed essential to her feelings of fulfillment. She believed everything she had done in her life had led her to this tremendous opportunity. If she didn't make her move now, she would always regret it. But Anthony saw the change as an extremely risky maneuver that would threaten their family's financial security. And because he and Teresa shared financial decisions, she would not change jobs without his approval.

The couple grappled with the decision for several weeks. During these discussions, Anthony brought up two characters from his childhood. One was his mother—a good-hearted but long-suffering woman who always subjugated her own needs to her husband's demands. Anthony felt his father often took advantage of his mother's submissiveness. "She was constantly being blindsided by him. He made a fool of her." And Anthony feared that someday he would be just like his mother—dominated, ineffectual, and foolish.

The second character was Anthony's grandfather, a man whom Anthony adored for his great wisdom and generosity of spirit. "My grandfather always saw right through people," Anthony said. "You could never fool him because he had his eyes wide open. He knew all your faults. Despite that, however, he would do whatever he could for you. He gave and he gave. That's just the way he was."

When the time came for Anthony and Teresa to make their decision, something surprising happened. Although he still felt apprehensive about it, Anthony decided to support his wife's dream.

"I can still see the potential for disaster," he explained in the session that followed. "But I also know how important it is for her to try this. And suddenly that seems more significant than anything else."

"That's an extremely generous thing to do," I told him. Then I asked, "Who does this remind you of?"

A smile spread across his face as he looked at Teresa. "This isn't like my mother, is it?"

"No," Teresa said, smiling as well. "It's not like your mother at all. It's more like your grandfather."

"You don't know what the future holds," I added. "But you're not about to be blindsided. You know exactly what Teresa needs, and you've got your eyes wide open."

"But I never thought I could be like my grandfather," Anthony said. "I never thought I could be that giving." Then, after a long silence, he added, "I've been very worried about this decision for a long time. Seeing it this way gives me a better handle on it. Now I know why I'm moving in this direction. I can see that there was a model for this in my life. I think everything is going to be okay."

The model—or framework—that Anthony refers to is what makes metaphors so valuable. In fact, therapists who want to help people solve problems or change their perspectives often start by helping them to change the metaphors they currently use to frame their lives.

Kopp tells of a patient who used the image of "a basket full of whips" to describe his habit of putting himself down. The patient's therapist suggested that he start imagining that he carried "a basket full of teddy bears" instead. Perhaps that could help him to be gentler with himself when he's under stress. A patient who felt his anger was "a teapot ready to explode" was advised to "lift the lid a little" and then his anger would not seem so dangerous.

**Putting metaphors to work.** You can enhance your emotional communication simply by listening and responding to the metaphors you hear in conversations—especially conversations about feelings. Certain metaphors may prompt you to ask questions that elicit more information about the feelings behind them. In this way the metaphor is a bid for understanding, while your question is a way of turning toward that bid with interest and concern. When you hear a metaphor, try to ask open-ended questions if you can, or just reflect back the information you're hearing. Doing so can help your conversation partner relax, knowing that you simply want to understand what's being said.

Here are a few examples:

> **A:** In this job, I'm just a rat in a maze.
> **B:** A maze, huh? What kind of a maze?
> **A:** A very confusing one. All I can see are dead ends.
> **B:** Sounds kind of frustrating. Like you need some help finding the right path.
> **A:** You're right. I need some guidance here.

> **A:** You always put me onstage in front of your friends.
> **B:** What do you mean by a stage? There's no stage here.
> **A:** But it's like I've got to perform all the time. Say all the right things.
> **B:** I didn't know you felt that way. I'm just so proud of you. I want my friends to know how great you are.
> **A:** But I feel like you're always feeding me lines. I feel so pressured!

**A:** After Sherry left, I lost my spark.
**B:** Do you mean "spark" like the energy you need to get started?
**A:** Yeah. I don't do anything all day. I just sit around and watch TV.
**B:** Sounds kind of dull.
**A:** It's worse than dull. Some days I don't even go to work.

To explore matters of emotional heritage, ask questions that elicit memories of childhood events or past relationships. Obviously, such questions work best in trusting relationships where people are used to sharing memories and being introspective. These questions don't need to be particularly probing or "psychological," however. You can simply ask, "Did anything like this ever happen when you were a kid?" Or, "Whom does your boss [your brother, your wife, etc.] remind you of when he acts like that?" Or, "Is there anybody else you're thinking of right now?" The answers you get may be good for all sorts of insightful conversation.

Once you hear somebody use a metaphor, it may be helpful to use that same figure of speech, or a comparable one, when addressing a similar concept later on. I once counseled an electrical engineer, for example, whose language about emotions was filled with allusions to wiring, charges, and circuitry. I soon realized that if I really wanted to connect with this man, the best way to do that might be to use the same lexicon.

You can take the same approach with friends and family. If your son is interested in the natural world, for example, talk to him about his cleaning his room in terms of maintaining a healthy "ecosystem." If your boss loves baseball, let him know that you're ready to "step up to the plate" on the next project, and that you really hope he'll "go to bat" for your next raise. If your brother loves to go to Reno, tell him that his "odds" of inheriting much from Dad are poor unless he does his part to keep the old man out of a nursing home. Noticing and then adopting another person's metaphor helps you to build a smooth, intimate connection. Metaphorically speaking, you're both "on the same page."

## Exercise: Log What You Hear in Metaphors

You can use your Emotion Log to document the emotional information you learn from people's metaphors. Here are some questions to consider and write about as you listen for the metaphors people use to express their feelings:

- What metaphors have you noticed yourself using recently?
- What do these metaphors tell you about the way you're feeling?
- Did you use them to express specific emotions?
- How did others react to your metaphors?

- What metaphors have you noticed others using?
- Think about a person with whom you've been in conflict lately. What metaphors does this person use?
- What do these metaphors tell you about the way this person has been feeling?

## Above All, Just *Listen*

While understanding metaphors and all the various forms of nonverbal communication can boost your ability to connect with others, you won't get far without a strong foundation of good, basic listening skills. Your knack for drawing others out and expressing genuine curiosity about their lives can be a real boon to bidding for connection and establishing satisfying relationships. Good listening skills can help you to feel easy in all sorts of social situations, and to build the kind of rapport that leads to solid emotional bonds.

**Focus on being interested, not interesting.** That's the counsel Dale Carnegie offered in his 1937 classic, *How to Win Friends and Influence People,* which is still a top seller more than six decades later. And after my three decades of observational research, I have to say that it's still some of the best advice available. Carnegie was right when he wrote, "You can make more friends in two months by becoming genuinely interested in other people than you can in two years by trying to get other people interested in you."

Although Carnegie's advice centered on friendship and salesmanship, my research shows that you can apply the same principle to building better relationships with your spouse, your siblings, your children, your boss—with anybody who plays a significant role in your life. That's because everybody wants to feel valued and appreciated. And nothing fosters such goodwill as your ability to pay sincere attention to the details of another person's life.

**Start by asking questions.** Don't ask the kind that can be answered with simple one-word responses. Instead, ask questions that allow people to explain their points of view and elaborate. Questions that begin with the words "Why do you suppose . . ." and "How do you think . . ." are good for this. Avoid questions that are too open-ended—questions like "What's new?" or "How's it going?" Too often, people give pat responses to such queries, perhaps because they're not sure you really want to know. But if you can ask the same type of question in a more tailored way, you're sure to get meatier answers. Examples: "So what's your latest project [at school, in your department, around the house, etc.]?" "How's your summer going? Got any vacation plans?"

It's good to ask specific questions, but it's usually not good for a relationship to pry, or to manipulate people into telling more about themselves than they're comfortable revealing. To find the right balance of disclosure, let the other person take the lead as you ask open-ended questions related to information that person has already revealed.

Say, for example, that a new acquaintance has alluded to using drugs while in college. If you wanted to pursue that line of conversation, you could say, "Was there a lot of drug use where you went to school?" Then, depending on his level of comfort, he could choose to speak from personal experience or to talk more generally. This would probably work better than a pointed probe, such as, "Did you ever feel addicted to smoking pot?" which might get to a point of interest more quickly, but you'd risk losing the connection.

**Ask questions about people's goals and visions of the future.** Such queries can be a great way to connect. I'm reminded of the way some couples in our apartment lab use the view outside the window as a way to launch conversations about one another's shared dreams and fantasies of the future. "Look at that boat," one husband said. "If you could sail away to anywhere in the world, where would you go?" Another asked, "If you had that kind of money, what would you spend it on? A boat, a cabin in the mountains, or what?"

**Look for commonalities.** People are attracted to those with whom they have things in common, so make it a point to let others know when you share similar views or backgrounds. At the same time, don't try to make yourself the focus of conversation. Say enough to establish common ground and empathize, but always remember to share the floor.

When you want people to disclose information about themselves, it can help to reveal details about your own life first. Be sure to aim for balance, however. Sharing too much personal information too early can be harmful to relationships. Your conversation partner may feel overwhelmed by the intensity of what you're sharing, or feel pressured to become too close too soon.

Be sparing, also, when sharing past experiences with teenagers or children. Young people often have a hard time imagining that their elders were ever as young as they are. And it's especially hard for them to imagine that older people ever encountered challenges similar to the ones they're facing. Such lack of imagination is not their fault; it's just a normal part of being young. You can still let youngsters know that you understand what they're going through, however. The best way is to engage them in friendly conversations about their own experiences. Ask pertinent questions, reflect back what you're hearing, and empathize.

Say, for example, that you're visiting your twelve-year-old niece, who has just gotten braces.

You could say, "I had braces when I was your age."

To which she might reply, "Oh."

Then you might say, "We didn't have those fancy colored braces back then."

To which she might reply, "Oh."

Or you could ask her questions about her own unique, current experience, resulting in a much more direct emotional connection. That conversation might sound like this:

"How do your braces feel?"

"They're okay now. But the first night was really painful."

"I'll bet. Did you take something for it?"

"Yeah, some ibuprofen."

"And how did it feel to wear them to school for the first time?"

"I felt so weird!"

"I think I know what you mean—like self-conscious?"

"Yeah."

"Did any of your friends tease you?"

"My friends didn't, but there's this guy in my math class and he was like, 'Hey, Metal Mouth.' And I was like, 'Oh, my God!' "

"So you felt kind of embarrassed?"

"Yeah."

"But you're smiling when you tell me about it. Did you feel kind of glad that he noticed?"

"Yeah. I guess so. Because he's real funny and smart. And I didn't even think he knew my name."

"But now he can call you 'Metal Mouth.' "

"Yeah, cool, huh?"

The difference in the two conversations is focus. The adult lets the preteen know that she's understood without taking the spotlight off the girl's present situation. As a result, the girl feels that she has an engaged, sympathetic listener, so she continues revealing more about her life.

**Tune in with all your attention.** Once you've encouraged somebody to talk, the next step is to listen—*really* listen. This probably sounds simpler than it is. Many people have an unfortunate habit in conversation of planning the next thing they're going to say rather than tuning in to what the other person is saying. It may help to think of your conversation as a tour of some aspect of this person's life. Be willing to go along for the ride, asking questions in ways that show your sincere interest and natural curiosity.

Listen in a way that feels natural, not forced. Your expressed interest ought to be genuine and consistent with your own personality.

**Respond with an occasional brief nod or sound.** This indicates that you're paying attention. Research shows that candidates who nod during interviews get the job more often than those who don't. Verbal cues such as "mm-hmm," "yeah," or even a grunt serve a similar purpose.

**From time to time, paraphrase what the speaker says.** Doing so tells the speaker that you're still interested, especially when you can restate the important parts. This also serves to ensure that you understand what's been said. A good time to paraphrase is when you introduce a question. For example: "You say you'd really love to go to Africa. Why do you think it would be a great place to visit?" Or, "It sounds like school has been really frustrating for you this spring. How is it harder for you now than last semester?"

**Maintain the right amount of eye contact.** Allow the speaker to catch your eye. Studies show that we tend to look more while listening, less while talking. We look away when we first start talking during a conversation. We look back when handing the conversation back to a partner. Avoid staring, which can be interpreted as a sign of hostility or intrusiveness. But don't be afraid to look at the speaker. Avoiding eye contact altogether gives the impression of disinterest, nervousness, or lack of confidence. Be aware also that holding eye contact with a warm smile for several seconds may be interpreted as flirtatious or seductive.

**Let go of your own agenda.** It's hard to be a good listener when you're struggling to direct the outcome of a conversation. Listening—especially when a friend or loved one is trying to work though a difficult emotional experience—requires instead that you let go of your desire to control the situation. In such instances it may be best to follow the maxim, "Don't just do something, stand there." Such passive, openhearted listening is rarely easy. More often, when loved ones are upset, people get the notion that they should "fix" what's wrong and "make it all better." There are many drawbacks to this approach. First, it falsely presupposes that people can know and determine how others should live. Second, it can be overwhelming to believe that you have to come up with all the solutions to another person's pain. Faced with such a burden, many people simply avoid the person who's having difficulties, or try to minimize or deny the negative feelings the other person expresses. And, finally, the optimum solutions to an individual's emotional problems rarely come from the outside; the best answers are usually the ones individuals discover for themselves. Although we can't eliminate all the pain life presents our friends and loved ones, we can offer one another immeasurable support in difficult times simply by listening in authentic, empathetic ways. Often it comes down to developing the kind of mindful presence I mentioned in chapter 3. The key is to look for those "emotional moments"—those unpredictable but golden opportunities we have to simply stop and say to another, "I understand how you're feeling right now."

**Turn off the television.** TV often interferes with people's ability to listen to one another. We haven't done an official study of the frequency with which people choose the television over social interaction, but time and again in our marriage lab, we have observed one partner make a bid for connection only to have the other partner "turn away" because he or she was more interested in the action on the television screen.

TV interferes with children's ability to connect, as well. A 1999 Kaiser Family Foundation study showed that American kids watch an average of two hours and forty-five minutes of TV a day. Some 17 percent watch over five hours daily. Compare this with other studies that show that kids spend just forty-five minutes a week talking to their parents.

More than two-thirds of kids over age eight in the Kaiser study said their families kept the TV on during meals, the times when you'd most expect kids and parents to be talking to each other. But with the families' eyes glued to the set, the quality of interaction can only deteriorate. Indeed, indicators of discontent—such as not getting along with parents, being unhappy at school, and getting into trouble a lot—are strongly associated with high media use, the study's authors say.

So, for the sake of your family relationships, limit TV watching. Be aware of occasions when TV gets in the way of your ability to respond lovingly to one another's bids for connection. And when you do watch television, try to choose programs you can enjoy watching together. Then talk about the TV programs afterward. Ask one another open-ended questions about what family members liked best and liked least about the program. How did the show make you feel? Did it remind you of any similar situations in your own life? If so, how? In other words, use the TV as a way to connect with one another, rather than as a means of isolation.

## *Exercise: The Emotional Communication Game*

Communicating well emotionally requires more than saying the right words; we also need to send and receive nonverbal messages accurately. This game gives you a chance to practice these skills by using various tones of voice and body language to express different meanings. You can play the game alone or with a spouse, friend, relative, or coworker.

To play with another person, designate one of you as the sender and the other as the receiver. Taking one question at a time, silently read each question, followed by three possible ways to interpret that question.

The sender then chooses one of the three interpretations and reads the question aloud, using the tone of voice and gestures he or she believes most accurately convey that meaning. The receiver must then guess which meaning the sender intended to send. The questions are divided by type of relationship, but you can try all of them if you'd like. After you've practiced each question, switch roles and do them again.

To play alone, take the part of the sender and practice saying the question aloud in three different ways to convey the three different meanings.

Whether you play alone or with a partner, the game can help you become more aware of the ways you send and receive emotional messages.

## Questions Among Coworkers

1. **Are you sure you can get this done?**

   **Meaning A.** Your colleague has a way of agreeing to things, but not making them a top priority. You're worried that he or she will not get the task done on time.

   **Meaning B.** You're pleasantly surprised and grateful that your colleague has agreed to do this job for you.

   **Meaning C.** You're simply asking for information.

2. **So, what did you think of my presentation today?**

   **Meaning A.** You did your best, but you were not quite sure how well the complex information you had to present came across. You can always rely on your friend to give you honest feedback.

   **Meaning B.** You think your presentation was terrific and you're hoping for some approval and celebration.

   **Meaning C.** You were very nervous and you think that you might have made a bad impression. You're looking for reassurance and support.

## Questions for Parents to Ask Children

1. **Are you going to clean your room?**

   **Meaning A.** You are pleasantly surprised because it looks as if your child is going to spontaneously do the cleaning. You don't even have to ask.

   **Meaning B.** You think it's time for your child to clean the room, and this is a gentle reminder.

   **Meaning C.** You've asked your child to clean the room a number of times, and you have been continually ignored. Now you're angry.

2. **Do you want your allowance?**

   **Meaning A.** If your child doesn't become more cooperative, the allowance is in jeopardy. You want your child to remember that this is the case.

Meaning B. You're wondering if your child even needs allowance this week, since he or she received so much money from Grandma.

Meaning C. You're about to leave for work and you just recalled that you have not yet given your child his or her allowance for the week. You're reaching into your wallet to draw out some money.

## Questions Between Friends

### 1. Are you going to wear that?
Meaning A. You think your friend's clothes look terrible.

Meaning B. You're wondering if the dinner party you're going to attend together is formal or casual, and you're looking to your friend's outfit as a clue.

Meaning C. You think your friend's clothes are cool and creative. You admire your friend's bold sense of style.

### 2. What do you want to do tonight?
Meaning A. You're asking for information.

Meaning B. Your friend has said no to all your suggestions, and you're exasperated.

Meaning C. You're tired of doing the same thing all the time, and tonight you have a new idea.

### 3. Are you okay?
Meaning A. Do you feel hurt by that awful phone call you just received?

Meaning B. That's the most bizarre plan you've ever concocted. Are you nuts?

Meaning C. Are you ready for the physical challenge you're about to take?

## Questions Between Spouses

### 1. Do you think it's going to storm?
Meaning A. You hope it will storm so that the two of you can enjoy watching the lightning together.

Meaning B. You hope it won't storm and ruin your plans for tomorrow's outing.

Meaning C. You're asking for information. Did he or she see a weather forecast?

### 2. Are you going to work on Thursday night?
Meaning A. You're expecting houseguests this weekend, and you would like help getting the house ready. You don't want your spouse to work that night.

**Meaning B.** You're anxious because you were thinking you could use the evening to work, but somebody's got to watch the kids.

**Meaning C.** You're reminding your spouse of his or her commitment to get a certain project done by Friday.

3. **Is it cold in here?**

**Meaning A.** You're wondering if the room is cold, or if you've got the chills from an oncoming virus.

**Meaning B.** You want the heat to be turned up, and you want your partner to do it.

**Meaning C.** You want to snuggle.

In this chapter we have examined several different components of emotional communication, including facial expression, movement, gesture, touch, tone of voice, descriptive words, and metaphor. But as you may have noticed while playing the Emotional Communication Game, we rarely use these elements in isolation. Most of the time we use them in combination, and almost unconsciously, to express what's happening in our hearts. You can improve your skills at sending and receiving emotional messages, however, by becoming more conscious of the way you communicate through sound, movement, and so on. As you do so, you'll be in a better position to bid for emotional connection and to turn toward other people's bids.

# 7

# Step Five:
# Find Shared Meaning

*W*hen Brian and Ron moved their families onto the same cul-de-sac a few years ago, neither man was looking for a new best friend. And even if they had been, they'd never have chosen each other. Brian is an oil company executive who frequently refers to environmentalists as "tree huggers." Ron is a lawyer for an environmental group. He calls the oil industry's environmental policies "despicable." But, as luck would have it, the men's young sons have become best buddies. That means Brian and Ron often find themselves sitting shoulder to shoulder at birthday parties, Scout meetings, soccer games, and more.

Over time, the pair learned they had a few things in common: a passion for spy novels, woodworking, and folk music. But, more important, they discovered they see eye to eye when it comes to raising boys. They agree, for example, that it's important to take your son to baseball games, to help him learn about computers, and to limit the time he watches TV. Because they agree on what it means to be a good dad, it's easier for them to tolerate their differences in other areas. Maybe they don't concur on environmental policy, but together they're creating the social environment they want for their kids. And this shared meaning gives them the incentive to extend repeated bids for connection to one another. ("Have you read the latest John Le Carré?" "Say, I've got an extra ticket for the folk music festival. Do you want to go?" "Come take a look at this cabinet I'm building." "Hey, how about those Cubs?")

This ability to discover shared meaning in our lives is the fifth and final step to building better emotional connections. It leads to greater stability in our relationships with friends, family, and coworkers. It helps people settle conflicts and collectively pursue the goals that really matter to them—goals like raising a healthy child, building a successful business, or helping an elderly relative die peacefully at home. When two people find meaning, they're willing to support each other's dreams, even when there's little to gain personally from doing so. All of this is very good for relationships.

We see examples everywhere of the way shared meaning bolsters relationships. Think about the politicians who run our government, for example. Their relationships are often some of the most contentious I can think of. And yet they keep coming together year after year to hammer out compromises that ensure the survival of social institutions like schools, courts, roads, the military, and so on. Why do they do it? Cynics might say it's for personal power or financial gain. But on another level, legislators and council members must agree that their work is meaningful. They share the feeling that debating issues, finding compromises, and making laws makes a positive difference in people's lives.

The same thing happens in positive work environments and healthy families. When people agree that their relationships lend meaning to their lives, they keep coming together, turning toward one another, and strengthening those relationships—even in the face of conflict.

How do we achieve shared meaning in our relationships? One way is to recognize that conflict often stems from people's idealism. If we can uncover the ideals hidden within another's position in a conflict, we can often find common meaning. Another way to achieve shared meaning is to talk about our dreams and aspirations, fostering one another's support for these quests. And, finally, we can achieve shared meaning through the use of ritual—that is, regularly engaging in meaningful activities that draw people together emotionally.

## People in Conflict as Idealists

In our culture, many people believe that having a conflict with another person indicates there's something fundamentally wrong with the relationship. Marriage is a good example. A husband and wife who are having irresolvable conflicts show up in a therapist's office feeling demoralized and saying, "We're screwed up. We can't figure out why we keep fighting about such ridiculous stuff." And the therapist thinks, "They're right. They're screwed up." He's immature. Or she's manipulative. He's power-hungry. She's mean-spirited. There's something pathologically wrong with one or both of them, and we have to fix it.

This approach fails to recognize how common and normal it is to have irresolvable conflicts. Our studies, for example, reveal that a full 69 percent of all marital conflicts never go away. So, if a couple has an ongoing clash over a particular issue—money, housework, and sex are common—they're likely to have that same conflict forever. If the husband's spending was a sore spot in a couple's relationship early on, it may well be an issue twenty years later. If they disagreed often about housework in 1982, they're likely to be having the same dispute in the year 2022. If one spouse complains that there's not enough sex and the other disagrees, they may keep disagreeing for many years to come.

This leads me to believe that most conflicts don't arise from pathology. I believe they develop because people attach different meaning to the same situations, which gets in the way of their ability to bid and respond to one another's bids for connection. But if they can keep talking to one another and describing how they find meaning in their positions, they may reach some common ground, a place where meanings merge and compromise is possible.

Consider these disagreements:

> EMPLOYEE: I can't work late tonight. My daughter has a recital.
> BOSS: Then maybe you don't understand what this project means to us.

> MOTHER: I always assumed that you'd marry one of our kind.
> SON: But, Mom, she *is* one of "our kind." She's a member of the human race.

> HUSBAND: How can you expect me to go to your cousin's wedding? I've got tickets to the World Series that day!
> WIFE: That's easy. Family means more than baseball!

Such differences may be based on any number of factors—diverse emotional histories, for example, or reliance on dissimilar emotional command systems. But just because they have these differences doesn't necessarily indicate that one or the other is screwed up. Dissimilarities may simply indicate that they're trying to live according to what they find meaningful. They're *idealists* who choose to take different stands based on different understandings of what things mean. In the above examples, for instance, the wife believes that loyalty to family makes life meaningful, while the husband believes that loyalty to a baseball team gives life meaning. Although these ideas are in conflict, they both can be seen as idealistic.

Recognizing the idealism in one another's positions and talking about it can be a tremendously helpful way to build emotional connections. Think of all the relationships that might be forged if people in conflict could say, "I know that we don't agree on this one issue, but I understand that you're as committed to your vision as I am to mine. Therefore I respect you."

All of this comes from each person sharing the meaning he or she holds within the conflict. Such sharing allows people to recognize the source of their conflicts as idealism—a recognition that leads them to turn toward one another and to connect emotionally.

## Become a Dream Detector

My research also shows that people form much more positive emotional connections when they encourage one another's dreams and aspirations. In this way, shared meaning provides the common emotional ground that motivates people to stay in a relationship or a job even when those bonds are wracked with conflict and struggle. People "hang in there," continually bidding and responding to bids for connection, because the relationship is part of what makes their lives significant.

Focusing on dreams can also help people find shared meaning within a conflict. The idea is to focus less on the conflict itself and more on the dreams, goals, or wishes that underlie each person's fixed position within that struggle. Some might call such dreams "hidden agendas." And indeed, the issues involved are often the most contentious and least discussed. Take the example of the worker who wanted to leave work to go to his daughter's recital, for instance. The employee may have a hidden agenda, or a hidden dream, of finding a better balance between the demands of work and family. But he doesn't talk about it for fear that his boss might think he's lazy and unworthy of a raise. Meanwhile, the boss's agenda, or dream, might be to increase productivity so that the business will become more successful and benefit everybody. But he doesn't overtly press this issue with his workers for fear that he'll lose the workers he values.

There's a good reason for people in conflict to try to view one another's perspectives in a more positive light: Digging into each other's hidden agendas or hidden dreams offers a tremendous potential for intimacy and emotional connection.

The trick to uncovering that potential is to stop trying to resolve the conflict. Instead, talk about the *meaning* your position holds for you.

The worker, for example, might tell his boss what it means to him to hear his daughter play piano. He might even tell a story or two that supports that meaning. Perhaps the man's own father was always too busy working to attend his football games when he was kid, and that hurt. So, when the man became a father himself, he vowed that he would always be there for the special events in his child's life. If he shares this story with his boss, his boss might gain a better understanding of what the recital means to the man.

Sharing such anecdotes gives people an alternative to simply arguing the pros and cons. So, when you're faced with a conflict, you might ask yourself, "What are the stories that support my ideas of what this situation means to me? What are all the feelings that I have about this issue? What are my dreams, goals, or wishes related to those feelings?"

I've found that when people in conflict start sharing their answers to such questions, they're no longer trying to stake out one true position in an argument. Instead, the conversation becomes a revelation of what really matters in their lives. It becomes a bid for connection, an opportunity to turn toward one another with statements like "Now I understand," or "I can see why you feel that way," or "If I were in your shoes, I'd feel that way, too."

Here's an example: Nancy and Amanda were administrative assistants who shared a small office in an accounting firm for more than three years. After spending so much time together in such intimate quarters, they got to know each other quite well and became close friends.

Still, they had an ongoing conflict over one particular issue: clutter. Amanda's habit of leaving junk mail, office supplies, and soda cans wherever she finished using them drove Nancy crazy. "How long would it take you to walk over to the cabinet and put this stuff back where it belongs?" Nancy often muttered.

Meanwhile, Nancy's penchant for constant straightening drove Amanda up a wall. "The minute I put something down, it disappears!" Amanda would gripe. "I feel like I'm working with Felix Unger!"

Amanda was referring, of course, to the ridiculously fastidious character in Neil Simon's play *The Odd Couple*, and the comparison didn't make Nancy feel good. Indeed, she found it so hurtful that she once retaliated by writing a memo to their boss in which she called Amanda a "slob." Ouch!

Such verbal warfare is common when people get entrenched in their positions, when they take a stand and refuse to be influenced by one another. They become increasingly defensive, and their attacks get more pointed, more destructive. In fact, my marriage research shows that when husbands and wives do this, it often leads to divorce. Of course, you can't divorce your coworkers. And for Nancy and Amanda's small company, moving them to separate offices was not an option. So the two women just continued complaining and bickering about their differences.

Then, one autumn, something surprising happened. Just for fun, Nancy took a community-college course on interior design. No, it's not a form of conflict resolution I normally recommend. But it did create a shift in the women's relationship that proved helpful. That's because Nancy started talking to Amanda in new ways about her love for visual order and beauty in her environment. In other words, she started telling Amanda about the *dream* that existed beneath their argument about the clutter. She loved art. She loved design. And she wanted to see that passion reflected around her. She wanted to create it out of the chaos they called their workspace.

Fortunately, Amanda understood. The reason Nancy kept insisting on having a neater office was not that she wanted to control Amanda, put her down, or make her work harder. It was that an uncluttered environment would fulfill in her a long and deep-seated need to express herself visually.

Realizing this didn't turn Amanda into an instant neatnik. But it did take the sting out of their clutter argument. In the past, when Nancy had complained, Amanda had automatically taken her words as criticism. Indeed, Nancy's complaints often brought up childhood memories for Amanda of being harshly reprimanded for messiness. "You are so sloppy and so careless," Amanda's mother used to say. And, as children often do, Amanda translated her mother's criticism as, "I am so worthless and so unlovable." In fact, if you were to ask Amanda about the dream beneath *her* position in the clutter argument, she might say, "I just want to move about my workspace peacefully. I want to stop feeling like I'm not doing things the right way, that I'm not good enough."

Amanda made it a point to share this insight with Nancy. And now, whenever Nancy's complaints feel hurtful, Amanda asks her friend to soften her tone and to remind her that she's appreciated—even if she is a bit messy.

By talking about the dreams behind the argument, Amanda and Nancy have been able to establish common emotional ground around the issue of clutter. Now Amanda can say to Nancy, "I understand what it means to you to have a neat environment, and I'll try to help." And now Nancy can say to Amanda, "I understand what it means to you to work with somebody who's less critical and more reassuring. I'll do my best to be that way for you."

## Sometimes Dreams Are Hidden

It's easy to see the connection between Nancy's dream of working in a well-ordered environment and her conflict with Amanda over clutter. Unfortunately, the link between dreams and conflicts is not always this clear. That's because people often keep certain dreams and wishes hidden—sometimes even from themselves. Unacknowledged dreams can still influence relationships, however, causing tension, resentment, and irritation.

If you're in a relationship where dreams are kept hidden, the two of you may find yourselves having the same arguments over and over, rehashing the same tired issues without ever reaching a satisfying resolution. You may try a broad range of problem-solving techniques, but it always feels as though you're just spinning your wheels. Or you may negotiate a solution, only to find that you never follow through with the settlement.

But once you stop trying to solve the problem and start uncovering the dreams hidden within it, progress is possible. Suddenly, you have the opportunity to address feelings woven into the fabric of that dream. These may be emotions that were never revealed before, feelings that are quite precious and deeply held. Two brothers, for example, might discover that their long-term bickering over the family business has less to do with money than with one brother's dream of finally feeling loved by his father. A woman and her teenaged daughter might learn that their arguments over piano lessons have little to do with the girl's skills. Instead, the conflict reflects the woman's own unfulfilled aspirations of becoming an artist.

As long as dreams stay hidden, people in conflict never get to explore the true meaning of their differences. They may also miss a chance for profound emotional connection.

How do you sense the presence of such hidden dreams? As we discussed in chapter 6, paying close attention to the metaphors used in conversations can help. What stories and symbols do you and others use when discussing conflict? What unspoken wishes or aspirations lie beneath these elements? What do their messages reveal about people's self-concepts and their roles in life?

It may take courage to broach such issues. But once people start talking about their dreams, they often discover the meaning in one another's positions, which can lead to compromise and stability in all kinds of relationships.

## Listening to Dreams

Michael and Leslie were a young military couple whose individual dreams were not easy to detect. When I first met them, they were very unhappy with their marriage. They were also at odds over whether to sell their house. But what most concerned me was how detached from each other they seemed to be emotionally—a clear sign that their relationship was in trouble.

At first they talked a lot about their bills and their belongings. Married just a few years, they had accumulated a new house, two new cars, a boat, a jet ski, a living room full of furniture, and a mountain of debt. Now they were preparing for a tough transition—Michael's discharge from the army. Their plan was to move to a new state and start new careers. But how would they finance it all? Michael's proposal was to sell the house and use their equity to pay their bills and buy a travel trailer. Then they could live in the trailer until they got resettled and out of debt, he said. But Leslie thought this was a terrible plan.

By the time the couple came to me, both were digging in their heels. But they had not explored the dreams that supported their entrenched positions. So I asked them, "What does this idea of selling the house and buying the travel trailer symbolize for you? Beyond the dollars-and-cents issue of whether it's a wise investment, what does it say to you about the way your life is going, how you're feeling about yourself as an individual, or as part of a couple?"

To Michael the answers seemed straightforward: The move would be a way for him finally to get control of the family's financial matters after their period of undisciplined spending. "Whatever we do, we've got to pay off the bills," he said with authority. I told him it sounded as if he felt the decision was part of what it meant to take charge as a husband and potential father, and he agreed. It might take some temporary sacrifice, but he believed that, in time, he could achieve his dream of financial security and get the couple's finances back on an even keel.

The matter wasn't so simple for Leslie. Having been raised in poverty, she saw the move from house to travel trailer as a giant step backward. "My biggest fear is that once we get into that lifestyle, we won't get out of it," she said. Michael tried to reassure her that he didn't foresee them living in a trailer for long. But Leslie was not to be consoled. Although she said she wanted to be a "good wife" and support Michael's decision, she suspected it was unwise. Then she started comparing the situation to an event two years earlier—the time he sold her sports car.

"That car was probably the most important thing in the world to me because I had been dirt poor," Leslie said, full of emotion. She turned to Michael and explained, "That was how I measured my success at getting out of the projects [public housing]. Then you sold it and you put me in a family car. I took that as a personal attack. And I took that as your way of controlling me."

"I didn't mean it as a personal attack," Michael responded. But he couldn't deny that control was his motive. "I wanted someone who would stay here forever . . . but you kept talking about how you can just dump a relationship without blinking an eye, how you always saved yourself an out. I was trying to eliminate those outs."

"You would have kept me regardless," Leslie insisted.

"Sometimes I'm not sure," said Michael. "Sometimes I look back at the car . . . It was a symbol of your freedom and how you could keep away from me."

Suddenly it was clear that the couple's most pressing problem had little to do with real estate or car deals. Rather, they needed to talk more deeply about Leslie's dreams of freedom, Michael's dreams of interdependence, and the conflict between those dreams. It wouldn't matter what kind of house they lived in; until they could find a way to honor one another's visions of the future, they were not going to be happy in their marriage. In addition, it was clear that they needed to get better at expressing their feelings, so it wouldn't take two full years before one could say to the other, "I took that as a personal attack."

Michael and Leslie talked about these issues often over the next few years. The last time I heard from them, they were still together, reporting high satisfaction in their marriage, and expecting their first child.

## Trust the Process and Offer Support

This strategy of discussing dreams when you encounter conflict does not come easily to many people. Perhaps that's because we're taught to stick to a narrow field of absolute facts when faced with opposition. If you believe there's got to be a winner and a loser in every conflict, then you try to make your argument as objective and highly accurate as possible; otherwise you'll be proven wrong. We lose a lot with this narrow approach—namely our ability to find shared meaning and connect emotionally. But once we broaden the landscape of our discussion to include dreams and hopes, we can see where our visions merge. We can find room for compromise.

Keep in mind that talking about your life dreams and what they mean to you requires some degree of trust. Such discussions can bring up issues so important and deeply felt that you feel exposed or vulnerable. But as with many high-risk propositions, there's also potential for high gain. So if you're willing to take the chance, talking about your dreams can be the bid that leads to stronger emotional connections with the people in your life who matter most.

Remember also that you can honor other people's dreams in many different ways. You can show your support and respect, whether or not you choose to participate in the dream—or even accept it. There's a broad range of alternatives. You can do any of the following things:

- Ask questions about the dream. One of my favorites is "What's the story behind that?" Usually dreams have a history and a narrative within them.
- Offer empathy. It can be helpful simply to say, "I may not agree with you on this, but I can understand why this seems important to you." Or, "Knowing you as I do, I can see why you feel this way."
- Offer emotional support and validation. You might say, "I'm proud of you for feeling so strongly about this matter," or "I may not be able to do this with you, but I'm behind you 100 percent."
- Participate in another's dream at a limited level, such as reading about the issue, helping to make plans, or offering advice.
- Offer some level of financial support or other resources, such as child care or transportation.
- Join in the dream on a trial basis.
- Join in the dream entirely, making it part of your own vision.

Below are a few more examples of the way that talking about dreams can reduce conflict, bringing about compromise and better relationships.

*Example 1*

**The conflict.**  Bob and Jill are siblings whose father has cancer. Recently informed that their dad may only live for another few months, Bob proposes that he and Jill sit down with their father and discuss end-of-life decisions. Bob wants to talk with their dad about his estate, funeral plans, and how he feels about artificial life support. But Jill resists. "Dad doesn't want to talk about these things with his kids," Jill says. "He wants to protect us from the pain of dealing with his death."

**Their dreams.**  Bob explains that he wants to look back on Dad's last days as a time of clarity and peace for everybody involved. He anticipates the family may face some tough decisions, and he believes they can approach them more calmly if they all understand Dad's wishes beforehand.

Jill says that her dream is to spare Dad as much pain as possible. But as she talks, she realizes that, barring miracles, she probably can't have her true dream, which would be to make his illness go away. In lieu of this, she would at least like to make their discussions as comfortable for Dad as they can. She figures there are counselors who might help.

**The compromise.**  Jill agrees to join Bob in discussions with Dad, but only after they consult with a hospice counselor for advice.

*Example 2*

**The conflict.**  Russ, a deeply religious man, has raised his son, Jason, to be a member of his liberal Catholic congregation. Once Jason reaches his junior year of high school, however, the boy seems increasingly drawn to more conservative thought, and starts attending Wednesday-night youth activities at a fundamentalist Protestant church. Now Jason wants Russ's permission to go on a monthlong summer missionary tour to inner-city neighborhoods with the fundamentalist group. Russ is opposed to the idea because he's afraid the experience will cause Jason to turn his back on his family and the Catholic Church. But Russ insists it's something he must do.

**Their dreams.**  Russ hopes that the family's Catholic church will be a compass and a comfort for Jason whenever he faces hard decisions or difficult times. He also dreams that the family's church and its leaders will be an inspiration for Jason, helping him to become a compassionate, open-minded adult.

When Jason talks about his dreams, he says he envisions himself following God's "calling"—to bring God's compassion and forgiveness to people in need, to help "save" them from the sins of the world.

**The compromise.** Russ agrees to let Jason go on the mission, asking that he keep two parts of his father's dream in mind: to be compassionate, and to stay open to new ideas. He also insists that Jason continue to attend Sunday services at the Catholic church after he returns. Jason agrees to all of this, and leaves on his mission.

*Example 3*

**The conflict.** Melinda and Debbie are two medical assistants who work full-time in a clinic. Both are mothers of small children, both love their jobs, and both want to work fewer hours. Why not job-share, they decide. So they take their proposal to Miles, the clinic manager, who says it won't work. Why not? Because the clinic would have to employ a third medical assistant instead of just two. The wages might be comparable, but the administrative costs would be higher.

**Their dreams.** Melinda and Debbie talk to Miles about their dream of a balanced life. They describe what it would be like to have enough time to really be there for their children during the week. They imagine arriving at the clinic feeling calm, rested, and better prepared to listen to patients and their concerns.

Balance is Miles's concern, as well. That's the sign of a solid administrator, he believes—somebody who knows how to balance the needs of patients, employees, doctors, and management.

Melinda, Debbie, and Miles all talk about their dream of working in an amicable place—a clinic where people care about one another's mental health as much as their economic well-being.

**The compromise.** Miles agrees to take another look at the actual costs involved. "Maybe we can juggle the numbers in some way to make it work for everybody," he says. Melinda and Debbie say they're willing to renegotiate their benefits if necessary to make it work.

Below is an exercise designed to help you talk about your dreams around a conflict and reach a place of compromise.

## *Exercise: Identifying the Dreams in Your Conflicts*

Here's an exercise you may want to try when you're having a conflict with someone close to you. The goal is to identify the dreams within your conflict and to determine how you can turn toward one another's dreams. If, after doing this exercise, you find that you still can't compromise, look at the next exercise, Ending Gridlock, on pages 219–221.

These exercises are designed to be done with the person with whom you're having conflict. But you can also do them on your own, using your Emotion Log and imagining how the other person might respond. Then, when the time is right, you can have a less formal conversation with this person about his or her dreams and the role they may play in your dispute. If that person will listen, talk about your dreams as well. Remember to put your primary focus on the dream and not on the conflict. You may want to tell the other person a story that illustrates what your dream means to you. You can ask the person with whom you're having conflict to do the same.

**1.** Working together, identify the problem that's causing ongoing conflict. Take five minutes to consider silently what life-dreams might be connected to your position in this conflict. They may be current dreams, or past dreams that have faded. Here are some possibilities:

- Having a sense of freedom
- Experiencing peace
- Feeling close to nature
- Having a sense of power
- Exploring who I am
- Experiencing adventure
- Experiencing beauty
- Taking a spiritual journey
- Experiencing justice
- Having a sense of honor
- Integrating my current life with my past
- Experiencing healing
- Knowing my family
- Becoming all I can be
- Aging gracefully
- Exploring a creative side of myself
- Feeling competent
- Feeling truly loved
- Getting over past injuries
- Asking God for forgiveness
- Exploring an old part of myself that seems lost
- Getting over a personal obstacle
- Having a sense of order
- Being productive
- Having the time and place to "just be"
- Being able to truly relax
- Reflecting on my life
- Getting my priorities in order
- Finishing something important

- Exploring the physical side of myself
- Being able to compete and win
- Experiencing travel
- Having solitude
- Achieving atonement
- Building something important
- Ending a chapter in my life
- Saying good-bye to something
- Having what I need

**Two examples of dreams within conflict:**
A couple disagrees about how to live in retirement. She wants to sell the house, buy a travel trailer, and hit the road because it's always been her dream to "just travel." He wants to stay home and turn his garage into a ceramics studio because it's always been his dream to "explore the creative side of myself."

A pair of business partners disagree over whether to expand the company. The one who wants to expand sees his dream as a chance "to build something important." The one who wants to keep the company smaller has the dream of "being able to truly relax."

**2.** Take turns talking about your conflict and how it relates to one or more of your life-dreams. Each person should talk for about twenty minutes while the other listens. Then switch roles.

**When you're speaking:** Remember that your goal is to clarify your dream and to be understood. Don't try to solve your main conflict as you talk. Just talk honestly about your dreams that are related to the conflict. Don't censor yourself, or downplay your description to please the person listening or to avoid resistance. Instead, talk as you would if you were talking to one of your best friends.

**When you're listening:** Remember that your goal is simply to understand the other person's dream. Don't try to solve the main conflict as you listen. And don't spend time thinking up counterpoints or rebuttals to what you're hearing. Just encourage the speaker to fully explore his or her dreams. Ask questions for clarification and to express interest. Try to suspend judgment. Listen as you would to a dear friend.

**Here are some questions for the speaker to consider:**

- What are your life-dreams related to this issue?
- What do you believe about this conflict and its relationship to this dream?
- What do you want?
- What do you need?
- What are *all* your feelings about our choices here?

- What is the meaning of this issue for you?
- What is the meaning of the decisions you're facing?
- What is the meaning of the position you're taking?
- Is there a story behind your dream? What is that story? Where does the story come from in your life?
- What does this issue symbolize to you?
- How do you think your goals related to this issue can be accomplished?
- Do you believe there are hidden dreams for you within this issue? What are those hidden dreams?

**3.** After each of you has fully expressed your dream within the conflict, you should each consider the following questions:

- Can you turn toward the other person's dream?
- Are there aspects of the other person's dream that you fear might come true?
- If you can't turn toward the other person's dream, can you at least support part of it?

Now take ten minutes each to answer the three questions above. As before, designate one person to speak and one person to listen. Then switch roles. As you discuss these questions, remember:

- Don't give up *your own dream* for the sake of peace between the two of you.
- State what you really want.
- If you feel your partner's dream will affect you in a way you can't accept, say so.

If you and your partner find that you're not moving any closer to a compromise, consider trying the next exercise. It's designed to move people from gridlocked conflict into dialogue.

## *Exercise: Ending Gridlock*

When two people find that they just can't compromise no matter what, it's often because their conflict involves issues that are much deeper than they initially recognize. Such conflicts often entail issues for one or both people that are central to the way they think about themselves. But as I explained earlier, the tougher the conflict is to solve, the greater is the potential for increased closeness in a relationship.

The key to unlocking that potential may be to approach the problem using small, temporary compromises. This gives each party a chance to "try on" the other person's point of view—an exercise that often leads to incremental advances in understanding. In addition, each party gets a chance to see the other honor his or her own dream within the conflict, a move that begins to loosen the gridlock. Below are the specific steps to follow when working with another person. Again, you may do the exercise alone, writing about the issue in your Emotion Log, imagining the other's response, and then incorporating your insights into a more informal discussion with the other person.

**1.** Working together, identify the problem that's causing ongoing conflict.

**2.** Each person makes a list of his or her "bottom line" issues. These are the issues about which you just can't compromise. Make this list as short as you can. The idea is to include only those things about which you absolutely can't be moved; to change your mind about these items would be intolerable.

**3.** Each makes a list of issues about which you might have some flexibility, even if it's just a little. Try to make this list longer than the previous one. Keep in mind that the more you're willing to give, the better you'll be at persuading the other person to give as well.

**4.** Show each other your lists.

**5.** Working together, come up with a temporary compromise that allows both of you to have your dreams, at least to some extent.

Here's an example of how this exercise worked for one family:

**1.** Ken and Evelyn are a middle-class Caucasian couple who disagreed about where to send their daughter, Madeline, to school. Evelyn had her heart set on Forest Side, the same expensive private school she had attended as a girl. Evelyn's research showed that Forest Side definitely had a better academic record than the public school. But Ken believed Forest Side would teach their daughter materialistic and elitist values with which he didn't agree. He also worried about money; he was afraid that if they spent money on high school tuition, it would hamper their ability to save for Madeline's college expenses.

**2.** Both Evelyn and Ken had just one item on their list of no-compromise issues. For Evelyn it was academic standards. "Madeline should have every chance of getting into the college of her choice," she wrote. Ken's must-have issue was ethnic and economic diversity. "I don't want Madeline's world limited to a bunch of rich white kids," he expressed.

**3.** For the list of flexible issues, Evelyn wrote that she would be willing to explore schools other than Forest Side. Ken decided he could be flexible when it came to the money issue.

**4.** The couple shared their lists with each other and talked about them. "I'm sentimentally attached to Forest Side," Evelyn told Ken, "but there might be other, more affordable places that are just as good."

"There's no way we can afford Forest Side," Ken said to Evelyn. "But if we found the right environment, I'd be willing to at least look at the budget with you and see if we might find some extra money for tuition."

**5.** After some research, the family found a private school with a good academic record, a diverse student population, and tuition that was lower than Evelyn's alma mater. "It's not Forest Side," Evelyn conceded, "but I think Madeline is going to flourish there."

"I never thought I'd be sending my kid to private school," says Ken. "But after doing our research, I can see that she'll have advantages there that I never even thought of."

Evelyn and Ken decided to enroll Madeline at the alternative private school, with the agreement that they would reevaluate their decision after her first semester.

## Explore the Rituals You Share and Create New Ones

Just as sharing your dreams can lead to closer relationships, sharing rituals can help you to build stronger bonds. A ritual of emotional connection provides structure in your life to ensure that bids for connection happen on a regular basis. A ritual of emotional connection is the one place you can count on having a significant exchange with somebody you care about. A regular evening meal with your family can be a ritual of emotional connection. So can a couple's annual romantic getaway, or the office staff's quarterly retreat. A ritual can be as casual as saying hello to your coworkers each morning. Or it can be as elaborate as a royal wedding.

Like routines, rituals are repeated over and over, so they become predictable. Everybody knows what to expect, and everyone knows what his or her responsibilities are in the ritual. But there's an important difference: Rituals have symbolic meaning. Brushing your teeth in the morning is a routine, kissing your kids good-bye as you leave is a ritual. The difference is, the kiss carries the meaning, while the tooth-brushing does not. The kiss says, "I love you, and I'll think about you, even when we're apart."

People typically build rituals of connection around such informal activities as sharing lunch or greeting one another at the end of a workday. They also have more formal rituals, such as birthday parties, prom dates, or victory celebrations. Then there are very formal, scripted rituals such as the celebration of weddings, funerals, or holy days like Christmas, Passover, and Ramadan.

Rituals are important in all kinds of relationships. Feeding and bedtime rituals are a fundamental way for parents to bond with their newborns. And such activities, when done with intention, can continue to be an important way for families to connect well into a child's adolescence.

Couples may establish rituals around lovemaking, taking vacations together, or relaxing over a glass of wine at the end of a long week.

Extended families often have their own unique rituals around the celebration of birthdays, Thanksgiving, Christmas, and religious holidays.

Rituals also serve to bond individuals with larger communities, such as their schools, sports teams, employers, unions, or political institutions. Singing the fight song at a high school football game is a way to say, "We belong together. We're all Central High School Wildcats and we're proud of it."

The rituals that people celebrate in churches, mosques, synagogues, and temples can be especially significant because they help individuals affirm their connection to a supportive community and to God. Many people find such rituals especially supportive and healing during times of transition, mourning, and crisis.

Why do rituals have so much potential power in our relationships? For many reasons:

**Rituals symbolize cultural identity and values we share with our families, friends, work groups, or a larger community.** They provide a focus whenever two or more people come together around a common activity, belief system, or cause. People may profess to believe in the same things, but rituals give them a way to put those shared beliefs into action.

Think of the choice of rituals the Roth family might regularly share on Saturday mornings:

- Maybe they all rise early to gather their ski equipment, pack up the SUV, and head for the mountains. If so, the children will know, "We're the Roths, a family who values adventure, activity, and the great outdoors. We like to ski and we like to do it together."
- On the other hand, they may routinely attend synagogue on Saturday so the children can say, "We're the Roths, a family who always honors our Jewish traditions. We find meaning in worshiping God together, and we do it in this community."
- If the family typically heads for the shopping mall on Saturday mornings, the children might learn, "We're the Roths, a family who likes nice, new things and we don't mind spending our hard-earned time and money to get them."
- And if everyone scatters and goes his or her own way? Perhaps the family will gather together at other times, for other rituals—bedtime stories, Sunday supper, or breakfast on weekdays. But if the family never comes together in a ritualized way, they may miss out altogether on that feeling of being emotionally connected to one another.

**Rituals ensure that people take time for emotional connection.**
Lack of time is one of the most common reasons people say they don't form
deeper connections with their families, friends, and communities. Ritual can
help to solve this problem because it adds the elements of predictability and
intention to our lives. When we make a commitment to participate regularly in
some form of ritualized connection, we're less likely to lose touch with the people who matter most. It's the difference between saying, "Let's do lunch sometime," and "Let's plan to take a walk together every Wednesday afternoon."

The "scripted" or predictable nature of rituals also makes them easy to
execute. If we always meet in the same place and do the same thing, we
don't have to spend time researching new sites. We don't have to come up
with a new plan of action each time we come together.

But what if you've already got a full schedule? The solution is to create
an informal ritual out of activities you're already doing together on a routine basis—activities like watching TV, leaving for work, exercising, commuting, helping the kids with homework, or caring for each other when
sick. Many parents of school-aged kids, for example, find they spend increasingly more time in the car, driving kids to soccer practice, ballet lessons, and
the like. You can make the best of that time by building a special ritual
around it. "Tell me the silliest thing that happened at school today," Mom
might say, inviting each child in the car to share a story. That might be followed with a round of "best things," "worst things," or "saddest things" that
happened that day.

Remember, also, that rituals don't have to be complex or time-
consuming; they only have to be repeated and predictable. The husband
who always brings his wife a cup of coffee in bed each morning is performing a thoughtful ritual. So is the boss who always starts the weekly staff
meeting with acknowledgments for work well done. Ditto for the church
congregation that always ends its Sunday service with a chorus of "Happy
Birthday" to members who've grown another year older. All of these are
quick and meaningful ways that people use ritual to connect. (For more
ideas of rituals for connection, see chapter 8.)

**Some rituals help us to process our feelings as we move
through life's transitions.** The transition may be a minor one, like
Mom's daily departure from the day-care center, or it may be a major one,
like a wedding. Either way, rituals give us a way to acknowledge that things
are changing and to express our feelings about it.

Small, simple rituals of transition—such as saying good night to
coworkers or tucking a child into bed—may seem inconsequential at the
time. But they can give people an extra feeling of trust in the relationship
and in the world around them. The child can fall asleep feeling secure that
all is right in her relationship with the most important person in her life. The

coworker knows that when he gets back to the job the next day, relationships are on an even keel; work will resume in a calm, collegial manner.

Big public rituals such as bar mitzvahs, graduations, weddings, and funerals can be especially helpful as we adjust to life's major transitions— changes like growing up, leaving home, starting a new family, or dealing with the death of a loved one. By celebrating such transitions in the company of friends and family, we ask for and receive the emotional backing of our community. It's a way to feel connected to a large community of support at a time when we need it most. If the ritual takes place in a spiritual or religious community, a person may benefit from feeling spiritually connected as well.

**Rituals can help us to stay connected despite our conflicts.** Have you ever had an argument with your spouse, your child, or your parent just a few minutes before you had to leave for the day? With your feelings still stinging from the fight, you faced a choice: Did you (a) offer the hug or kiss that's always been a ritual of departure in your relationship; or (b) just walk away without a gesture or word? If you chose answer *a*, your ritual of affection provided an opportunity for you to turn toward one another and begin a repair process, despite your conflict. Even in the midst of battle, your ritual can communicate, "I may be mad at you, but I still value our relationship. I think we can work this out." If you don't have such ritualized ways of expressing affection or respect, it might take a lot longer before such feelings are expressed.

Our culture is filled with examples of other rituals that help to bridge the differences of opposing factions. Think of the way sports teams shake hands at the end of a game. Or the way disparate factions of a church community might come together to share communion. Athletes from around the world compete in the Olympics despite their political and cultural differences. In U.S. political races, when the election is over, the losing candidate typically delivers a concession speech in which he pledges to help citizens come together in support of their new leader. Following the disputed and highly contentious election of U.S. President George W. Bush in the year 2000, his opponent Al Gore delivered a concession speech that was characterized as an important step toward healing and unifying the country. That's the value of such rituals. Whether the dispute involves a couple, a family, a work team, or an entire country, certain rituals can help us to maintain important relationships even in the face of tremendous conflict.

## Consider Emotional Command Systems

As you think about rituals you'd like to have in your life, keep in mind that different kinds of rituals may appeal to different people, depending on the emotional command systems they rely on most. The Nest-Builder, for example, might best enjoy rituals that involve outward expressions of belonging and support. A game that explores what everybody has in common comes to mind, or an exercise in which people share compliments with one another might be appealing.

The Commander-in-Chief, on the other hand, might prefer rituals that help the group move closer to achieving some collective goal. Many work groups, for example, hold annual retreats at which they review the group's mission statement and then set the next year's objectives, goals, and strategies, based on that assessment. Those with a highly activated Commander-in-Chief might appreciate rituals that move this task forward.

The Jester might like rituals that provide entertainment and diversion, while the Explorer might enjoy those that help the group discover new realms of adventure. The Energy Czar might appreciate ritualized relaxation exercises, while the Sentry prefers rituals that help the group feel safe and secure. The Sensualist? Activities such as massage, aromatherapy, or hands-on art projects come to mind. The point is, if you're creating rituals of connection to use in your family, work group, or circle of friends, it may help to consider the types of command systems that are prominent in the group, and plan accordingly.

## Re-create and Update Rituals in Healing Ways

Rituals have the potential to be an extremely positive force in people's relationships. But they can also have a negative power—particularly if somebody uses rituals to manipulate others unfairly, or to cause a rift.

In one Jewish family I recently counseled, for example, the husband constantly chided his wife for not performing the rituals of their Orthodox traditions in the proper way. Even though he was inconsistent in his own religious practice, he expected her to follow the rules perfectly. But no matter how hard she tried, he always found flaws. Soon she began to feel that she could never be "Jewish enough" to please him, and this was causing a great deal of pain in their marriage.

In this way, becoming overly rigid about manners, holiday celebrations, religious rites, and the like can harm a relationship far more than it can help.

Perhaps you've seen the Coca-Cola television commercial where five generations of one family are gathered in a bucolic setting for a family reunion. Just as the photographer is about to snap the family portrait, an ancient matriarch asks her great-great-granddaughter for a Coke. "I'm sorry, Grandma," the young woman says, "but we don't have any." At this, the old woman is outraged. "What?" she scolds. "I'm 101 years old and this is probably the last time we'll get together. We're supposed to have Coca-

Cola!" She backs up her motorized wheelchair, knocking over tables and yelling, "Get away from me! Get away from me!"

The ad strikes me as both funny and tragic. In its overblown way, it shows what can happen when people cling so tightly to tradition and ritual that it harms their relationships.

Another hazard occurs when one person bears too much responsibility for making a ritual happen. The administrative assistant who single-handedly prepares a huge holiday party for the staff every year is a classic example. Not only does she feel overburdened and resentful, but the work team misses out on the fun of preparing the holiday party together.

To remedy or avoid such problems, I often encourage people to take a careful look at the rituals in their lives and what these activities mean to them. I counsel them to explore their childhood memories of rituals surrounding mealtimes, holidays, and such. Most people bring up at least a few sorrowful recollections, such as evening meals fraught with conflict over a child's refusal to eat what's served. Or holiday celebrations ruined by a belligerent alcoholic relative. Forgotten birthdays. Turbulent bedtimes. Religious ceremonies that were painfully long and excruciatingly boring.

Examining past rituals may help you to uncover unresolved feelings and hidden dreams. It's also a great way to discover traditions that you want— or don't want—to re-create in your current life. A woman raised as an only child remembers stuffy Christmas dinners surrounded by boring, aging relatives who drank too much, then fell asleep. To ensure that her children's holidays will be much more lively, she's developing Christmas rituals that involve families with children her daughter's age, and with plenty of child-centered activities. A man who remembers falling asleep at night to the sound of his parents' violent arguments goes out of his way to make bedtime peaceful for his own son. First there's a warm bath, followed by a light snack and a bedtime story. Then it's lights out while the rest of the family settles into quiet routines. In ways like these, you can create new and healing rituals of connection that celebrate your current dreams and values.

If you decide you want to change existing rituals in your life, be sure to discuss those changes with others involved well in advance. Remember that your goal is to discover shared meaning and connection through ritual. Making changes on your own without the support of others will defeat that purpose.

Don't be surprised if you encounter resistance to change. That's human nature. Older children and young adults in particular may balk at changes, particularly if such changes threaten to impinge on their sense of freedom. One way to soften resistance is to suggest instituting whatever change you have in mind on a trial basis. ("Let's turn the television off during dinner for the next week and see how that feels." Or, "Let's skip the gift exchange this year and give the money to charity instead. If we like the way that feels, we can do it again. If not, we'll go back to the way we've always done it.")

## *Exercise: Examining Your Rituals*

On the following pages you'll find a list of various activities around which people commonly create rituals. You'll also find a list of questions to ask yourself about those activities. Using your Emotion Log to capture your ideas, brainstorm new rituals as well as new ways to handle your current rituals. In chapter 8 you'll find descriptions of many rituals that help to strengthen various types of relationships.

You can also do this exercise with the people with whom you share these activities. Take turns answering the questions and listening carefully to one another's responses.

### *Types of Rituals*

- Waking up, waking one another up
- Breakfast
- Lunch
- Dinner
- Snacks
- Bedtime
- Leaving one another
- Reuniting
- Handling finances
- Hosting others in your home
- Special days (birthdays, anniversaries, miscellaneous celebrations)
- Taking care of one another when sick
- Renewing your spirit
- Taking vacations or getaways
- Traveling
- Recreations, games, and play
- Dates or romantic evenings
- Attending sports events
- Participating in sports events
- Watching television
- Attending movies
- Attending concerts, plays, and other cultural events
- Religious festivals and holidays
- Regular religious services
- Rituals of transition (funerals, weddings, bar mitzvahs, etc.)
- Attending another's performance or sports event
- Doing hobbies
- Creating art

- Running errands
- Doing household chores
- Participating in community events or politics
- Doing charity work
- Doing schoolwork
- Soothing other people's feelings
- Apologizing or repairing feelings after an argument
- Arriving at your job
- Doing your job
- Leaving your job

## Questions to Consider

- What was this activity like in your family or with your friends when you were growing up?
- Did you have rituals surrounding it?
- What were those rituals like?
- What did you enjoy about this ritual?
- What did you dislike about it?
- What would have made it better?
- What's this activity like in your life today?
- Do you have rituals surrounding it?
- What are those rituals like?
- If you have rituals surrounding this activity, how satisfied are you with them?
- What does this ritual mean or symbolize for you?
- Does this ritual help you to feel more connected or less connected to the important people in your life?
- Does this ritual foster positive feelings or negative feelings toward others?
- What could be done to make this ritual a more positive experience for you? For others?

# 8

# Apply What You've Learned

*M*arriage counselors, labor negotiators, and kindergarten teachers have known it all along: Whenever two or more people get together to accomplish *anything*, sooner or later there's bound to be a conflict. Building better emotional connections doesn't change this, but it can help you to maintain happy, stable relationships as you discover ways to live with your differences.

In this final chapter, we'll revisit the five steps to making your relationships work, exploring examples and exercises for applying them in specific types of relationships—those between spouses, parents and their children, friends, adult siblings, and coworkers.

## Building Better Emotional Connections in Marriage

### Step 1. Look at Your Bids for Connection with Your Spouse

My research clearly shows that if you want to improve your marriage, you should work on improving that fundamental unit of emotional connection, the bid. Remember: Happily married couples extend bids and respond to one another's bids for emotional connection at a much higher rate than unhappily married couples do. They make a habit of constantly turning toward one another's attempts to connect. They avoid turning away or turning against each other. This habit has a remarkable payoff: It allows spouses to be affectionate to one another and maintain their interest and sense of humor, even when they're in conflict.

## Exercise: Look for Opportunities to Turn Toward Your Spouse

Husbands and wives who live mindfully together find a seemingly infinite number of ways to turn toward each other and connect emotionally. Mostly, this is a matter of noticing and responding to their partners' bids for connection. But husbands and wives can also be proactive, creating increased opportunities in their shared lives for turning toward one another. On the next few pages you'll find a list of concrete, action-oriented opportunities for connecting.

There are two parts to the list: things you can do *for* your partner and things you can do *with* your partner. You can do these activities sporadically or you can build them into recurrent rituals. If you ritualize the opportunities, you can ensure that you'll make the connection, without having to remember just when and how to do it.

First, read the list to see how many of these activities you did in the past week. Are there items on the list you'd like to do more often? Are there things you'd like to make a regular part of life together? Circle three of those items and then decide together how and when you can make them happen in the week ahead. When the week is over, evaluate how you did. Were you successful at incorporating the new activity? If so, what difference did it make in your relationship? Did it change your feelings toward your partner in any way? Did you feel a shift in the emotional climate of your home?

If you were not able to incorporate the activity into your week, what obstacles got in the way? Are there ways to eliminate those obstacles?

Review the list again and repeat the exercise on a weekly basis.

You can read and contemplate this list on your own, but it makes a lot more sense to do it with your spouse. That way, each of you has the chance to state your personal needs and desires, enhancing your potential for connection.

As you do this exercise:

- Don't set high standards for your spouse's turning. Accept whatever effort you see. Just trust in this basic rule of nature: Successful turning toward leads to more turning toward. When a person improves in this area, that improvement builds on itself.
- Don't interpret your spouse's request for turning toward as an accusation that you've done something wrong in the past. Just take it as a compliment that your partner wants to see more of you.
- Don't make turning toward a competition; that would be counterproductive. Instead, think of the way that one kind act leads to another.

And what if you don't see an immediate improvement in your relationship? That's not unusual, either. In fact, just discussing some of the items on this list may stir up conflict. Nevertheless, try to stay engaged in the process of finding ways to connect emotionally. If both partners are committed to improvement, your efforts will pay off.

## Things to Do for Your Spouse

- Fix coffee, a snack, or a meal for your partner.
- Wait on your partner when he or she is ill.
- Compliment your partner's accomplishments, efforts, and looks.
- Ask your partner about his or her day.
- Praise his or her efforts around the house.
- Say "thank you."
- Listen. Listen. Listen.
- Run errands for your partner.
- Put a loving note in your partner's lunch or briefcase.
- Call or send e-mail during the workday.
- Do one of your partner's chores.
- Do something kind for your partner's friends and family.
- Buy a silly card or gift.
- Write a poem or song for your partner.
- Make a drawing, painting, or craft for your partner.
- Give flowers or balloons.
- Write a love letter.
- Offer your partner a massage or back rub.
- Ask about your partner's important childhood memories. Listen.
- Ask about your partner's fears. Listen.
- Ask about your partner's dreams, goals, visions. Listen.
- Ask your partner the Bugs Bunny question: "Eh, what's up, doc?" It's a way to say, "How are you?" or "Tell me all about what's going on inside you these days." Then listen and even take notes.

## Things to Do Together

- Hug.
- Kiss.
- Hold hands.
- Wrestle.
- Cuddle.
- Have a snowball fight.
- Sit down to breakfast on a weekday.
- Eat breakfast and read in bed on weekends.

- Read the paper.
- Kiss upon parting. Make it at least a six-second kiss.
- Kiss upon reuniting.
- Meet for lunch during the workday.
- Reunite at the end of the day and talk about how it went.
- Cook meals.
- Bake.
- Clean house.
- Fold laundry.
- Make a grocery list.
- Go grocery shopping.
- Plan a getaway or trip somewhere.
- Go shopping for clothes, housewares, or gifts.
- Help with school projects.
- Plan and host holiday celebrations.
- Learn a new language together (and plan a trip to the place where that language is spoken).
- Bathe the kids together, and help them get ready for bed.
- Take the kids on outings (museums, movies, the zoo).
- Attend school events together (PTA meetings, teacher conferences).
- Plan and host the kids' birthday parties.
- Attend your child's sports events and performances.
- Keep in touch with and/or visit with extended family.
- Exercise; go to a fitness club.
- Take a class (like ballroom dancing).
- Do yard work or gardening.
- Do home repairs.
- Maintain the car.
- Pay bills; manage the finances.
- Help care for sick or aging relatives.
- Commute.
- Walk the dog; care for a pet.
- Run errands.
- Do volunteer community work.
- Go on a picnic or a hike, or go camping.
- Take a vacation.
- Go out to brunch, dinner, or your favorite pub.
- Stay overnight at a romantic getaway.
- Plan and host a dinner party.
- Plan and take a vacation.
- Watch TV or videos. Talk to each other about them.
- Go to plays, concerts, or readings. Talk about them.
- Go to movies. Talk about them.

- Go to sports events. Talk about them.
- Go to art galleries or museums. Talk about them.
- Share a favorite recreational activity (bowling, skating, fishing, skiing, etc.).
- Read silently. Talk about what you're reading.
- Play a board game or a card game.
- Play computer games, surf the Internet.
- Reminisce.
- Make and maintain a family photo album.
- Build a fire in the fireplace and read or talk.
- Gossip, not in a mean way, but to try to understand another person.
- Philosophize.
- Remodel or redecorate your home.
- Hunt for a new house or apartment.
- Test-drive new cars.
- Sing or play music.
- Read plays, poetry, or novels aloud to one another or with kids.
- Create art or crafts (e.g., paint, sculpt, do woodwork).
- Listen to music.
- Take a shower or bath.
- Shampoo each other's hair.
- Make love.
- Talk over drinks (alcohol, coffee, tea).
- Go dancing, or to a nightclub or a comedy club.
- Go to a community event (auction, public forum, political meeting, etc.).
- Plan and celebrate milestones (birthdays, graduations, promotions).
- Help each other develop a self-improvement plan (career, health, fitness, etc.).
- Plan your future; dream.
- Go to a religious service.
- Meditate or pray.
- Other: _____.

## Step 2. Discover How the Brain's Emotional Command Systems Affect Your Marriage

In chapter 4, you had the opportunity to complete a series of questionnaires that assess your brain's emotional command systems, the nerve-based circuits that coordinate the emotional, behavioral, and physical responses needed for various life functions. As we learned, people differ in how much they like to have those systems stimulated, and such differences can influence our ability to connect emotionally with others.

By completing those questionnaires, you had a chance to explore your own preferences related to these systems, as well as the preferences of those around you. While the chapter 4 questionnaires allow you to assess possible changes in your own individual life, they can also point to changes a couple might make in their lives together. If you haven't done the questionnaires yet, you may want to do them now, focusing on how your emotional command systems influence your marriage. You'll also want to complete the exercise titled Your Emotional Command System Score Card, on pages 119–120, which can show how you and your spouse differ in relation to various systems.

Because spouses typically relate to one another in so many different ways, it's good for couples to find a comfortable balance in all seven emotional command systems described in this book. There are no universal formulas to follow. Every couple needs to find the balance that works best for them in each system. The three that are especially important in marriage are the Nest-Builder, the Commander-in-Chief, and the Sensualist.

The Nest-Builder is significant in marriage because it helps people to regulate issues of autonomy and independence. It's the area that's activated when couples answer certain questions: How much intimacy or interdependence will we have in this marriage? How much freedom and autonomy do we each need? Will we allow others to become as close to us as we are to each other? If somebody comes between the two of us in some way, will one of us feel jealous?

When a husband and wife answer these questions differently, it may indicate that they have different levels of comfort within the Nest-Builder system, and such differences can be a major source of conflict. By acknowledging and accepting differences, however, couples can either avoid or begin to resolve conflicts.

Another system that commonly causes concern in marriage is the Commander-in-Chief, which has to do with issues of power and control. When power issues come to the fore, husbands and wives grapple with these questions: Who's going to have the most influence in this marriage? Which of us is going to take the lead, and for which areas of our relationship? Can we split this up in ways that reflect different interests and talents? Can we share responsibility for important decisions, or divide them in a fair way? Or are we more comfortable with just one of us calling all the shots?

Conflicts can arise around such issues, particularly if husband and wife both have highly activated Commander-in-Chief systems. But again, acknowledging and accepting this similarity helps couples to avoid or to solve problems that have to do with power and control.

Understanding your similarities and differences within the Sensualist system is also important for a happy marriage. Problems often arise when one partner is more interested in sex or sensual pleasure than the other. Knowing that such differences could be based on an individual's brain circuitry can help. With this understanding, one partner is less likely to feel personally rejected when the other acts uninterested. Rather than judging themselves or each other as "cold" or "rejecting," "too horny" or "overindul-

gent," partners can see their differences in a more objective light and begin
to negotiate solutions.

In all relationships, couples have conflicts when partners are relying on
totally different emotional command systems in the same situation. For
example, the Explorer in one partner thinks the two can ski down unmarked
slopes, while the Sentry in the other argues that it's just too dangerous. The
Jester in one partner thinks they should both spend Sunday at a jazz festival,
while the Energy Czar in the other thinks it's time to catch up on sleep.

Understanding how you and your spouse use your emotional command
systems can improve your ability to bid and respond to one another. The section titled Bidding Across Emotional Command Systems, starting on page
124, may help.

### Step 3. Examine How Your Emotional Heritage Affects Your Relationship with Your Spouse

In chapter 5 we explored how a person's emotional past can impact current
relationships. Your emotional heritage includes lessons you learned about
feelings in childhood, your family's philosophy of emotion, and the enduring vulnerabilities you may still carry as a result of painful events. All of
those things can affect your ability to connect with your spouse today. Being
aware of such aspects of your partner makes all of this public between the
two of you; it gives you a language for talking about these things, making it
possible to honor and respect your differences.

## Exercise: How Does Your Past Influence Your Marriage?

To gain more insight, look back at the exercises in chapter 5. If you haven't
completed the questionnaires, do so now. Then, using your Emotion Log,
answer the following questions, which are designed to explore how your emotional heritage may affect your marriage in particular. You can do this exercise
with your spouse, or you can do it on your own, imagining how your spouse
might respond. Either way, look for opportunities to discuss these issues with
your partner. A better awareness of the way your emotional past affects your
marriage may improve you ability to bid and respond to one another's bids.

**1.** Review your scores on the exercise What's Your Emotional History? on
pages 140–145. Look carefully at your scores in each category: pride, love,
anger, sadness, and fear. Think about how comfortable you are with expressing each of these emotions to your spouse. Then answer these questions,
thinking about each emotion separately.

- How does your comfort level with this emotion affect your ability to feel close to your spouse?
- When you experience this emotion, are you usually able to explain to your spouse how you're feeling?
- Do you feel that your spouse understands how you're feeling?
- Do you feel guilty or self-conscious expressing this feeling?
- Is your spouse likely to turn toward you, away from you, or against you when you express this emotion?
- How would you like your spouse to respond when you express this feeling? Can you tell your spouse the kind of reaction you'd like?

Now think about your comfort at hearing your spouse express these emotions. Then answer these questions, again thinking about each emotion separately.

- How does your comfort with hearing your spouse express this feeling affect your ability to connect with him or her?
- Do you feel that you're able to empathize with your spouse when he or she is feeling this way?
- Do you feel embarrassed, frightened, or angry when your spouse expresses this feeling?
- Are you likely to turn toward, turn away, or turn against your spouse when he or she expresses this feeling?
- How would you like to improve your ability to share such feelings with your spouse?

**2.** Review the results of your responses to the exercise What Was Your Family's Philosophy of Emotion? on pages 146–150, and answer these questions.

- Was your family's philosophy primarily emotion-coaching, emotion-dismissing, emotion-disapproving, or laissez-faire?
- How does that affect the philosophy you express in your marriage?
- In relating to your spouse, what is your philosophy of emotion? How does this affect your marriage?
- In relating to you, what is your spouse's philosophy of emotion? How does this affect your marriage?

**3.** Review the results of your response to the exercise What Are Your Enduring Vulnerabilities? on pages 164–165. Answer the following series of questions for yourself. Then answer the questions once more, this time putting yourself in your spouse's place.

- How do your enduring vulnerabilities affect your ability to connect emotionally with your spouse?

- Do you feel that past injuries interfere with your ability to bid for emotional connection? In what way?
- Do you feel that past injuries interfere with your ability to respond to your spouse's bids? How so?
- Do past injuries ever get in the way of your ability to feel included by your spouse?
- Do past injuries interfere with your ability to express affection, or to accept affection from your spouse?
- Do you sometimes feel that you're struggling too hard to control your spouse because you feel vulnerable?
- Do you sometimes feel that you're struggling too hard to resist being controlled because you feel vulnerable?
- Are there ways that your spouse could help you to heal from past injuries? What healing thing would you like your spouse to do or say? Have you expressed this to your spouse?

## Step 4. Sharpen Your Skills at Emotional Communication with Your Spouse

Words alone can't express all we feel. That's why couples need to be attuned to one another's facial expressions, movement, gestures, tones of voice, and so on. In chapter 6 we explored the broad range of ways that people express and read one another's feelings. Then we practiced those skills with the Emotional Communication Game, an exercise designed to show how nonverbal cues can change the meaning of various phrases. Here's another chance to practice your emotional communication skills with your spouse, this time using scenarios common to marriage.

### Exercise: The Emotional Communication Game in Marriage

To play the game with your partner, silently read each item and its three possible interpretations. Arbitrarily pick a particular meaning for each item. Then take turns reading each item aloud, as you or your partner tries to guess which of the three meanings you're trying to convey. You can also practice the game on your own, but I encourage you to do it as a couple, if possible, because it will help you to learn more about the unique ways each of you expresses feelings.

1. Are you going to do the dishes?
   a. You're angry that you did them every night last week, and you think it's your partner's turn.

    **b.** You're pleasantly surprised that your partner seems ready to do the dishes.

    **c.** You're just asking for information because you're not sure whose turn it is.

2. Will you answer the phone?
    **a.** You're trying to avoid an incoming phone call, so you want your partner to answer the phone as a favor to you.
    **b.** You're busy, you don't want to be distracted, and you're irritated that your partner seems to be ignoring the ringing.
    **c.** You'd like to answer the phone, but your hands are full of cookie dough. You need your partner's help.

3. I'm scheduled to work Labor Day weekend.
    **a.** You're disappointed because you had both hoped to get away alone together that weekend.
    **b.** You're pleased because you'll get paid overtime and you need the money.
    **c.** You're just passing this information along to your partner. It doesn't matter that much to you one way or the other.

4. Oh, are we having tuna casserole?
    **a.** You like tuna casserole and are pleasantly surprised.
    **b.** You're disappointed because you've had this for dinner a lot lately.
    **c.** You're neither positive nor negative about it, but just asking for information.

5. My mother is coming for a visit.
    **a.** You are dreading the visit and want your partner's support and comfort.
    **b.** You are genuinely excited that she is coming.
    **c.** You are neither excited nor worried, just informing your partner about the visit.

### Step 5. Find Shared Meaning in Marriage

Our research shows that couples form happier, more stable marriages when they find common meaning in their life together. Doing so requires you to be mindful of one another's dreams and visions for your marriage, and to communicate your values about these issues to one another. Rituals that draw husbands and wives together emotionally can also help.

    Below is a list of questions designed to explore meaning in your marriage. That's followed by suggestions for rituals that can enhance your sense of shared meaning.

# *Exercise: What Does Your Marriage Mean to You?*

Some of the questions that follow deal with the marriage itself, and roles you may want to have within your partnership. Others deal with goals that you have for yourself and your family. And still others address sensitive issues like sex, money, and religion—issues that often require a great deal of negotiation in a marriage.

I suggest that couples read these questions together and discuss just a few of them at a time. Your goal is not to reach agreement, but simply to express your feelings as individuals, and to listen to one another with open hearts. Doing so may help you to better understand each other's perspectives, which is absolutely necessary when it comes time to deal with conflict. Such understanding also serves as the foundation upon which to build your rituals for emotional connection.

Don't try to answer all these questions in one sitting; that would be too hard. Instead, consider discussing them over a period of weeks. Then revisit the questions from time to time to see how your perspectives have changed. The important thing is that you maintain an open dialogue so that such heartfelt discussions can become a foundation from which you build your lives together.

- How do you feel about your role as a husband or wife? What does this role mean to you in your life?
- How did your father or mother view this role? How are you similar or different?
- Are there ways you'd like to change your role in your marriage? What are they?
- How do you feel about the balance in your life between your role as a spouse and your other roles, such as parent, worker, friend, or adult child?
- What does your home mean to you? What qualities must your home have for it to be a safe, satisfying place for you to spend your time? Think about the home where you grew up. How do you want your home to be similar or different?
- What does money mean to you? How much is enough for you? How much prominence should the acquisition of money and possessions have in your life? Think about the role money and possession had in the home where you grew up. How do you want the role of money to be the same or different in your life?
- What does extended family mean to you? How close do you want to be to your extended family? To your spouse's extended family? Think about the role of extended family in the home where you grew up. How do you want this to be different or similar in your life?

- What is the role of ethics, morality, spirituality, or religion in your life? What does it mean to you to have a purpose in life? What role did these issues play in your family as you grew up? How should this be in your family now?
- What does sex mean to you in your marriage? What should it mean? What do you find most satisfying about sex with your spouse? Are there ways to make it even better?
- What goals do you have in life for yourself, your spouse, and your children?
- What do you want to accomplish in the next five to ten years?
- What is one life dream that you want to fulfill before you die?
- How does your marriage help or hinder accomplishing these life goals? How could it be better in this regard?
- Imagine seeing your epitaph or obituary. What would you like it to say? What legacy do you want to leave? What changes would you have to make in your life today to make that vision come true?
- Like many people, you may spend most of your time tending to immediate demands—"putting out fires," so to speak. But are these activities truly important to you? What activities serve as sources of energy, pleasure, intimacy, or meaning in your life? Are you sharing these kinds of activities with your spouse? Do you make enough time for these important things, or do they often get postponed and crowded out? How can the two of you make more time for the things that genuinely give you pleasure?

## Rituals of Connection in Marriage

As you may recall from chapter 7, rituals are repeated, predictable events that have symbolic meaning. A ritual can be really simple, like a peck on the cheek as you rush off to work, or quite elaborate, like a wedding.

When rituals of emotional connection are done well in a marriage, they help married couples celebrate their bond and stay together through all kinds of trials and triumphs. Below are some suggestions about rituals that pertain to family relationships, and to marriage in particular.

**Morning rituals.** To reduce morning stress, prepare the next day's sack lunches, clothes, backpacks, and so on the night before. This will leave more time to do nice things like pouring your spouse a cup of coffee or chatting over the morning newspaper.

**Leave-taking.** Before you part company, find out at least one thing that's going to happen in your partner's life that day. That will give you something to ask about when you get home.

**Affectionate greetings and partings.** Share a loving kiss when departing or coming back together again. A peck on the cheek is okay, but a warm, mindful kiss is so much better. It says, "I'll think of you while I'm gone," or "I'm glad to be back together again."

**Calling or sending e-mail.** Brief phone conversations or funny notes via the Internet during the day say, "You're on my mind."

**Mealtimes.** Sit down at the table to share your meals. Turn off the television. Make the table attractive with softened lights, candles, and soothing music. Soften the conversation as well—talk about the events of the day in ways that are supportive, affectionate, and encouraging. Save the more difficult conversations for another time.

**After-dinner coffee.** Here's a ritual that's especially good for couples with children. Once the entire family finishes their meal and their dinnertime conversation, the kids are excused to play, do homework, or watch a video. This gives Mom and Dad time for a one-on-one conversation over coffee or tea. Describing this ritual in his book *Intentional Families,* the psychologist William Doherty said it became so important to him and his wife that they continued it long after their grown kids left home. He also suggests doing the ritual over a hot beverage. This ensures that you'll sit still long enough for it to cool and for you to drink it. But it also provides a definite end to the ritual (when the drink is gone) in case one or both of you have other things to do.

**Eating out.** Going to a favorite romantic restaurant can be a great way to acknowledge a special event like a birthday, anniversary, or job promotion. It can also make an ordinary night feel special. It's a way to say, "Let's treat one another well; we deserve it." If money's tight, consider going out just for dessert or a glass of wine. The point is to celebrate the relationship, not to run up a big bill.

**Bedtime.** What could be more symbolic of the trust and intimacy in marriage than the act of taking off your clothes, lying down, and falling asleep under the same blanket with another person? Celebrate this nightly ritual by being mindful of its refuge. Try to let go of the tension of the day. If you've felt angry or irritable toward your spouse during the day, don't dwell on the feeling. Instead, think of this time as a temporary ceasefire—an interval to just be together and relax.

**Dates.** Get out and do something enjoyable as a couple, without kids or other adults around. Make sure that at least part of the date includes time for talking. For couples with children, I recommend one evening date weekly and three weekend getaways a year. To make sure dates happen, book standing reservations at a restaurant or a bed-and-breakfast. This takes the work out of deciding where and when to go. Like all good rituals, it happens automatically. If paying for a baby-sitter is a problem, consider trading child care with another family. Or, if you can get the day off, schedule dates during a weekday when the kids are at school or day care.

**When one spouse is sick.** Because people often feel vulnerable and childlike when they're ill, how one spouse takes care of another at such times can be quite important. Of course, individuals can have very different ideas about how they want to be cared for. Some want solitude in a dark, quiet room, while others long to have company and lots of attention. Be sure to talk with your spouse about this. Find out what gives your partner comfort. Ask about his or her family's rituals around caretaking. Were there special foods, home remedies, or expressions of affection that seemed especially soothing? What could really make a difference today?

**Rituals of triumph.** Whether you say it with balloons, a banner, a bottle of champagne, or plane tickets to Maui, the important thing is to celebrate your partner's successes. It's all part of developing that habit of praise and appreciation, which I described in chapter 3 as an antidote to the "crabby habit of mind." When you create hoopla over your partner's triumphs—large and small—you demonstrate your support for his or her goals and visions, which contributes to the stability of your marriage. So look constantly for opportunities to say, "I'm so proud of you. You've worked so hard for this. And I'm your biggest fan."

**Rituals surrounding bad luck, failure, or fatigue.** In moments of deep discouragement, it can be extremely comforting to have a reliable outward sign that your spouse stands by you. Again, such rituals can be very simple. "Let me draw you a hot bath." "Lie down and I'll give you a back rub." "You go to bed early tonight, honey. I'll give the kids their baths." "Let's just call out for Chinese food, rent some videos, and forget about the rest of the world for a while. We don't even have to answer the phone." The important thing is to let your spouse know that despite disappointments in the outside world, your marriage is a place of safety and support.

**Rituals around initiating and refusing sex.** Some people believe that lovemaking has to be spontaneous to be sexy, so they try to avoid any kind of rituals or preplanning. The trouble is, a married couple's life can get so busy with work and family responsibilities that unless they plan a time to make love and have a ritual surrounding it, the lovemaking never happens.

Or it only happens late at night when both partners are exhausted and it's not so much fun. So I recommend that couples ritualize lovemaking to make sure that it happens regularly and in a way that both partners find exciting.

Think about the effort you made early in your relationship to make sex as pleasurable as possible. Perhaps certain music, perfume, lingerie, or candlelight helped you to set the mood. If you've let such preparations fall by the wayside, bring them back to your relationship. If there are elements you'd like to incorporate into your ritual, try them out, talk about them with your partner, and plan to use them again.

Pay attention to the rituals your partner finds most exciting, and use those often. Remember that learning to make love to someone is much like learning to give the ideal back rub. You may start off using techniques that you'd most like to receive, but with experience and feedback, you make adjustments and use techniques your partner likes best. Don't take your partner's feedback as rejection; see it as useful information instead. Being a great lover is all a matter of learning what turns your partner on.

Is there a specific, regular time during the day when you can plan to be alone together? Maybe it's on the weekend, when your kids are off at music lessons. Or maybe it's during a lunch hour, if you can arrange to meet at that time of day. If you have the opportunity for spontaneous lovemaking sometime, by all means take it! But don't let your lack of unstructured time be a drain on your love life.

Some kind of ritual for talking about sex can also help—especially considering how shy some people are on the subject. Many couples have an interval in their lovemaking ritual that's considered "uncensored." That's the time when it's okay to reveal whatever desires or fantasies they have. That's not to say that partners are required to always fulfill one another's fantasies. But the most fulfilling sexual relationships are those in which couples feel free to at least share their most private thoughts.

Couples often develop their own code words or signals for initiating or refusing sex as well. The psychologist Lonnie Barbach suggests that couples talk about sexual interest in terms of a nine-point scale; when you're a "nine," you feel extremely lusty, and when you're a "one," you're not in the mood at all. That way, one person can say, "I'm an eight tonight, how about you?" And the partner can reply, "I'm a nine" or "I'm a two." This helps the individual to communicate how he or she is feeling about sex at the moment, without making a low interest seem like personal rejection.

**Vacations.**  What's the first thing most married couples do once they tie the knot? Take a honeymoon vacation, of course. It's our society's way of saying, "Take some time alone together in a romantic spot and get this relationship off to a good start." I recommend that couples continue to honor their marriages by repeating this ritual as often as possible. Find a destination that's both romantic and pleasurable. Leave the kids, pets, and other relatives at home. And don't bring the office pager.

**Handling finances.** Because money can be such a source of conflict for couples, it can be a real blessing for couples to find a sane way to negotiate issues like spending, saving, and investing. Rituals that help a couple to mesh their shared life goals with a financial plan can help. Books such as *Your Money or Your Life*, by Joe Dominguez and Vicki Robin, or *The Mindful Money Guide*, by Marshall Glickman, provide advice and exercises for doing just that.

**Apologizing or repairing feelings after an argument.** Some couples have ritualized ways of saying "I'm sorry," "I screwed up," or "Let's try again." The classic ones involve flowers, candy, or greeting cards. In fact, Hallmark now has a whole line of cards just for this occasion. But many of the everyday rituals mentioned earlier can double as rituals of apology and forgiveness as well. That's one of the wonderful things about incorporating rituals into your relationships. They ensure that when things get rocky and feelings get hurt, it won't be long before partners will have a chance to come together and express their feelings. Let's say you squabble with your spouse over the phone bill just before it's time to leave for the office. If you have a ritual of kissing one another before you depart, that's your golden opportunity. Standing face-to-face near the door, one of you can say, "I'm sorry I was so testy." And the other can reply, "It's okay. I understand. I was a little crabby myself."

## Building Better Emotional Connections Between Parent and Child

### Step 1. Look at Your Bids for Connection with Your Child

To make the most of your connection with your child, understand that in childhood, bidding for emotional connection is not an optional event. Children are designed by nature to behave in ways that attract attention from adults. From infancy on, a child's very survival depends on adults noticing them and taking action. If children *can't* connect with parents through positive behavior, they will do it by acting up. For little ones, this may mean lots of fussy, whining, annoying behavior. Older children may become obstinate or defiant, just to get their parents' attention. But when parents turn toward their children's bids for connection in consistently positive ways, children are less likely to act up. Whether they're conscious of it or not, they know their parents are there for them emotionally, and they don't have to behave badly in order to prove it. The key, then, is to look constantly for opportunities to turn toward your children and to connect emotionally with them.

Here are a few things to keep in mind as you do so.

**Take your time.** Children generally process feelings more slowly than adults do. So, when you talk to kids about emotions or emotional topics, give them plenty of time to digest and think about things. Don't expect immediate answers.

**Be prepared for emotional honesty.** Studies show that most kids are pretty poor liars. In fact, until the age of eleven or so, most don't master the art of the "white lie"—that is, hiding the truth in order to spare others' feelings. So if you ask your child how he or she is feeling about something you've done, for example, be prepared to hear and respect the honest truth.

**State your goals clearly when you make a bid for connection.** Subtler bids can go right over a young child's head, causing hurt feelings as the family misses its opportunity to connect. Here's an example of a bid that may seem straightforward, but is actually too subtle for this nine-year-old child.

> DAD: Want to go bowling?
> JEREMY: Nah, I'd rather read my Harry Potter book right now.

Jeremy, a concrete thinker, interprets Dad's bid as a simple request for information, and he provides an honest answer. Jeremy may not realize that Dad's after more than just a bowling partner—that he wants to connect with his son. But if Dad gets more explicit about his goal, Jeremy can see that the issue is spending time together, not bowling right this minute, and he may respond more positively to his father's bid.

Here's what happens when Dad is more clear.

> DAD: I haven't seen much of you this week. Would you like to do something together this weekend? We could go bowling. What do you think?
> JEREMY: I'm reading my Harry Potter book right now. Could we do it tomorrow?
> DAD: Sure. Let's do it after lunch tomorrow.
> JEREMY: Great!

**Use your child's expression of feelings as an opportunity for intimacy or teaching.** When your child opens up to you with expression of fear, sadness, or anger, try to validate those feelings by saying that you understand why he or she might feel this way. Then work with your child to solve the problem that's causing the sadness, anger, or fear.

246 THE RELATIONSHIP CURE

**Understand that emotions can be extremely intense for children.** That's because they lack the life experience that teaches, "This too shall pass." They may not understand that the sadness, fear, or anger they're feeling is not going to last forever. So, when you talk to kids about their feelings, don't underestimate or dismiss the intensity of what they're going through. If you do, you may blow an important opportunity to connect with them.

**Notice, validate, and name your child's emotions.** Help your child to find words for what he or she is feeling. Then, without dismissing the feelings, offer some guidance on how to cope. ("Are you disappointed that Laurel didn't invite you to her skating party? I'll bet it hurts to feel left out. Let's talk about it for a while. Then, later on, maybe you could invite Nicole to go to a matinee with you on Saturday.")

**Set limits on misbehavior.** As the child psychologist Haim Ginott taught, all emotions are acceptable, but some behaviors are not.

## *Exercise: Look for Opportunities to Turn Toward Your Child*

Below is a list of activities that afford the chance to turn toward your child in ordinary but important ways. The list is presented in two parts, things you can do *for* your child and things you can do *with* your child. Read the lists and consider which activities you did in the past week. Are there activities on the list that you'd like to try in the weeks ahead? Are there some that you'd like to make part of your daily interactions together? Circle those activities and try them out in the coming week. When the week is over, look back and see how you did. Consider how new efforts to turn toward your child affected your feelings of emotional connection with him or her.

### *Things to Do for Your Child*

- Pay attention to what's going on in your child's day-care center or school. Talk to teachers. Read newsletters. Show interest.
- Attend your child's sports activities, performances.
- Attend school events, open houses, parent/teacher conferences.
- Sit down with him or her at mealtimes, including breakfast. Turn off the TV and talk.
- Pack your child's lunch. Include healthy treats and a friendly note.
- Take photos of your child.

- Praise positive behavior in specific ways. Instead of saying, "You're a great artist," describe how the drawing makes you feel: "This picture makes me want to go out into a forest."
- Show affection by touching your child gently and often. Cuddle and stroke smaller children. Offer your hand to bigger kids as long as they'll take it. Make hugs a habit. Pat your child on the arm, head, or back when he or she is behaving well.
- Offer choices whenever possible. Within reason, let your child decide what to wear, what to eat, what activities to pursue.
- Pay attention to your child's likes and dislikes. If he likes crunchy peanut butter rather than smooth, buy crunchy peanut butter.
- Show interest by asking your child questions about her day.
- Take interest in your child's friends. Ask questions about them.
- Be kind to your child's friends.
- Show interest in your child's creative projects.
- Express gratitude.
- Ask your child what she wants to be when she grows up. Listen.
- Ask your child about his fears. Listen.
- Ask your child what she would wish if she could have three wishes. Listen.
- Apologize when you're wrong. Doing so teaches that it's okay to make mistakes and to admit to them.
- Monitor your child's activities.
- Always know where your child is.
- Keep asking questions about your child's experiences and thoughts.
- Other: _____.

## Things to Do Together

- Play games.
- Go for a walk.
- Take a nap.
- Make up stories.
- Cook a meal.
- Bake a treat.
- Share jokes.
- Have a "grug"—a group hug.
- Share "butterfly kisses" (with your eyelashes) or rub noses.
- Tickle, wrestle, and horseplay. (But be careful never to shake a small child or baby. This can cause brain injury.)
- Look at your child's baby pictures. Tell your child happy or funny stories about her birth and infancy. Let your child know how glad you are that he was born.

- Sit down together for meals.
- Watch his favorite TV shows and talk about them.
- Read the newspaper aloud and talk about it.
- Read the funnies aloud and talk about them.
- Read books aloud—even after your child is old enough to read to herself.
- Play catch, shoot baskets, kick a soccer ball around the yard.
- Do craft projects.
- Play make-believe.
- Redecorate or paint your child's room. Give him choices for colors, fabrics, and so on.
- Set the table. Make it a "fancy dinner" once in a while, with candles, good dishes, and cloth napkins.
- Plant a garden; designate one part as your child's.
- Shop for your child's clothes. Give your child choices.
- Start a savings account. Make deposits together. Calculate the interest.
- Buy your child a few shares of stock. Check the prices each day.
- Play computer games.
- Surf the Internet for cool kids' sites.
- Go to your child's favorite restaurant.
- Go to the park, playground, or children's museum. Crawl around on the equipment with your child.
- Go to a children's theater. Talk about the play.
- Go to a children's movie. Talk about it.
- Share a favorite recreational activity, like swimming, skiing, hiking, camping, bowling.
- Go to an art museum. Make up stories about the pictures.
- Go to "story hour" at the local library or bookstore.
- Build a fire in the fireplace and roast marshmallows.
- Turn off the lights, light some candles, and tell (not-too-scary) ghost stories.
- Plan and take a vacation.
- Make a scrapbook of vacation memories when you get home.
- Sing. Play music.
- Dance.
- Put up the tent in the backyard and have an overnight camp-out.
- Do conditioning exercises.
- Volunteer to go on field trips with your child's class.
- Volunteer to work in your child's classroom.
- Provide help with homework when appropriate.
- Make plans for the holidays.
- Plan birthday celebrations.
- Make packages of letters, drawings, and audiotapes or videotapes for out-of-town relatives.

- Research the family tree.
- Do a jigsaw puzzle.
- Videotape a "documentary" about your family or your child's life.
- Make a family photo album.
- Take a sex-education class together at your local children's hospital or Planned Parenthood office.
- Make a growth chart and check it often.
- Do community volunteer work together.
- Go to religious services.
- Meditate or pray.
- Other: _____.

## Exercise: Create Your Child's Love Map

Here's another exercise designed to help you turn toward your child. It's similar to the Love Map presented in chapter 2, but this one is specially tailored for use with kids. It's designed to help you explore the details of your child's daily life. The more you know about your child's experiences, feelings, preferences, and so on, the easier it will be to turn toward him or her and connect emotionally.

You can do this exercise alone, but it's even better to do it with your child's other parent (or other primary caregiver) and take turns answering these questions about your child. If either of you has trouble answering particular questions, circle those items and make a point to talk to your child about them. Then return to the exercise and try once more to complete the map together. Don't think of the exercise as a competition; that's not helpful. Instead, think of it as a game you can play together to benefit your child.

You may also want to return to this exercise at regular intervals as your child grows. Doing it each year on or near your child's birthday, for example, will help you stay up to date with important changes he or she is going through.

1. What are your child's two favorite foods?
2. What two foods does your child most dislike?
3. What are your child's two favorite kinds of music?
4. Who are your child's favorite singers?
5. What are your child's special hobbies and out-of-school interests?
6. Name all your child's friends.
7. Name all your child's enemies.
8. Who are two of your child's heroes and heroines?
9. Name two of your child's favorite videos or movies.
10. Name two of your child's favorite TV shows.

**11.** What two animals does your child like, and what two does your child dislike?

**12.** What would be your child's ideal vacation getaway?

**13.** Name two of your child's favorite bands.

**14.** What sports does your child especially like to play?

**15.** What sports does your child like to watch and follow?

**16.** Name one person your child has had a crush on.

**17.** What sports does your child find uninteresting?

**18.** If your child had a sizable sum of money to spend and could go shopping anywhere, what three things would he or she buy?

**19.** What is one thing your child would like to change about you?

**20.** What types of clothing does your child prefer to wear and hate to wear?

**21.** Who is your child's least favorite relative?

**22.** Name two people your child would pick for wall posters in his or her room.

**23.** Who is your child's most favorite relative?

**24.** What would be your child's ideal birthday party this year?

**25.** What are your child's favorite types of dessert?

**26.** If your child could design the ideal family, what would it look like?

**27.** What is one thing you would like to change about your child?

**28.** Name three preferences your child has about evenings at home. (For example, does your child prefer to spend time alone reading?)

**29.** What would be your child's least favorite kind of birthday party?

**30.** What would be your child's idea of a good way to spend a rainy day indoors at home?

**31.** Name three of your child's recent favorite books.

**32.** Name your child's three favorite and three least favorite teachers.

**33.** Name three preferences your child has about weekends. (For example, would your child like to go to a museum? A ball game?)

**34.** Name two of your child's favorite songs or pieces of music.

**35.** What are the main problems your child will have to overcome to have a successful and happy life?

**36.** What are two of your child's favorite musical instruments?

**37.** Describe two of your child's dreams that have yet to be fulfilled.

**38.** What occupations has your child seriously considered having when grown up?

**39.** What are two occupations that your child definitely would not want to have when he or she grows up?

**40.** What are your child's two favorite colors?

**41.** What three games does your child like to play, if any?

**42.** What color are your child's eyes?

**43.** Where would your child most like to travel, and why?

**44.** Name two of your child's favorite restaurants.

**45.** How does your child feel about reading?

**46.** Name two places or events that your child would find uncomfortable.

**47.** What does your child like for you to do when he or she is sick?

**48.** What are your child's comfort foods?

**49.** What was the saddest event in your child's life?

**50.** How does your child feel about mathematics?

**51.** What was the worst time your child ever had?

**52.** How does your child feel about writing?

**53.** What is your child's attitude toward crime?

**54.** What would be your child's ideal bedtime routine?

**55.** What are two of your child's favorite ways to exercise?

**56.** What would be your child's ideal birthday present?

**57.** Name two things your child fears.

**58.** How does your child feel about war?

**59.** What would be your child's ideal weekend?

**60.** Describe one great day your child recently had. What happened that day?

**61.** What two things make your child most angry?

**62.** How does your child feel about travel?

**63.** Does your child know the real difference between good and evil? How do you know this about your child?

**64.** Describe one heart-to-heart talk you recently had with your child.

**65.** Describe your child's ideal sack lunch. What would he or she like least?

**66.** What are two of your child's current stresses?

**67.** Name two lies your child has told.

**68.** What does your child think about hunting animals?

**69.** How does your child feel about the police?

**70.** Name three of your child's personality weaknesses that you worry about.

**71.** What are the worst and best parts of your child's current school year?

**72.** List your child's three favorite adults.

**73.** What is your child's attitude toward money?

**74.** How does your child feel about politics?

**75.** How does your child feel about popular animals like cats, dogs, horses, or whales? Why does your child feel this way?

**76.** How does your child feel about school tests?

**77.** How does your child feel about teasing?

**78.** What is your child's attitude toward poor people?

**79.** Describe one time when your child felt ashamed or humiliated.

**80.** What was the best time your child ever had, and why?

**81.** Name two things that your child is really worried about.

**82.** Who are your child's favorite painters?

**83.** What would be your child's idea of the "coolest" car to own?

**84.** What are your child's attitudes toward violence?

**85.** What is one thing you could do to improve your relationship with your child?

**86.** What would your child describe as the best experience he or she ever had?

**87.** What does your child most like to do with friends?

**88.** How does your child get over being sad?

**89.** What have been some of your child's ideal and worst summer experiences?

**90.** How would your child ideally like to decorate his or her room?

**91.** How does your child try to get your attention?

**92.** What is your child's attitude toward homework?

**93.** What are two things your child is proudest of about himself or herself?

**94.** Describe one bad day your child recently had. What happened that day?

**95.** What would your child choose to give you as a birthday gift?

**96.** Who was your child's favorite teacher, and why?

**97.** Describe one nightmare your child has had.

**98.** What are your child's feelings about nature?

**99.** How does your child feel about charity?

**100.** What would your child describe as the worst experience he or she ever had?

## Step 2. Discover How the Brain's Emotional Command Systems Affect Your Relationship with Your Child

A young father once told me this story about trying to put a new snowsuit on his three-year-old son while a neighbor was visiting. His son didn't like the snowsuit at all, and put up a mighty resistance.

Finally the neighbor dad asked, "Do you mind if I try?" A bit embarrassed, but grateful for intervention, the father released his son and said, "Fine."

As the little boy watched, the neighbor laid the snowsuit out on the floor and began fussing with its zipper and Velcro wrist straps. "Do you want to see how it works?" the man asked. The little boy nodded, approached the suit, and fiddled thoughtfully with the Velcro. After a minute or two, the man asked, "Do you want to put the snowsuit on—all by yourself?" The boy nodded again, and with the man's instruction, he stuck his feet into the legs of the suit. Then he wiggled his arms into the sleeves. Finally the boy pulled the zipper all the way up and announced proudly, "I did it all by myself!"

I like this story because it demonstrates what can go wrong when children and parents are operating from different emotional command systems. With his Energy Czar system fully activated, the father was thinking, "I must protect my child from the cold!" But the child longed only to activate his own Commander-in-Chief system and say, "I can do it myself!" He wanted to experience his Explorer system and say, "Look what I discovered!"

The neighbor succeeded in getting the boy to put on his snowsuit because he understood this. He could see the boy's desire to be independent and powerful. He looked at the situation from the child's perspective and he thought, "This boy hates the feeling that he has no control. But he would probably love to show his family and friends that he's capable of dressing himself—especially once he sees how cool the new snowsuit really is."

Dreams of being independent, skilled, adventurous, and powerful are important to most children throughout childhood and into adolescence. That's why preschoolers are so fascinated with cartoon superheroes. It's the reason young teens were so taken with the scene in *Titanic* where Leonardo DiCaprio stands on the bow of the boat and yells, "I'm king of the world!" It's also the root cause of many power struggles between parent and child. When they're little, battles may center on bedtime, eating habits, or getting in the car seat. When they're big, conflicts shift to issues like homework, fashion, friendships, and curfews.

Kids need much more than independence and power, however; they also long for security, protection, and a sense of belonging. They lack life experience and they need adult guidance. They need to know that we, as grownups, are there to set limits and to shelter and defend them if things get scary. We're there to give them nurturance and support. So while we need to allow children to activate their Explorer and Commander-in-Chief systems, we also need to stand beside them with our Sentry and Nest-Builder systems appropriately activated, setting limits, offering guidance and safety. We also need to pay attention to our Energy Czar systems, making sure that children get the rest and nutrition they need. As adults, our message is this: We believe in you and we want you to try your wings, but only when you're ready. And we'll do our best to catch you if you should fall.

What's the best way to achieve this balance? By allowing kids to make choices for themselves whenever it makes sense to do so. If you've got little ones, for example, you can take them to the grocery store and line up three types of breakfast cereal that fit your Energy Czar's nutritional criteria. Then say, "You decide." Let kids choose what color of shirt to wear, what book to read, what game to play. Having such choices, and learning to choose well, helps kids to feel competent and satisfied. Then, as kids get older, you can let them take responsibility for more important choices. For example, you can give them a clothing allowance and let them decide how to spend it. Let them choose their own elective classes, the sports they want to play, and the hobbies they want to pursue. All of this allows them to explore their own independent dreams and visions of the types of adults they want to become. It allows them to take responsibility for their choices in incremental steps. And by letting them make their own choices, you show that you care about their preferences, their hearts' desires. It's a way to show your willingness to understand them. It's a way to connect emotionally over and over again.

Although I've discussed some of the common conflicts that arise between parents and children here, the questionnaires in chapter 4 can give you a more individualized picture of the emotional command systems you rely on most. If you haven't completed these questionnaires, I encourage you to do so. You may even want to complete them as you think your child would. Then, using Your Emotional Command System Score Card on pages 119–120, you can see how you and your child differ and you can read about ways to negotiate interactions across those differences.

### Step 3. Examine How Your Emotional Heritage Affects Your Relationship with Your Child

Have you ever had this experience? You're talking to your child when you suddenly realize that the words coming out of your mouth are not your own, but words your mother or father said to you so many years ago. For better or worse, the way you connect emotionally with your child is influenced by the way your parents connected with you. That's why it's important to be aware of your emotional heritage. This includes the messages you heard as a child about expressing feelings, your family's philosophy of emotion, and your enduring vulnerabilities—that is, past emotional injuries that still feel sensitive to this day.

Understanding your emotional heritage is important because it can provide insight into the way you bid and respond to bids for emotional connection with your child. For example, if you had a strong-willed father who reprimanded you for not being cheerful, you may have a hard time responding well to your own child's sadness. On the other hand, if you had a dad who mostly empathized with your negative emotions and helped you to find solutions to problems, you've got a head start toward teaching your child to cope.

### Exercise: How Does Your Past Influence Your Connection with Your Child?

Below is a list of questions designed to explore the way your emotional heritage affects your ability to bid and respond to bids for connection with your child. Before you answer these questions, however, look back at the exercises in chapter 5. If you haven't completed them, you may want to do so now, because you'll need the results to answer the following questions.

You can write the answers to these questions in your Emotion Log. Sharing your answers with your child's other parent or a trusted friend may be helpful as well.

**1.** Look at your scores on the exercise What's Your Emotional History? on pages 140–145. Note your scores in each category: pride, love, anger, sadness, and fear. Think about how you feel when you hear your child express each of these emotions. Then answer the following questions, thinking about each emotion separately.

- How does your comfort with hearing your child express this feeling affect your ability to connect with him or her?
- Do you feel that you're able to empathize with your child when he or she is feeling this way?
- Do you feel embarrassed, frightened, or angry when your child expresses this feeling?
- Are you likely to turn toward, turn away, or turn against your child when he or she expresses this feeling?
- How would you like to improve your ability to be with your child as he or she is being emotional?

**2.** Review the results of your responses to the exercise What Was Your Family's Philosophy of Emotion? on pages 146–150, and answer these questions.

- Was your family's philosophy primarily emotion-coaching, emotion-dismissing, emotion-disapproving, or laissez-faire?
- How does that affect the emotional philosophy you express in your relationship with your child?
- In relating to your child, is your philosophy primarily emotion-coaching, emotion-dismissing, emotion-disapproving, or laissez-faire?
- What effect does your own philosophy of emotion have on your child?

**3.** Review the results of your response to the exercise What Are Your Enduring Vulnerabilities? on pages 164–165. Then answer the following questions.

- How do your enduring vulnerabilities affect your ability to connect emotionally with your child?
- Do you feel that past injuries interfere with your ability to bid for emotional connection with your child? In what way?
- Do you feel that past injuries interfere with your ability to respond to your child's bids? How so?

- Do past injuries ever get in the way of your ability to feel included by your child?
- Do past injuries interfere with your ability to express affection toward, or accept affection from, your child?
- Do you sometimes feel that you're struggling too hard to control your child because you feel vulnerable?
- Do you sometimes feel that you're struggling too hard to resist being controlled by your child because you feel vulnerable?

## Step 4. Sharpen Your Skills at Emotional Communication with Your Child

Emotional communication between parent and child begins long before kids learn to talk, and continues for the rest of the life of the relationship. You can hone your skills at emotional communication by practicing the Emotional Communication Game, which was first introduced in chapter 6 (see pages 202–205). Here are several more items geared to give you practice at reading and responding to emotional cues in parent-child conversations.

### Exercise: The Emotional Communication Game for Parents and Kids

You can play this game with another adult or with your child, if he or she can read. Start by silently reading each item and its three possible interpretations. Then take turns reading the items aloud, as the other person tries to guess which of the three meanings you're trying to convey. You can also practice the game on your own. Doing it with your child, however, may help you notice things about the unique ways he or she expresses feelings.

1. Are you going to practice your piano lesson?
   a. You see that your child is going to practice, and you're pleasantly surprised.
   b. You think it's high time that your child practiced, and you're afraid that he or she will never get around to it.
   c. You're just asking for information.

2. Are you going to eat that?
   a. Your child is very fussy, and has been playing with his or her food and you're annoyed.
   b. You understand that your child doesn't particularly like this dish, and you want to give permission to leave it unfinished.
   c. You're neutral about it, and just asking for information.

**3.** You left your game in the yard. If it stays outside all night, it will get wet and be ruined.

    **a.** You think your child is careless with toys, and that makes you angry.

    **b.** You know the game is precious to your child, and you want to let your child know that you're worried about its safekeeping.

    **c.** You're simply reminding your child where the game is and that it might rain that night.

**4.** Your friend Jamie called. Are you two getting together again this weekend?

    **a.** You like your child's friend, and hope they'll see one another again soon.

    **b.** You think your child has been seeing too much of this person, and you're worried.

    **c.** You're just asking for information.

**5.** Have you taken care of Max?

    **a.** Your child keeps forgetting to feed the pet, and you're angry about this kind of irresponsibility.

    **b.** You're pleasantly surprised that your child has taken the initiative to feed the pet.

    **c.** You're just asking for information about whose turn it is to feed the pet.

## Step 5. Find Shared Meaning in Parenthood

What does it mean to raise kids? By exploring this issue and sharing your insights with the important people in your child's life, you can help build a stable, committed social environment for your child. When parents and caregivers find common ground around child-rearing issues, they build stronger emotional ties and are less likely to engage in conflict—an obvious plus for kids. They're more likely to support one another's goals and visions for raising a child. In addition, exploring such issues gives you a better awareness of the values your child may be learning from others.

    Below is a list of questions designed to help you better define your vision for parenthood. That's followed by a list of rituals that can help you to find shared meaning and emotional connection with your child and others involved in your child's life.

### *Exercise: What Does Parenthood Mean to You?*

Here's a list of questions. You can write your answers down in your Emotion Log. It's also a good idea to share your answers with your child's other parent and/or caregivers.

If you have an older child, you may want to talk about these issues with him or her as well. The discussion might help the two of you to view your relationship from one another's perspective, enhancing your connection.

- What does it mean to you to be a parent?
- What's your definition of a good parent?
- How does your understanding of good parenting differ from your own parents' understanding?
- What does it take to provide a healthy, nurturing environment for a child?
- What qualities must a child have in a home in order to have a happy life? Did the home you grew up in have those qualities? How do you want your child's environment to be similar to, or different from, the home you grew up in?
- Who should be the most important influences in your child's life? How can you ensure that your child spends enough time with these people to make it so?
- What role should education play in your child's life? How will your child get the kind of education you want for him or her?
- What role should television, the Internet, popular music, advertising, and other forms of media play in your child's life? How will you help your child to interpret and understand things he or she learns through the media?
- What do you want your child to learn about ethics, morality, spirituality, or religion? What meaning or purpose should these issues have in your child's life? How will your child learn about these things?
- What are the most important things you want your child to know about friendship? About marriage? About family? About sexuality? About money? About making a living? How will your child learn these things?
- What is the meaning and purpose of discipline in your child's life? What's the best way to discipline your child? Does your current habit of discipline differ from this? If so, how can you change it? How can you ensure that your child receives consistent discipline?
- Imagine your child as an adult looking back on his or her childhood, long after you have died. What would you want your child to say about the kind of parent you were? What changes would you have to make in your life today to be that kind of parent?

## Rituals of Connection with Your Child

Rituals can enhance emotional connection in any relationship, but they're especially helpful for children, who often thrive on the comfort and security of knowing what's going to happen next. For small children—who often have trouble making the transition from one part of the day to the next—rituals can smooth the way. ("Go to the window and we'll do our special wave before I leave for work. Then I'll look in the window to find you when I come back.") For adolescents, rituals can be an anchor during changing times. ("Yes, you can take the bus to the mall with Frannie, but I expect you home for supper by six.") And for youngsters of all ages, rituals can be used to transmit a family's values and sense of belonging. ("We always have the Passover Seder with your grandmother. It means so much to her that we come together this way each year.")

On the next few pages you'll read suggestions for rituals that may enhance connections between parent and child. Some, like bath time, are geared toward very young children, while others appeal to kids of all ages. Whatever rituals you choose to do with your kid, try to make the activity appropriate for your child's age and stage of development. Keep in mind that kids may enjoy taking more responsibility for creating the ritual as they grow older. A three-year-old, for example, might enjoy folding festive napkins for the Thanksgiving Day feast, while a thirteen-year-old can help you bake the turkey, stuffing and all.

**Morning rituals.** If the kids have got to scoot to school or day care, wake them early enough so that they can calmly dress and eat breakfast. Sit down at the table together. Talk about the day ahead for each of you in encouraging ways. If you're spiritually inclined, say a short prayer together, or read an inspirational verse.

**Leave-taking.** Acknowledge older kids as you go your separate ways with a quick kiss, a hug, or affectionate words. Little ones may benefit from reassurances of how soon you'll be reunited. Special handshakes, silly waves, or funny sayings ("See you later, alligator!") repeated each day can help to seal the deal emotionally.

**Reuniting.** Let your kids know how happy you are to see them with a warm, affectionate hello. Ask specific questions about things that may have happened since you last saw them. "Tell me about the field trip." "What did you do at recess?" "Who brought snacks?" Vague questions like "How was school today?" are guaranteed to elicit vague responses—especially from teens. But if you ask more probing questions, like "What was the *dumbest* thing that happened in school today?" you're bound to make a connection.

Remember that kids preschool age and younger may need some transition time when they see you after hours of separation. So don't be surprised if your child is not ready to go the minute you arrive at the baby-sitter's house or day-care center. Spending a few extra minutes in their own world at the end of the day may help to make them feel more secure.

**Mealtimes.** Everybody's got to eat, so why not make dinnertime a shared pleasure—the focal point of your time together each day. Kids may benefit from involvement in the whole process—from planning to cooking to cleaning up afterward. But at the very least, make an effort to come together around the dining table at least once a day. If conflicting work schedules make a shared dinner impossible, find a substitute. Designate another gathering time—right after school or just before bed, for example—and stick to it. Then come together over a snack, a cup of tea, or cookies and milk. If even that's impossible, try to find at least a few times a week when you can all be together.

Talk about the events of the day and make sure each person—from youngest to oldest—gets a chance to talk. Because your intention is to connect, turn off the TV and try to eliminate other distractions; let the answering machine pick up the phone. The idea is to treat family meals as the great opportunity they are—your best daily shot at influencing your kids, showing them you respect and care about them.

Try to make the table a peaceful environment. If there's a problem brewing, set aside another time and another place to talk about it soon.

Power struggles over kids' eating habits are a common cause of mealtime tension in many families. You can avoid such problems by following this simple rule, recommended by many nutritionists: The parents are in charge of what's served; the child gets to decide how much of it he or she will eat. Some families also avoid food fights by offering picky eaters a healthy "default." ("If you don't like what we've prepared, you can have a peanut butter and jelly sandwich and a piece of fruit. But you fix it yourself and you don't complain.")

**Bath time.** With its warm water, sweet smells, bubbles, and rubber ducks, bath time can be one of the most pleasurable rituals small children share with their parents. You can make it all the more fun by incorporating songs and imaginative games into the routine of washing up. Approaching hygiene the same way each night can take the fear out of chores like shampooing. Also, avoid tears and power struggles by allowing plenty of time for play as well as for transitions in and out of the tub.

**Homework time.** You can let your child know how much education means to you by helping him or her to establish a structured ritual around studying. Designate a special time each day for homework, for example. And make your family's priorities clear. Some families, for example, make the phone and TV off limits until homework is done. Also, select a comfortable, quiet, well-lit place in your house where your child can sit each day to study. You can offer to assist in projects when that's appropriate, but don't hover. Kids need to learn to take responsibility for their own work.

**Bedtime.** Nighttime rituals provide some of the best opportunities to feel emotionally connected to children. They're groundwork for the separation that parent and child inevitably experience during sleep, and they can be a way to acknowledge and process the feelings that inevitably go along with being apart. It's almost as if family members are going away on a brief journey to wherever our dreams are about to take us, and bedtime rituals allow kids to feel better prepared for the journey. So take your time, and don't be surprised if your child likes to get ready for bed the same way every night. Rituals may include telling a story to your child or listening as your child tells you a story. Some kids like a small snack, such as crackers and milk. Others may involve their toys and stuffed animals in a litany of good-nights. A back rub, a prayer, or a song can be a soothing way to end the day. Affectionate hugs, kisses, and special handshakes are sometimes called for. And never underestimate the power of reading aloud to your child as a way to bond, to instill a love for good books, to share an adventure, and to drift peacefully into sleep.

And just because your child is growing doesn't mean that you have to let go of all your bedtime rituals. I know families who still enjoy reading aloud together just before bed well into their child's teen years.

**When your child is sick.** Like bedtime, childhood illnesses are golden opportunities to use ritual as a way to say you care. Here's a common, simple, and effective ritual: The parent drags pillows and a blanket out to the living room couch and urges the sick child to rest and read or watch TV. The child is then centrally located where all in the family can express their affection and concern. Common props may include the thermometer, the heating pad, orange juice, chicken soup, and piles of the child's favorite reading. Try not to worry about "goldbricking." A child who knows he'll be well cared for in illness won't need to test that theory. Concentrate instead on listening to your child's bid for connection, and turn your attention to helping him or her to get well.

**Support for sports, arts, and academic achievements.** At the end of every soccer game, parents join hands and form an arch for junior athletes to run through. Each spring, "Band Booster" parents hold an old-fashioned school carnival—complete with a cakewalk and a duck pond game—to raise funds for new musical instruments. Each fall, parents flock to their kids' classrooms and sit in undersized chairs to pore over test scores during parent-teacher conferences. Events like these all demonstrate to our kids that their achievements matter. When they see us joining other adults in ritualized support of their growth and development, our kids know their parents aren't the only ones behind them—the whole community cares.

**Holiday celebrations.** Holidays provide special opportunities for emotional connection in all relationships, and they can be especially meaningful for parents as a way to pass along family traditions and teach values to their children. We need to be vigilant, however, to keep commercial pressures from overwhelming our chances. With retailers feeling increasing pressure to make huge profits from holiday sales, our children may get the message that religious holidays like Christmas and Hanukkah are more about acquisition than connection. What's the solution? Take a look at your family's holiday traditions and weed out those that make you feel harried, worried, or put-upon. Cling instead to those rituals that leave family members feeling peaceful, emotionally satisfied, and closer to loved ones. Books like *The Intentional Family,* by William J. Doherty, Ph.D. (Avon, 1997), and *Unplug the Christmas Machine,* by Jo Robinson and Jean Coppock Staeheli (Quill, 1991), can be enormously helpful in finding ways to improve your emotional experience of the holidays.

One important point that the authors of both books stress: Don't leave all holiday preparations up to one family member (i.e., Mom). Involving the whole family in planning, decorating, cooking, and so on may take more time and patience than doing it yourself. But if your intention in celebrating the holidays is to draw closer to loved ones, then, of course, it's worth it to make these activities teamwork. Encourage children to express their ideas and add their own creative touches. Then, as kids grow up, they naturally may start taking on more responsibilities for holidaymaking, allowing the matriarchs of the family to relax through more of the celebration.

One more piece of advice: Create holiday rituals that express your family's own unique likes and dislikes. This adds to children's sense that their participation in the celebration strengthens their ties to the clan. ("Our family thinks having a dead tree in our house at Christmas is a dumb idea. We buy a live one in a pot, decorate it, and then plant it later on." "Our family loves animals. We always go to the zoo at Passover time and see the new babies.") Some families create rituals around their own idiosyncratic "holidays"—an annual drive to the country in the fall to view the autumn color, for example, or a trip to the ocean at summer solstice.

**Rites of passage.** Some religious traditions provide rites of passage for children as they move into their teen years. Rites such as the Jewish bar mitzvah and bat mitzvah give communities an opportunity to acknowledge and celebrate this passage in a formal and public way. It's a chance to say, "Our sons are growing into men and our daughters are growing into women. We as parents have powerful hopes, dreams, and expectations for them as they make this transition. We want them to become responsible, happy, successful adults. We intend to give them all the love, guidance, and support they'll need to make this transition successfully. But we also know that they'll need the guidance and support of others from our community, so we ask for your help and your prayers during this transition as well."

Unfortunately for too many teens, such truths are never spoken, never acted upon. Consequently they drift through their teen years without the emotional reassurances of support that such rituals can provide. Teens may wish, suspect, and believe that their parents are beginning to see them as responsible adults, but there's no moment for them to connect emotionally around this truth.

Whether you're religious or not, you may want to create some kind of personalized family ritual aimed at forming a stronger emotional bond with your child during this challenging life transition. Writer Celeste Fremon, for instance, described a "Not Mitzvah" she held for her non-Jewish son. She invited her son's closest friends and relatives and asked each of them to present a gift that would symbolize what he or she wished for his future. Gifts ranged from a worn Swiss Army knife to a new power drill. Each also brought along a wish or piece of advice that would help the boy along his way. Writing in the *Utne Reader*, Fremon said that on the surface, the ceremony didn't seem that significant. "And yet it was a very big deal that so many men in Will's life showed up to tell him that he mattered, that they took him seriously, that they were there for him if he needed them."

Other parents have described less formal celebrations. One dad taught his son to shave, then took him out for ice cream to celebrate. Another family held a bonfire on the beach at the end of elementary school, and burned a huge pile of papers their son had accumulated—minus the most treasured stories and artwork, of course. One mom celebrated her daughter's first menstrual period with a special dinner out for just the two of them. Another mom took her girl to a fancy hotel, where the two had facials in the spa and spent the night. Each parent valued the experience as a chance for one-on-one time, a time to acknowledge his or her child changing and to say, "I'm here for you."

**Family chores.** Washing dishes, raking leaves, folding laundry—such tasks can become rituals of connection if we do them side by side. The key is to make the activity a positive experience. While you work, chat with your child about topics he or she finds interesting and upbeat. Offer your child lots of praise for his or her efforts, as well. ("I like the way you stacked those towels." "When we weed the flower bed together, we get done in half the time.") It may take some cajoling to get children in the habit of doing chores together, but once they begin to experience them as positive activities in which they get emotional support, their resistance wanes.

**Discipline.** Your routine ways of responding to your children's misbehavior can be powerful rituals for teaching them what you truly value.

That's why it's so important to develop thoughtful, consistent habits for disciplining your child.

For small children, such rituals might include a short "time out" followed by a heart-to-heart talk about how to handle the problem differently in the future. This response teaches that it's important to understand one another and learn from our mistakes. For older children, the ritual ought to include consequences related to the misbehavior. Also, make sure that the consequences draw kids into family activities rather than excluding or isolating them. ("I asked you to be home for supper by six, and you were an hour late. So tomorrow night you need to be home by five. That way, you can help me cook and set the table.")

It may help to remember that the words *discipline* and *disciple* have the same Latin origin, *discere,* meaning "to learn." Your children are like your disciples, constantly looking to you for clues about how to live.

**Apologies and forgiveness.** As with marriage, parent-child bonds can benefit from rituals of emotional healing. What signals does your family typically use when one or more of you is ready to negotiate a cease-fire and start repairing hurt feelings? Are there words or gestures that everybody understands to mean "I'm sorry," "Let's talk," or "I forgive you"? Rituals of apology and forgiveness may include those very words, or they may be more subtle—a wisecrack or an offering of something to eat, for example. Gestures of apology might be a peck on the cheek, a hug, or a back rub. When your daughter has a temper tantrum, runs to her room, and slams the door, does it mean something to hear the door quietly open five minutes later? Is it an unspoken invitation for you to enter and begin peace talks? Pay attention to such rituals as they develop in your family, and honor them. They can be extremely helpful for children, especially very young ones who lack the verbal skills to express all the pain they may experience when family members fight. But children can easily understand the soothing effects of a hug or a few minutes together in the rocking chair.

## Building Better Emotional Connections in Friendship

### Step 1. Look at Your Bids for Connection with Friends

One of the most delightful—and volatile—aspects of friendship is the voluntary nature of it all. Whether it's a cup of coffee, a lavish gift, or an offer to stay by your sickbed, favors from friends are intentional acts of generosity. Friends are not obligated to us by law, economics, or family bonds. Our friends turn toward our bids for connection simply because they want to, and that's what makes those relationships so rewarding.

By the same token, our friendships often suffer from a lack of time because of all our other commitments and obligations. So it often takes a bit of extra effort and creative thought to find opportunities for turning toward your friends. The exercise below may help.

## Exercise: Look for Opportunities to Turn Toward Your Friends

Scan the following lists for ideas on how to turn toward your friends in new ways. Try out some of these ideas in the weeks ahead. Then look back and see how your efforts are affecting your friendship. Do you feel that you're growing closer, feeling more connected?

The exercise called Look for Opportunities to Turn Toward Your Spouse, on pages 230–233, provides ideas for lots of activities that would be fun to share with a friend as well. But some friendships—especially new ones and old ones that need rekindling—may require a different perspective or some fresh ideas for "turning toward." These somewhat shorter lists of activities may help.

### Things to Do for Your Friends

- Ask "How are you?" in a way that shows you'd really like to know.
- Listen to their stories and jokes (even if you've heard them before).
- Return the things you borrow.
- Say "thank you" for favors.
- Offer spur-of-the-moment invitations to coffee, dinner, or drinks (but don't be hurt if your friends can't come).
- Accept spontaneous invitations when you can. (But don't feel guilty if you can't make it.)
- Ask for advice, but don't feel obligated to take it.
- Ask friends if they'd like your advice before you offer it. If they say yes, share your wisdom. Don't be disappointed when they don't do what you suggest.
- Know when what you're asking for is too much.
- Ask your friend about his or her childhood. Listen.
- Remember his or her birthday with a card or a gift.
- Nod in agreement when your friend says good things about his or her spouse or lover.
- Notice and say positive things about your friends' children.
- Ask your friend about his or her dreams, goals, and visions. Listen.

- Offer compliments.
- Accept apologies.
- Ask your friends about their life stories. Listen.
- Ask your friends about their parents. Listen.
- Tell them it's okay to call anytime.
- Let them off the hook when they say, "I can't do it. I'm exhausted."
- Drive them to the airport when they're going away on a special journey or a difficult trip.
- Let them be as upset as they need to be.
- Support their efforts at health improvement.
- Encourage their efforts to build skills, learn more, become more.
- Offer to help out when your friend is stressed.
- Ask for help.
- Let them help you.
- Monitor your friend's well-being, and be there in good times or bad.
- When you lose track of each other over time, try to pick up where you left off.

## Things to Do Together

- Visit one another.
- Commute.
- Exercise.
- Volunteer.
- Share gossip, jokes, and news via e-mail.
- Phone one another often.
- Form a group of friends who share a common hobby or interest. Meet regularly. When you can't get together, discuss your common interests online.
- Confide in one another and keep each other's secrets.
- Swap baby-sitting, pet-sitting, house-sitting.
- Trade big favors like helping one another paint the house, move residences, or build a deck.
- Celebrate one another's successes.
- Host a party for a mutual friend.
- Share hugs, handshakes, pats on the back.
- Cry together.
- Be there for the big events in one another's lives—kids' weddings, parents' funerals, serious illnesses.
- Collaborate on a project.
- Show one another your baby pictures.
- Pray or meditate together.

## Step 2. Discover How the Brain's Emotional Command Systems Affect Your Friendships

A few months ago, I had a long visit with a close friend and professional colleague I had known for a long time. He came to see me at an extraordinary time in his career, a time when all of his life's work seemed to be coming to fruition. As the afternoon unfolded and I listened to him tell me about his success, I realized that I had two choices. One was to react the way I had often reacted in similar situations when we were younger: I could jump in and start telling him about all the projects I'd been working on. I could catalog my recent accomplishments to see if he might be as impressed with my work as I was with his. In other words, I could do what so many men are accustomed to doing in friendship: I could turn the visit into a contest. But my second choice was to react in a different way. I could simply relax, listen, and focus on my friend's story, sharing his sense of pride and happiness.

I chose the second response, and I'm so glad I did so. It was a wonderful experience just to be with him and to relish this time in his life. I asked him to describe his thoughts and feelings about his work. By the end of our visit, I think we were both feeling very good about our friendship and this time we'd shared. And what about my stories? God willing, my friend and I will have many more good visits to come, and all that information can keep for another time.

Looking back, I can see how the choice I made in that situation relates to the concept of emotional command systems. I chose during the visit to activate my Nest-Builder command system rather than my Commander-in-Chief. I consciously decided that it was more important to feel close to my friend at this time than to engage in a competitive game of "who's up and who's down." It's not that competition doesn't have its place in friendship. Friendly, supportive rivalries can be very invigorating as we encourage and inspire one another to keep growing and improving our lives. And at different times in our lives, this had been true for my friend and me as well. But this time we chose to take our friendship down a different path.

Staying aware of the way you activate your various emotional command systems can be helpful in any relationship, but I think it's especially important in friendship because of the voluntary nature of such bonds. Compared with a marriage or parent-child relationship, it's relatively easy to walk away from a friendship gone sour. You don't have to file for divorce or relinquish custody to end a friendship. You can simply stop responding to phone messages and e-mail from a friend.

Sustaining a mutually satisfying friendship, on the other hand, requires special care and many subtle negotiations—both spoken and unspoken. On the Nest-Builder front, friends need to establish how close the friendship will become. How much time will they spend together? Will they share true feelings? What happens when other commitments, such as work and family, get in the way? How will your Commander-in-Chief systems find a suitable balance? Will one person always take the lead? Will the other be perfectly happy in a supporting role?

Friends who become sexually attracted to each other have to make decisions about managing (or not managing) their Sensualist command systems. Will they acknowledge the sexual energy between them? Or will they stay silent on the matter, allowing the energy to simmer on the back burner while dabbling in flirtation and fantasy? If they acknowledge the attraction, will they act on it, or will they set boundaries to keep it in check? And what becomes of the friendship if the two disagree?

Friends who travel together may need to find the right balance between their Explorer systems in order to have a rewarding trip. Negotiations between Energy Czars will be required when one or both begin to grow tired and hungry. And if that trip includes risk, the two may have to get their Sentry systems aligned or go their separate ways. Aligning Sentry systems often requires negotiation whenever two families with children start making plans together. ("You're not going to let them go down to the beach alone, are you?" "I don't care if it is New Year's Eve. Our Melissa is *not* going to drink champagne!") And if two friends' Jester systems aren't in balance, a friendship may wither from a simple lack of fun.

That's not to say you're going to find the perfect balance in all these areas with all your friends. To the contrary, no single relationship can meet all your emotional needs. In fact, it would be a mistake to invest that much expectation into any relationship, including marriage. It's better instead to focus on building congenial bonds with a variety of people who bring different gifts to your life. That way, you can revel in your friendships with a diverse group of friends. You can appreciate your friendship with competitive Charley, for example, who inspires you to boost your heart rate every time you go out for a run together. But you'd never tell Charley about your problems with your boss. You save those conversations for Chris, who hates to run but is always so compassionate, understanding, and insightful. Chris also has a great sense of humor, so you love to go see comedies together. But he's not much of an Explorer. You'd rather travel with Esther, who . . . I'm sure you get the picture.

If you completed the Emotional Command System questionnaires in chapter 4, you'll have a picture of your preferences related to these systems. You may want to ask a friend to complete them as well, or you can answer them as you imagine your friend might. Then, using Your Emotional Command System Score Card on pages 119–120, you can compare your preferences with those of your friend.

## Step 3. Examine How Your Emotional Heritage Affects Your Relationships with Friends

Friendship, like other relationships, is affected by our emotional heritage. The messages you heard in childhood about the expression of feelings, your family's emotional philosophy, and past emotional injuries can all influence how you connect emotionally with friends.

If you've completed the exercises in chapter 5 on emotional heritage issues, you should have a general sense of what these matters mean for your relationships. By completing the exercise below, you can focus on how such issues impact particular friendships. This increased awareness may help you improve your ability to bid and respond to bids for connection with friends.

### Exercise: How Does Your Past Influence Your Friendships

Take a look at you responses to the emotional heritage exercises in chapter 5. Then, thinking of a particular friendship, answer the following questions in your Emotion Log. If you're particularly close to this friend, you might want to do this exercise together. Or you can do it on your own, imagining how your friend might respond. Either way, look for opportunities to discuss these issues with your friend.

**1.** Review your scores on the exercise What's Your Emotional History? on pages 140–145. Look carefully at your scores in each category: pride, love, anger, sadness, and fear. Think about how comfortable you are with expressing each of these emotions to your friend. Then answer these questions, thinking about each emotion separately.

- How does your comfort level with this emotion affect your ability to feel close to your friend?
- When you experience this emotion, are you usually able to explain to your friend how you're feeling?
- Do you feel that your friend understands how you're feeling?
- Do you feel guilty or self-conscious expressing this feeling?
- Is your friend likely to turn toward you, away from you, or against you when you express this emotion?
- How would you like your friend to respond when you express this feeling? Can you and your friend talk about it?

Now think about your comfort at hearing your friend express these emotions. Then answer these questions, again thinking about each emotion separately.

- How does your comfort with hearing your friend express this feeling affect your ability to connect with him or her?
- Do you feel that you're able to empathize with your friend when he or she is feeling this way?
- Do you feel embarrassed, frightened, or angry when your friend expresses this feeling?
- Are you likely to turn toward, turn away from, or turn against your friend when he or she expresses this feeling?
- How would you like to improve your ability to share such feelings with this friend?

**2.** Review the results of your responses to the exercise What Was Your Family's Philosophy of Emotion? on pages 146–150, and answer these questions.

- Was your family's philosophy primarily emotion-coaching, emotion-dismissing, emotion-disapproving, or laissez-faire?
- In relating to your friend, what's your emotional philosophy? What effect does your emotional philosophy have on this friendship?
- In relating to you, is your friend primarily emotion-coaching, emotion-dismissing, emotion-disapproving, or laissez-faire? How does your friend's emotional philosophy affect your relationship?

**3.** Review the results of your response to the exercise What Are Your Enduring Vulnerabilities? on pages 164–165, and answer the following series of questions for yourself. Then answer the questions once more, this time putting yourself in your friend's place.

- How do your enduring vulnerabilities affect your ability to connect emotionally with your friend?
- Do you feel that past injuries interfere with your ability to bid for emotional connection with this friend? In what way?
- Do you feel that past injuries interfere with your ability to respond to your friend's bids? How so?
- Do past injuries ever get in the way of your ability to feel included by your friend?
- Do past injuries interfere with your ability to express affection toward, or accept affection from, your friend?
- Do you sometimes feel that you're struggling too hard to control your friend because you feel vulnerable?
- Do you sometimes feel that you're struggling too hard to resist being controlled by this friend because you feel vulnerable?

- Are there ways that your friend could help you to heal from past injuries? What healing thing would you like your friend to do or say? Can you express this to your friend?

## Step 4. Sharpen Your Skills at Emotional Communication with Your Friends

Good friends can become quite adept at reading one another's feelings through facial expressions, tones of voice, gestures, and the like. We explored such nonverbal forms of communication in depth in chapter 6. Below is a reprise of a game designed to help you practice your emotional communications skills. This time around, all the items are geared toward situations involving friends.

### *Exercise: The Emotional Communication Game with Your Friends*

To play the game with a friend, start by silently reading each item and its three possible interpretations. Then take turns reading the items aloud as your friend tries to guess which of the three meanings you're trying to convey. You can also practice this on your own. But playing it with a friend may help you to gain special insights into the unique ways your friend expresses emotions.

1. Do you want to have lunch this week?
    a. You're angry that you always have to make all the suggestions about getting together.
    b. You're pleasantly surprised that your friend seems to have time available, and you think it's a great idea to have lunch together.
    c. You're just asking for information about whether your friend has time for lunch.

2. Are you busy right now?
    a. You sense that this might not be the right time to talk, and you don't wish to intrude.
    b. You want to discuss an issue that your friend keeps avoiding, and that makes you feel irritated.
    c. You're just asking for information.

3. What do you think of this new suit?
    a. You love this new suit and think you look great in it; you're fishing for a compliment.

    **b.** It was an overpriced suit, and you're not sure it looks good on you. You're thinking of returning it.

    **c.** You hate this suit, and you want support for returning it.

4. Did you make the reservations for Amy's birthday party?
    **a.** You're tired of having to remind your friend of things he or she agreed to do.
    **b.** You're just wondering how the arrangements for the party are going.
    **c.** You're happy that it was possible to make arrangements at such a great restaurant.

5. Are you going to talk to your boss about a raise?
    **a.** You think your friend should ask for a raise, and you're worried that he or she is being too meek about this important issue.
    **b.** You think this is the wrong time to push for a salary increase, and you're worried that your friend may be acting too pushy.
    **c.** You're just asking for information.

### Step 5. Find Shared Meaning in Your Friendships

Friendships based on shared meaning are probably the richest friendships of all. How satisfying it is to know that you and your friends have interests and values in common, that you understand one another's aspirations and dreams. You can foster this sense of shared meaning by completing the exercise below and by participating in the rituals of connection described after that.

### *Exercise: What Does Friendship Mean to You?*

Below is a list of questions to help you clarify the meaning of friendship in your life. As you read these questions, think about particular friends and the way those relationships are currently unfolding. Your answers may point to the strengths and weaknesses of those bonds. The exercise may help you to see new directions you can take to strengthen your emotional connections with friends. If you feel especially close to a particular friend, you may want to read and consider this list together. But you can also use the list on your own, simply imagining how your friends would answer these questions. Then, if you get the chance, you may want to bring up individual topics mentioned here, and see if your perceptions match their ideas.

    Keep in mind that no single friend can fulfill all of your emotional needs. Still, in answering these questions, you may identify areas you'd like to pursue with a particular friend—areas of untapped potential in your relationship.

On the other hand, you may see the limitations of your relationship more clearly, in which case you might do better to turn to other people for various emotional needs.

- What does it mean to you to be a good friend? Do you feel that each of you is a good friend in this relationship?
- Is it important to have a balance between giving and taking in this friendship? How are you doing in that regard?
- How important is it for you to be able to express your true feelings to one another? Is it okay if you and your friend tell each other when you feel angry, sad, or afraid?
- What's the role of acceptance in this friendship? Can you rely on one another to feel affirmed? Supported? Valued? Is that important to you?
- Is it important to offer advice to one another? Is it important to be willing to listen to each other's counsel? Does this differ from topic to topic? Are there certain areas where you're not open to advice from this friend—your marriage, for example, or your career or your children?
- What's the role of truthfulness in this friendship? Is it important for you to share honest opinions? Is it okay to disagree?
- Is it okay in this friendship to be jealous or resentful of one another's success? Is it okay to express those feelings?
- Is it okay to feel jealous or resentful if this friend has close relationships with other people? Is it okay to express those feelings?
- How important is trust and confidentiality in this friendship? What happens if you or your friend betrays that trust?
- How important is it for you to support the commitments each of you makes outside the friendship? For example, how should you support one another's commitments to marriage, career, or children?
- How much time should you make for each other? What if one or both of you have family obligations that get in the way? What if either of you has job responsibilities that steal time away from the friendship?
- What's the role of intimacy in this friendship? How much sharing is enough? How much is too much?
- How dependent should you be on one another? When asking for a favor, how much would be too much?
- What's the role of adventure in this friendship? Are you both satisfied with where it stands?
- What's the role of entertainment or amusement in this friendship? Are you both satisfied with where it stands?
- How important is reliability in this friendship? Do you see it the same way?
- How important is affection in this friendship? Are both of your needs being met?

- How important is intellectual stimulation in this friendship? Are you both satisfied in this regard?
- If one of you acquires a lot more money or status than the other, how would that affect your relationship?
- How important is it to you to have the same philosophy of family life or parenting? Do you share the same values in this area?
- How important is it for you to have the same ideas around monogamy and commitment to marriage? Do you have this in common?
- How important is it for you to agree about spiritual matters or religion? Do you agree on these topics?
- How important is it for you to agree about politics? Do you agree?
- How important is it for you to pursue the same recreational or leisure-time activities? Are you both satisfied with where this stands?

## Rituals of Connection with Friends

**Exercise buddies.** Name the two activities that fall to the bottom of your to-do list most often. If you're like many people, they're "exercise" and "spending one-on-one time with friends." But if you link the two with a regularly scheduled fitness ritual, you may find you're more likely to do both. When you know that your friend is waiting for you at the corner each morning for your 6:00 A.M. walk, you're much more likely to get out of bed and do what's best for your health—and your friendship. It's also a nice way to show your concern and affection for one another. The ritual says, "We choose to be active together because we care about each other's health and well-being."

But what if your schedules are too unpredictable? Then make a pact to touch base each Monday—or even each morning—just in case the two of you have time to spare for walking, running, or shooting baskets together.

**The standing date.** Anybody who's read the runaway best-seller *Tuesdays with Morrie,* by Mitch Albom, will understand the power of promising to meet a dear friend weekly, no matter what. It's the true story of a sports columnist who travels halfway across the country each week to meet with his old college professor, who is dying from Lou Gehrig's disease. But we don't have to wait for terminal illness to make this kind of commitment to one another. Pick a place (a diner, a park, a tavern, your home) and set a time (once a week, once a month, once a quarter, or once a year). Make that time inviolate. Then show up with your ears and heart open to each other's wisdom and influence.

**Volunteer together.** Like setting aside time to exercise with a friend, volunteering in tandem allows you to do two important things at one time—

nurture your friendship and serve the greater good. I've heard of friends who work at food banks together, sit side by side at the polls on election day, or volunteer to co-lead committees at church. Doing this kind of work together reinforces shared values, which form the foundation of great friendships.

**Support groups, book groups, and more.** Find some friends with whom you share an obsession, a problem, a craft, or a hobby, and form a group that meets regularly to pursue your interest. Read books about it, share what you're learning, invite guest speakers, go on field trips. If your interest involves an activity, like quilting or playing cards, that you can do together at your meetings, have at it. If it's a seasonal activity like skiing, gardening, or salmon fishing, get together in the off-season to make plans for next year.

Most groups do well by sticking to their original mission when they get together, lest they lose members for lack of focus. It also helps to place a strong emphasis on the friendships and emotional support that sustains the group. Let the group evolve and go in new directions, as well. I heard of a bridge club, for example, that started pooling its winnings to finance trips together. Then there was the men's spirituality group that got tired of discussing the work of Robert Bly and the like, and decided to just watch *Monday Night Football* instead. One book group could never agree on what to read, so they just discarded that aspect of their regular gatherings. Now they just come together to talk about their struggles with job and family.

Six to twelve people are a good number for such groups. This makes a group small enough to allow everybody to participate, but if a few folks can't make a certain meeting, the group doesn't lose momentum. When discussion and support is key to your purpose, a casual ritual, like giving everybody ten uninterrupted minutes to talk, can help.

**Commuting time.** Board a ferry in the Pacific Northwest on any weekday morning and you'll find them—the "ferry friends." They're people whose bonds are forged by saving seats for one another on the crowded boats that carry passengers from their island homes to Seattle each morning. I know of one woman who passed up a higher-paying job for one reason: Her new schedule would prevent her from visiting each morning with three women who always shared her booth on the boat. Another woman had a friend who suffered from episodes of depression and was sometimes so despondent that she could hardly speak. "But my friend always arrived early and she always placed her briefcase in the next chair so that I would sit next to her," the woman explained. "Some days it was hard to sit with her in the silence, but I knew she wanted me there, so I would do it. Then a few days would pass, and everything would be just fine." In this way, the seat-saving ritual sustained their relationship when words could not.

Ferryboats aren't the only places where commuters meet and hatch such loyal bonds. Friendships are also formed and strengthened by the forced intimacy of carpools, express buses, and commuter trains. If you travel the same direction on the same schedule day after day, you're bound to meet others with whom you can share the ride. And if you take the chance of turning toward those familiar faces on a regular basis, within time you may find friendships that enrich your life.

**Holiday celebrations.** When we think of traditional holidays like Thanksgiving, Christmas, or Hanukkah, we usually think of spending that time with relatives, celebrating "the way we've always done it." And yet, people's most precious holiday memories often involve times when they were separated from family and were forced to celebrate with whatever rag-tag group of "orphans" they could gather together. ("It was my first year studying abroad, and I thought I'd be alone on Thanksgiving. But then I met this couple . . ." "It was during the war, and I was stationed in Korea . . ." "Remember the first Christmas we were married? We couldn't afford to fly back home to Minneapolis, so we . . .") Two factors make such celebrations special: One is that we're forced to take an active part in actually creating the ritual rather than depending on others to create it for us. The other is one I mentioned earlier: the very voluntary nature of friendship. In other words, the participants in these celebrations come together because they *want* to do so, rather than out of a sense of obligation.

We don't have to wait until life circumstances separate us from our relatives to have this experience, however. We can simply make the choice to be more conscious about the way we celebrate holidays, and with whom. Inviting friends to mix with your family during the holidays can be a great way to liven up tired holiday rituals. It gives us an opportunity to see our customs with fresh eyes and consider why we do things the way we do them. It can also be fun to invite friends from different religions or cultures to share our traditional holidays. Doing so gives us a chance to remember what our traditions mean to us. ("What *is* the significance of eating bitter herbs at the Passover Seder?" "Why *do* we bring these dead trees into the living room every December and decorate them with all these gaudy baubles?")

**Spiritual practice.** Whether we form friendships in traditional churches, mosques, synagogues, and temples, or via pursuits like yoga and transcendental meditation, the emotional connections we make with others around religion and spirituality can be quite strong. It only makes sense. In most cases we're drawn to particular communities of worship because we agree with that group's beliefs and values. In fact, many of us are attracted to the same denominations to which our families belonged—sometimes for generations. Once embraced by a particular group, we're invited to engage in ritualized communal activities like song, prayer, meditation, sacraments, and service to others. By design, such activities help us feel connected to something much larger than our individual selves—namely, a community of spirit. When that connection is authentic, the quality of unconditional acceptance and friendship that we find in such settings may be unsurpassed. That's why I often encourage people with an interest in religion or spirituality to seek friends in such organizations, and to strengthen those bonds through communal worship.

## Building Better Emotional Connections in Adult Sibling Relationships

### Step 1. Look at Your Bids for Connection with Siblings

Ask people about their feelings toward their brothers and sisters, and you rarely get a neutral response. Whether we view our siblings as a source of delight or heartbreak, it is clear that sibling bonds are often the most emotionally charged relationships in our lives.

Why is that? For one thing, people typically spend an enormous amount of time with siblings at a very impressionable age. According to one study, 80 percent of Americans and Europeans have at least one sibling with whom they spent more time during their formative childhood years than they did with their parents.

Consequently, these relationships become interpersonal "learning labs"—a place where children first experiment with behaviors and roles they can use later in life. The assertive older brother, for example, gets to wear the mask of benevolent (or malevolent) boss, while his little brother experiments with being alternately compliant and rebellious. An older sister, acting as baby-sitter for her younger siblings, finds out how it feels to be a loving, nurturing parent or an abusive, raging one. In learning to fight and reconcile, to cooperate and manipulate, to compare and compete, children use their sibling relationships as a key element for determining who they will become. And in so doing, they develop patterns of interaction that may affect their feelings toward one another for the rest of their lives.

Because these patterns of interaction are set at such an early age, it's sometimes hard to stay present in your relationships with siblings. In adulthood, you find yourself relating to brothers and sisters as you remember them—"the gullible little one," for example, or "the stronger, smarter one." If you want to connect emotionally, however, you've got to be able to see and understand one another as you are today. This often takes an extra measure of effort, attentiveness, and curiosity—a willingness to ask, "How are you *now?* What's your current life about? And where are you headed?"

Expanding your view of your sibling in this way will provide you with a much broader and deeper terrain upon which to connect.

At the same time, acknowledging your shared history is also important. It's what makes our relationships with our siblings so unique, and talking about the past is certainly one way to connect emotionally. But if you want your relationships with siblings to grow and evolve, try not to focus exclusively on yesterday's issues.

## Exercise: Look for Opportunities to Turn Toward Your Siblings

Below are lists of activities for building better emotional connections with your brothers and sisters. Scan the lists for ideas about how to converse and interact. Circle those activities that you'd like to try, and make a conscious effort to incorporate them into your life over the next several weeks. Then look back to see whether you notice any shifts in your relationship. Don't expect to see any drastic and immediate changes; instead, look for subtle shifts of energy—slightly more enthusiasm for the conversation, perhaps, or more expressions of interest in one another's current lives.

Remember also that people with truly satisfying sibling relationships often treat one another as they would their friends. So, when you're thinking about ways to turn toward a sibling, take a look at the lists of suggestions for marriage (pages 231–233) and for friendship (pages 265–266). They may provide ideas for staying present with your siblings as well.

### Things to Do for Your Sibling

- Visit one another.
- Ask your sibling about his or her job. Listen.
- Ask your sibling about his or her hobbies or interests. Listen.
- Ask about his or her spouse and kids. Listen.
- Be kind and accepting to his or her spouse—even if it's a second marriage.
- Be kind and accepting to his or her children—including stepchildren.
- Offer advice if your sibling asks for it. But remember, it's best to offer words of understanding before words of advice.
- Refrain from offering advice when you know your sibling's had enough.
- Listen to your sibling's memories of childhood—even when they're hard to hear or different from your own.
- Share your own memories of childhood—even when they're hard to talk about, or different from what your sibling remembers.
- Write a letter of apology for things you're sorry about. Then let it go.

- Accept your sibling's apologies. Then let it go.
- Show a continuing interest in your nephew or niece.
- Host your niece or nephew for a long weekend or spring break.
- Support your sibling's efforts to improve his or her life.
- Remember birthdays and other important events.
- Accept invitations to weddings, graduations, funerals.
- Let your sibling tell his or her own news to other family members.
- Offer help in hard times.
- Accept help in hard times.
- Buy candy from your niece or nephew's Scout troop (or basketball team, jazz band, etc.).

## Things to Do Together

- Share jokes, gossip, and news via e-mail.
- Phone one another often.
- Give one another pictures of your kids.
- Host a party for another relative.
- Pool your family pictures to create a "family archive." Make copies of the good ones so that everybody can have one in their own home.
- Interview elderly relatives about their life stories. Record the interviews on audio- or videotape.
- Research the family tree. (Local librarians can point you to great resources on genealogy.)
- Talk about your perceptions of the past. (Who was favored? Which parent was the more involved one? How was your parents' relationship?)
- Be there for the big events in one another's lives—weddings, graduations, funerals, serious illness.
- Hand down the baby clothes.

## Step 2. Discover How the Brain's Emotional Command Systems Affect Your Sibling Relationships

In chapter 4, you had a chance to assess how you use your brain's emotional command systems, the various circuits that carry your emotional responses to life experiences. Using Your Emotional Command System Score Card, on pages 119–120, you can compare the way you and your siblings use these systems, which may provide insights about ways to connect emotionally.

As you become more conscious in your sibling relationships, know that it's common for the competitive Commander-in-Chief operating system to be hard at work in sibling relationships. While this is true of many peer relationships, with siblings it's likely to be even more intense. For example, you may have some feelings of jealousy or envy left over from the days when you vied for the same space on Mom's lap or for the last cookie in the cookie jar. In addition, as adults you may or may not have the same values and lifestyle. After all, you don't choose your brothers and sisters the way you choose your friends. Unlike friends, your relationship is not centered on living in the same neighborhood, belonging to the same social circle, or working at the same types of jobs. So chances are greater that you'll be on uneven ground, with one of you having more wealth, more accomplishments, or better luck than the other.

Comparison and competition also stems from natural curiosity about the road not taken. We look at our siblings, who came from the same parents, the same homes, and we wonder, "How could life have been different for me if I had taken the path my sibling took?" "What if I had married earlier, as my brother did?" "What if I had inherited Dad's long legs instead of Mom's squat stature?" "What if I had gone to college as my sister did, instead of joining the military?" "What if I had used my inheritance to invest in the stock market instead of buying this house?" Although such comparisons are normal and may give you some insights into your own life, they're usually not very helpful for developing better feelings toward your siblings. That's why I advise people to accept their differences and to acknowledge any feelings that may result—feelings like jealousy, envy, pride, sorrow, or resentment. But try not to dwell on the inequalities you may perceive. Give your attention instead to the task of trying to understand your sibling and his or her experiences, and you can look forward to a much richer relationship.

## Step 3. Examine How Your Emotional Heritage Affects Your Relationship with Siblings

It's easy to understand why issues of emotional heritage loom so large in our sibling relationships. Growing up in the same family, brothers and sisters often presume that they were affected in the same way by parental attitudes toward emotions, that they carry the same emotional philosophy and enduring vulnerabilities as a result. But sibling studies actually show that such factors as birth order, variations in temperament, and simple differences in perception can leave siblings with vastly divergent ideas of what went on in their home, and what it means to be a family. As Susan Scarf Merrell writes in *The Accidental Bond: The Power of Sibling Relationships* (Times Books, 1995), "Siblings can be discomforting reminders that each person grows up in a family that is his and his alone. Thus, one adult sibling's memory of an overwhelming and unsympathetic mother can be difficult to reconcile with another's recollection of a loving caretaker. Each person's truth is valid, a function of the unique individuals doing the perceiving and of the particular life phases and experiences of each. This is one reason that, so frequently, grown brothers and sisters go through uncomfortable phases in their relationships." Discovering that there are unshared—even misunderstood—memories of what happened "may make it easier to part ways, rather than to acknowledge that every family exists at multiple points of reality," Merrell concludes.

Seeing and understanding your differences with siblings can be hard, especially if you always believed that you experienced the same things in childhood. But once you can acknowledge that you may have different perceptions of the past, you're in a better position to connect with one another today. You're less likely to second-guess what your siblings are thinking or how they're feeling about various family matters. You start making an effort to treat them just as you would other peers whom you'd like to know better. You start paying more attention to one another, listening more closely, turning toward each other's bids for connection in a more conscious way. And the great thing is, when you do connect, you have a relationship with one another as you really are today, not as you remember each other from childhood.

Developing a solid personal understanding of your own emotional heritage is a good place to start. That's where the exercises in chapter 5 may be useful. Doing them may help you to identify in a general way how your family's attitudes toward emotion and your own vulnerabilities affect your ability to connect with others. By completing the exercise below, you can explore how these issues affect your relationship with siblings in particular.

## *Exercise: How Does Your Past Influence Your Bonds with Siblings?*

Though it's important to stay current in your relationships with your brothers and sisters, your bond may also benefit by thinking about what you learned about emotions in childhood. If you haven't completed the questionnaires on emotional heritage in chapter 5, do so now. Then, thinking of a particular sibling, answer the following questions in your Emotion Log. If you're particularly close to this sibling, you might want to do this exercise together. If that's not possible, then see if you can find opportunities to discuss these issues with your sibling informally sometime.

**1.** Review your scores on the exercise What's Your Emotional History? on pages 140–145. Look carefully at your scores in each category: pride, love, anger, sadness, and fear. Think about how comfortable you are with expressing each of these emotions to your sibling. Then answer the following questions, thinking about each emotion separately.

- How does your comfort level with this emotion affect your ability to feel close to your sibling?
- When you experience this emotion, are you usually able to explain to your sibling how you're feeling?
- Do you feel that your sibling understands how you're feeling?
- Do you feel guilty or self-conscious expressing this feeling?
- Is your sibling likely to turn toward you, away from you, or against you when you express this emotion?
- How would you like for your sibling to respond when you express this feeling? Can you and your sibling talk about it?

Now think about your comfort level at hearing your sibling express these emotions. Then answer these questions, again thinking about each emotion separately.

- How does your comfort level with hearing your sibling express this feeling affect your ability to connect with him or her?
- Do you feel that you're able to empathize with your sibling when he or she is feeling this way?
- Do you feel embarrassed, frightened, or angry when your sibling expresses this feeling?
- Are you likely to turn toward, turn away from, or turn against your sibling when he or she expresses this feeling?
- How would you like to improve your ability to share such feelings with this sibling?

**2.** Review the results of your responses to the exercise What Was Your Family's Philosophy of Emotion? on pages 146–150, and answer these questions.

- Was your family's philosophy primarily emotion-coaching, emotion-dismissing, emotion-disapproving, or laissez-faire?
- In relating to your sibling, is your philosophy primarily emotion-coaching, emotion-dismissing, emotion-disapproving, or laissez-faire? What effect does your own philosophy of emotion have on this relationship?
- In relating to you, what's your sibling's emotional philosophy? How does this affect your relationship?

**3.** Review the results of your response to the exercise What Are Your Enduring Vulnerabilities? on pages 164–165. Then answer the following questions.

- How do your enduring vulnerabilities affect your ability to connect emotionally with your sibling?

- Do you feel that past injuries interfere with your ability to bid for emotional connection with this sibling? In what way?
- Do you feel that past injuries interfere with your ability to respond to your sibling's bids? How so?
- Do past injuries ever get in the way of your ability to feel included by your sibling?
- Do past injuries interfere with your ability to express affection toward, or accept affection from, your sibling?
- Do you sometimes feel that you're struggling too hard to control your sibling because you feel vulnerable?
- Do you sometimes feel that you're struggling too hard to resist being controlled by this sibling because you feel vulnerable?
- Are there ways that your sibling could help you to heal from past injuries? What healing thing would you like for your sibling to do or say? Can you express this to him or her?

## Step 4. Sharpen Your Skills at Emotional Communication with Your Siblings

Members of the same family often use a complex vocabulary of nonverbal signals to communicate their feelings to one another. In chapter 6, you learned about the many forms of emotional communication, and practiced reading one another's signals with the Emotional Communication Game. Here you'll have another chance to play the game, this time portraying situations common among adult siblings.

### Exercise: The Emotional Communication Game with Siblings

To play the game with your sibling or another adult, silently read each item and its three possible interpretations. Then take turns reading the items aloud, as the other person tries to guess which of the three meanings you're trying to convey. You can also play it on your own, though I encourage you to do it with a family member because it provides an opportunity for noticing one another's gestures, facial expressions, vocal qualities, and so on.

1. Have you called Mom lately?
   a. You're just asking for information.
   b. You're annoyed that your sibling ignores your mom.
   c. You know that your mom has some good news that you're dying to tell your sibling but can't.

**2.** When are you going to come visit us?
   **a.** You're just asking for information.
   **b.** You've done all the visiting over the past few years, and you're annoyed about this.
   **c.** You hope that your sibling will be considerate about the timing of this next visit, and that he or she won't show up without calling first.

**3.** Let's talk about who's paying for the next dinner out.
   **a.** You're tired of paying for the dinners, and you wish your sibling would offer to pick up the tab once in a while.
   **b.** You want to pay for the next dinner, and your sibling wants to pick up the tab.
   **c.** You're just trying to see whose turn it is to pay.

**4.** Which one of us do you think our parents favored when we were growing up?
   **a.** You're angry that your sibling was favored, and you want to talk about old grudges you have.
   **b.** You're just wondering what your sibling thinks about this issue.
   **c.** You're anxious talking about this, but you think it's important to discuss because you think your sibling has some strong feelings about the issue.

**5.** Are you going to buy a new car?
   **a.** You think that a new car is incredibly extravagant, and that your sibling shouldn't make this purchase.
   **b.** You're excited that your sibling is finally doing something nice for herself or himself.
   **c.** You're just asking for information.

## Step 5. Find Shared Meaning with Your Siblings

As people grow up and leave home, sibling relationships typically take a backseat to other bonds like marriage, friendship, and parenthood. But as we approach middle age, two things typically happen that bring our siblings back into the forefront of our lives. First, our parents grow old, requiring siblings to come together around such issues as long-term care, their parents' end-of-life decisions, and healing from the grief of a parent's death. And, second, we start to think more deeply about the stories of our own lives: how our childhood relationships with parents and brothers and sisters affected us; what the bonds of extended family mean to us today. Our adult relationships with our siblings loom large as we grapple with these issues and questions.

That's certainly the way it was for me and my younger sister, Batia. For most of our adult lives we were happy to live quite independently of one another, in different parts of the country. But something shifted in our relationship after my father died in 1987, and this caused a falling out. It's still hard for me to say how the trouble started. I think Batia had the feeling that I wasn't taking leadership in the family and that I wasn't looking out for her feelings. It wasn't that she needed me to do much. But this was a difficult time for all of us, and she just wanted me to show that I really cared about her and would be there for her if she needed me. Unfortunately, I mistakenly took this as an unreasonable request for me to be a parent for her. I later learned that this wasn't her request at all, however. She just wanted me to be more present in her life—to not be so aloof.

Sorting through all of this took time—years, in fact. For me, the slow process of gaining a better understanding started when my older cousin suggested that I write a letter to Batia, apologizing for any pain I might have caused her, and asking her to drop past grievances. She agreed to do that, which was a great gift. After that, we both began learning to identify the old hurts and trying in good faith to heal them. Our most important differences concern our ideas of what it means to be a family and to be able to count on one another. My wife, Julie, has been very helpful to us in this process, in part by helping Batia and me to smooth over issues—sort of translating for each of us so that we can be empathetic to one another. And now that we've been able to hear each other out on this issue, I feel that we've reached a new level of understanding and a much more respectful relationship. It's definitely a work in progress. And keeping the lines of communication open will continue to be important—especially as our family deals with the next chapter, which is providing for our aged mother, who's becoming increasingly dependent on others for care.

On the next few pages you'll find an exercise for exploring meaning within your sibling relationships. You'll also find suggestions for family rituals that may help you and your siblings to connect emotionally.

## Exercise: What Do Your Sibling Relationships Mean to You?

Below is a list of questions to consider regarding your relationship with brothers and sisters. You can answer them on your own, or, if you've got an open, trusting relationship with a sibling, you may want to answer them together, discussing the places where you agree and disagree. Whether you discuss them openly or not, don't be surprised if this exercise makes you more aware of your differences. That's the point. We can't accept our differences until we acknowledge what those differences are. Then, if we decide to strengthen our connections despite our differences, we can express that desire to one another, creating a much deeper, more meaningful relationship.

- What does it mean to you to be a good sibling?
- What qualities should a family of adult siblings have in order to help its members lead happy, fulfilling lives?
- Do you feel that you're a good sibling in this relationship? Do you feel that your brother or sister is a good sibling?
- What does family mean to you? What qualities should a family of adult siblings have in order to help its members lead happy, fulfilling lives?
- How close or distant do you think an extended family should be? Think about the role of extended family in your home when you were growing up. How do you want your family to be the same or different?
- How important is it for brothers and sisters to provide emotional support for one another? What does good emotional support between siblings consist of? Do you feel you get what you need from your sibling?
- How important is it to you to be able to share your true feelings with your sibling?
- How do you and your sibling show that you care about one another's current lives?
- What does your sibling not understand about you that you wish he or she would understand?
- How much time should siblings make for one another? Are you happy with the amount of time you spend with your sibling?
- How important is it for siblings to share responsibility for their aging relatives? How should these responsibilities be shared? What role does each of you want to have?
- How do you each view your parents?
- How important is it to be able to talk openly about the past?
- What were your separate perceptions of your family growing up?
- Is it okay to talk about memories of difficult times, or about how family members were hurt?
- What if you disagree about what happened during your childhood?
- Are there remaining hurts and grievances that need to be discussed?
- What values, philosophies, or points of view have you adopted from your family of origin in building your own families? Which values, philosophies, or points of view from your childhood family have you rejected?
- What if there's a big difference in the amount of money or success you and your sibling have had? How does this disparity affect your relationship?
- How important is affection, gratitude, and appreciation in your relationship? Are these elements that you'd like to change in your relationship? In what way?

- How important is it for siblings to celebrate holidays together? If it's important, which holidays matter most? Are there ways you'd like to change the way you come together (or not) during the holidays?
- How important is it for siblings to acknowledge one another's birthdays? Are you happy with how this works in your relationship?
- How important is it for relatives to be at such ceremonies as weddings, graduations, and funerals? Do you agree with your sibling about this?
- How important is it for siblings to have fun together? Are you satisfied with this aspect of your relationship?
- How important is it to have the same philosophy of raising kids? Do you share the same values in this area?
- Are there ways that you'd like to change your relationship with your sibling? In what way? What would it take to make those changes? What would your relationship look like once those changes took place?

## Rituals of Connection with Siblings

**Family reunions.** In some clans, the term "family reunion" means scores of distant cousins getting together annually for a weeklong jamboree under the family crest. For others it's a more intimate gathering—just one family, perhaps, consisting of a couple and their grown children whose careers have carried them to far-flung corners. Either way, the act of planning, or simply attending, a regular family reunion is a common ritual that often strengthens bonds between adult siblings.

Since the whole point of a family reunion is to connect, it makes sense to plan a variety of activities that help people of various ages and interests to interact in enjoyable and stimulating ways. Experts at planning successful reunions give this advice: Keep activities lighthearted and optional. Nobody wants to play volleyball or charades with unwilling participants. Board games like "Family Stories" and "Cranium" are great for getting people to talk with one another. And be sure to spread the work around. Involve lots of people in the planning, cooking, and cleanup.

Some families plan their reunions on "neutral turf"—a hotel or country resort, for example. That way, no single household feels overburdened by hosting the whole family. It also helps to make everybody feel welcome, regardless of tensions that may exist between particular family members. If cost is a concern, you may want to consider a family camp-out, possibly renting just one cabin for cooking and to house Grandma.

**Sibling getaways.** You may also want to consider hosting getaways or mini-reunions for you and your siblings. I know one group of three sisters who gather for a weekend retreat at a cabin on the Washington coast each winter. There are no husbands or kids allowed—just plenty of time to talk and to walk on the beach. Of course, lots of men have been getting away with this sort of thing for generations—they call it "hunting season" or "a fishing trip." But you don't need to be an outdoorsman to take off with your brother for a few days. You can take a trip to another city to catch a concert or visit an old friend. The point is to spend some time together away from the distractions of your everyday lives.

**Holidays.** Holiday rituals ought to enhance our relationships with relatives rather than to detract from them. So think about the way you've typically celebrated Thanksgiving, Christmas, Hanukkah, and so on. Do holidays leave you feeling better about your siblings or worse? Does one sibling carry more than his or her fair share of the work of making holiday celebrations happen? Do other siblings feel left out? Does holiday spending get out of hand as you try to buy presents for all your brothers and sisters and their growing families? Is overeating or overdrinking weighing down your sense of joy? Do you long to make some changes, but not know where to start?

To start making positive, conscious changes in the way your extended family celebrates holidays, discuss the issue with your siblings and other relatives. It would be best to have this discussion long before the holiday happens. Get together and brainstorm. Talk about the rituals that still hold their meaning for you, and those that feel obligatory, burdensome, or hollow. You may find that others feel just as ready for change as you do, and they're relieved that somebody is taking the lead.

Be careful as you make changes, however, to retain those elements of the holiday that help individual family members to feel connected to one another. This sense of belonging is often enhanced through celebrations that emphasize a family's shared ethnic heritage or religious beliefs. Just think of religious holidays like the Jewish Passover, Christian Easter, or Muslim Ramadan, or ethnically based holidays like the African-American Kwanzaa, the Irish Saint Patrick's Day, or the Swedish Santa Lucia Day. Such holidays can be a terrific opportunity for siblings to gather and focus on unique traditions that connect them with each other and with values that transcend their individual interests—values that are important to family, culture, and community.

**Birthday celebrations and anniversaries.** Hosting parties for your parents takes on added significance as the folks grow older. Living a long life in the company of your children is certainly something to celebrate. Many siblings collaborate on special celebrations around milestones like Mom and Dad's fiftieth wedding anniversary, or Dad's seventy-fifth birthday. Siblings may invite relatives and longtime friends to come and publicly share their favorite memories of the honorees. Handmade, personalized gifts that express the giver's feelings are also common. One family I know presented their parents with a quilt, each of its twenty-eight squares decorated by a child, a child's spouse, or a grandchild.

**Caring for a sick relative.** Perhaps nothing can strain or strengthen connections between siblings the way that caring for a seriously ill relative can. The burden of labor and responsibility is often overwhelming, requiring an extraordinary amount of cooperation and negotiation among siblings, most of whom want desperately to "do the right thing." All of this is especially true when it involves a parent with a long, debilitating illness such as cancer, stroke, or Alzheimer's disease. Such situations require a whole host of difficult decisions regarding long-term care, life support, financial planning, and, if the illness is terminal, funeral planning. Despite having to face such tough issues, however, some families find that they feel more emotionally connected than ever as a result of coming together to care for a sick loved one. Whether or not families can afford professional nursing care, siblings often find themselves collaborating in the intimate rituals of bathing, feeding, and comforting a dying parent, and it changes their relationships with one another in unimagined ways. "I will never forget the tenderness with which my brother cared for Mom during her last days at home," a friend once told me, "how he read to her, held her hand, fed her ice chips with a spoon. I had never seen that side of him before."

A photo taken at the reception after her mother's funeral tells the story. In it, the woman, her two sisters, and this brother stand with their arms around one another's shoulders. Looking exhausted, bereft, and yet peaceful, they manage to muster weak smiles for the camera.

"We were terribly sad that day," the woman remembers. "But we also felt proud of the way that we had pulled together and made it possible for her to die quietly at home. We'll never be the same."

**Funerals.** Although it's hard to think about, our loved ones' funeral rituals are among the most powerfully emotional events of our lives. And when it's the funeral of a parent, our siblings are usually the ones with whom we most closely share that experience.

Often, a tremendous amount of decision-making must be done when a family member dies. Arrangements need to be made that involve emotionally charged issues like cremation, caskets, burial plots, eulogies, religious ceremonies, and more. Experts in funeral planning advise discussing these issues well before anyone dies or becomes terminally ill. That way, family members won't have to grapple with such difficult decisions while coping with intense feelings of loss and grief.

With funeral arrangements made beforehand, family members can turn their attention to the ritual itself, so that everyone can benefit from the help that such rites are designed to provide. Ideally, funerals help grieving people to share a sense of support and connection during a time of tremendous emotional upheaval. They give us a chance to collectively honor the person who has died. They're also an opportunity for families to focus on the values and traditions that bind us together. When a eulogist at a funeral says, "Mary was devoted to her children, her nursing career, and her church community," it's a way for her relatives to acknowledge their common beliefs about what makes life meaningful.

In addition, funerals can help families to strengthen old ties or to reestablish broken ones. Friends and relatives often travel a long way—both in terms of miles and pride—to be present at the burial of a loved one. In fact, it's not unusual for an estranged family member to come back to the family when a parent or sibling dies. And the reception that long-lost relative receives may set the course of his or her relationship with the family from that moment forward.

Families often benefit from creating a memorial ritual that allows anyone who wants to participate to do so. For example, friends and family members might be invited to share a memory or impression of the person whose life is being honored. This communal act contributes to a family's sense of connection as they're saying good-bye to a loved one.

Funerals are not easy. But this much I know: If you set your intention on connecting emotionally with other survivors, the support you give and receive will go a long way toward healing relationships and healing from grief.

## Building Better Emotional Connections in Coworker Relationships

### Step 1. Look at Your Bids for Connection with Coworkers

When I was a young man attending MIT, one of my favorite diversions was to spend time with my older cousin Kurt. He was a garment salesman from New York, and twice a year he would come to the Boston Statler Hotel to show his company's line of children's clothes. One day when I was visiting him, a woman came in whom Kurt greeted warmly. After chatting informally for a very long time, the woman finally said to him, "What have you got for me this season, Kurt?" And my cousin answered matter-of-factly, "Nothing, Dorie. Not a thing."

"All right, then," she replied, squeezing his arm. "I guess I'll see you in the fall." Then she got up, kissed him graciously on the cheek, and left.

"What are you doing?" I asked him, astounded. "You're supposed to be a salesman! You just told her to go away without buying anything!"

Kurt looked at me for a moment with a kind smile. Then he said, "Let me explain something to you. I have known this woman for a long time. I know her store. I know her clientele. And the line I've got this year just won't go over there. But next season I may have a better fit. If I do, I'll tell her so, and she will trust me. That's what business is all about—relationships. Building long-lasting, trusting relationships."

It was such a revelation to me. I had always assumed that if Kurt was a salesman, his job must involve lots of high pressure, fast talk, and snowing people. But here he was behaving in much the same way he would with my mother, my sister, or me. His success in business came from getting to know people, listening carefully to their needs, and responding to them accordingly.

That was almost forty years ago. So you can imagine how amused and delighted I am to hear business gurus of the last decade talk about the importance of "relationship marketing"—that is, designing business strategies that emphasize keeping customers as much as attracting them. Relationship marketing says you may have to invest a lot of time and resources into identifying and responding to customers. But over the long haul, that investment will pay off in terms of loyalty and commitment.

I'm also gratified to hear employees at large companies and institutions refer to the people within their own organizations as "our customers." The payroll clerks, for example, call the employees they serve their customers. The purchasing agents have customers, too—the workers down the hall who send them purchase orders. This tells me that everybody is practicing "relationship marketing" with everybody else. It says that organizations are beginning to see that what matters most are the workers' relationships—their ability to recognize and respond to the needs of people with whom they do business.

Paying attention and turning toward one another's needs clearly has a positive impact on workers' lives and the organizations that employ them. Studies show that an employee's perception that he or she works in an emotionally supportive environment increases job satisfaction, lowers stress, decreases the likelihood of quitting, and improves team performance. Yale University researchers who conducted a study of service workers found that workers' ability to talk with one another about their stress helped them to cope, and even protected them against health risks. Another one of their studies showed that work groups' performance suffered when members didn't communicate well or didn't pay attention to one another's feelings, or when individuals became so controlling that they didn't allow others to contribute. In contrast, when people in these work groups got along with one another, the positive results were synergistic—that is, peers in the group motivated each other to do better, and the sum of their combined efforts ended up being greater than if each person had been working alone.

A responsive attitude is also an advantage in relationships between supervisors and workers, especially in a tight labor market when employers are struggling to retain valued staff people. A recent Gallup poll of two million workers at seven hundred companies revealed that most workers rate having a caring boss even higher than they value money or fringe benefits. A similar study conducted by Lou Harris found that workers who didn't like their bosses were four times more likely to leave their jobs than were people who thought their bosses were nice.

## Exercise: Look for Opportunities to Turn Toward Your Coworkers

Bidding and responding to bids for emotional connection is probably not an explicit requirement of your job description. And yet, if you work with other people, you undoubtedly need these skills to form effective relationships with your coworkers. Much of the work of emotional connection happens in informal ways, in the way we talk with one another as we congregate around the coffeepot or share information *before* the meeting starts. While it would be impossible to catalog all the ways people in various jobs have for turning toward one another, the list of activities below may give you ideas about opportunities for emotional connection on your job.

Scan the list and circle those new activities that you'd like to try. After a few weeks, look back and see if those efforts have made a difference in your work environment and in the way you're feeling about your coworkers.

### Things to Do for Your Coworkers

- When you go for a snack or a cup of coffee, offer to bring something back for someone else.
- Say hello and good-bye each day.
- Share information that's vital to both your jobs.
- Be open to laughing at your coworkers' jokes.
- Turn away from your computer (or other equipment) and look at the person who's talking to you.
- Say thanks when somebody does something for you.
- Return favors.
- Return things you borrow.
- Minimize distractions when your coworker needs to concentrate.
- Turn down your music if he or she asks.
- Refrain from wearing perfume or cologne if he or she is allergic to it.
- Look for things to appreciate in others, creating a climate of appreciation on the job.

- Remember his or her birthday with e-mail or a card.
- Send a note of praise to your coworker's boss acknowledging a job well done.
- Offer similar praise at staff meetings for hardworking peers.
- Notice photos, signs, posters, and other personal expressions in your coworker's environment. Ask about them. Listen.
- Decorate your own environment with things that interest you, if possible. Let these things be a way of helping others get to know you.
- Take photos at work just for fun, and post them, if possible. Make copies for people who appear in the photos.
- Ask your coworker about his or her weekend, holiday, or vacation. Listen.
- Be sympathetic when folks are sick. If they come to work feeling lousy, tell them to go home and rest.
- Ask your coworker why he or she chose this job. Listen.
- Ask your coworker about his or her goals and aspirations. Listen.
- Remember personal things about your coworker, and refer to these in future conversations.
- If you have resolved a conflict, recall the resolution in the future.
- Pay attention to your coworker's special interests and needs. Honor them.

## Things to Do Together

- Go to lunch.
- Take a coffee break.
- Host a potluck lunch.
- Take walks.
- Join a gym.
- Go out for drinks or coffee after work.
- Swap recipes.
- Swap information about other shared interests (music, politics, sports, etc.).
- Take a class or workshop relevant to your job.
- Take a class or workshop on stress management or healthy lifestyles.
- Take a class or workshop that's just for fun.
- Volunteer for a community project.
- Join a professional association and go to meetings and conferences together.
- Start a group at work related to a common hobby such as hiking, theater, or bowling.
- Plan your work group's holiday party.
- Plan a celebration for another coworker who's retiring, having a baby, getting married, or has won an award.

- Swap resources for child care or elder care.
- Go get a flu shot.
- Go shopping at lunch.
- Organize a blood drive.
- Commute.

## Step 2. Discover How the Brain's Emotional Command Systems Affect Your Coworker Relationships

To understand how the brain's emotional command systems affect your relationships at work, take a look back at chapter 4 and consider all the characters involved in the wilderness adventure trip described there. Do any of them remind you of your coworkers or yourself at work? Do the conflicts that arise because of their differences sound familiar?

The emotional command systems questionnaires you completed can also help you to see which systems you're most likely to have highly activated in the work you do. This awareness could help you to develop insights into why you sometimes have conflicts with certain people on the job. (Your Energy Czar, for example, can't stand the way his Jester wastes precious time socializing on the job. Or your Jester just wishes the boss's Commander-in-Chief would slow the pace of production during summer vacation time.)

If you want to gain deeper insights into the way your emotional command systems are activated at work, complete the questionnaires in chapter 4 once more, this time keeping work-related situations in mind specifically as you answer them. Then you can see how your results differ from the first time you completed the questionnaires. This may tell you which of your systems are more exclusively activated in the workplace. You may also want to complete the questionnaires with coworkers and then use the Emotional Command System Score Card on pages 119–120 to compare results.

It may also be helpful to consider how group dynamics in many organizations often resemble family dynamics. Here's an example: Organizations typically have finite resources to distribute among workers in the form of pay, benefits, and amenities such as window offices or parking spaces, so managers have to decide how those resources are distributed. As a result, staff relationships begin to feel like family relationships, with the boss in the role of parent, and peers acting like rival siblings. With their Commander-in-Chief emotional operating systems fully activated, coworkers compete for money, power, and influence. The Nest-Builder system also comes alive as workers try to strengthen bonds with the boss and win management's favor. When managers develop and communicate fair ways of compensating their workers, all this rivalry can work in an organization's favor and benefit employees who are willing to play. But if workers perceive that the systems are unfair or nonexistent, they may experience lots of conflict and dissension. They may also feel demoralized, and angry with their managers and coworkers.

All of this is human nature, as old as the story of Cain and Abel. In fact, because our behaviors are partly based on biologically wired, emotional command systems, such habits are probably even older! What does this mean for forming trusting relationships on the job? Are all workplace friendships doomed to be sullied by office politics and cutthroat competition? Of course not. In fact, people often find some of their closest, lifelong friends on the job. This only makes sense—particularly if you work in a profession you like. On the job, you're likely to find people with similar interests, lifestyles, and values. Friends at work can give you advice, help you to improve your performance, open doors to better jobs, or simply help you to get things done. Friends can be a great source of information about opportunities or threats in the work environment. And if you establish a high level of trust, they can also be a great source of social support, helping you deal with stress on the job.

The key is establishing that trust—which is what naturally occurs when two people develop a solid habit of bidding for connection and turning toward one another's bids in positive ways. But this process can take some time, especially in an environment where ambition can cloud people's intentions. In her book *Toxic Friends/True Friends* (William Morrow, 1999), Florence Isaacs suggests that it's best to go slowly as you make friends at work. To save your job and your reputation, don't reveal too many vulnerabilities until you're sure the other person will protect your interests, she advises. And if you're feeling uncomfortable about what you can and can't confide in one another, say so. Don't be afraid to talk about the boundaries of your friendship and why you may feel a need for more or less distance at times. It also helps to have a good network of friends outside the job. That way, you won't feel the need to rely exclusively on your work buddies for emotional support—which can get difficult, especially if you're having problems on the job.

### Step 3. Examine How Your Emotional Heritage Affects Relationships with Coworkers

Like all relationships, your bonds with coworkers may be affected by your emotional heritage—i.e., your family's attitudes toward emotional expression, their emotional philosophy, and the enduring vulnerabilities you may retain from past injuries.

As we discussed in the preceding section, workplace relationships often resemble family dynamics. So it's not surprising that emotional situations in the workplace can cause you to react the way you might have in the past. A woman who was taught in childhood always to sublimate her anger, for example, might have a hard time standing up to injustices in the workplace.

People's work relationships may also be affected by traumatic incidents that occur inside or outside the family. You may remember, for example, the story in chapter 5 of the executive who had suffered traumatic wartime experiences as a young man. He then carried the "enduring vulnerability" of often feeling tense and fearful, particularly if he thought his coworkers might "ambush" him with surprising information that could damage his career.

These are just a few examples of why it's good to be aware of your emotional heritage and how it can affect your current work life. Completing the following exercise may help you see how these issues relate to your own coworker relationships.

## Exercise: How Does Your Past Influence Your Connections with Coworkers?

**1.** Review your scores on the exercise What's Your Emotional History? on pages 140–145. Look carefully at your scores in each category: pride, love, anger, sadness, and fear. Think about how comfortable you feel when you experience those emotions at work. Then answer these questions, thinking about each emotion separately.

- How does your comfort level with this emotion affect your ability to get along with coworkers?
- When you experience this emotion at work, are you usually able to express it in a productive way?
- Do you feel that your coworkers understand how you're feeling?
- Do you feel guilty or self-conscious expressing this feeling?
- Are your coworkers likely to turn toward you, away from you, or against you when you express this emotion?

Now think about how comfortable you feel when you recognize these emotions in your coworkers. Then answer these questions, again thinking about each emotion separately.

- How does your comfort level with your coworker's emotions affect your ability to connect with him or her?
- Do you feel that you're able to empathize with your coworker when he or she is feeling this way?
- Do you feel embarrassed, frightened, or angry when your coworker expresses this feeling?
- Are you likely to turn toward, turn away from, or turn against your coworker when he or she expresses this feeling?

- How could you and your coworkers do better at responding to one another's feelings in the workplace? Is this something you can discuss as a group or with an individual coworker or supervisor?

**2.** Review the results of your responses to the exercise What Was Your Family's Philosophy of Emotion? on pages 146–150, and answer these questions.

- Was your family's philosophy primarily emotion-coaching, emotion-dismissing, emotion-disapproving, or laissez-faire?
- How does that affect your own philosophy of emotion?
- In relating to your coworkers, what's your emotional philosophy? How does this affect your job?
- If you could characterize the emotional philosophy of your work team as a whole, would you say that it's primarily emotion-coaching, emotion-dismissing, emotion-disapproving, or laissez-faire? How does this philosophy affect your team's performance?

**3.** Review the results of your response to the exercise What Are Your Enduring Vulnerabilities? on pages 164–165. Then answer the following series of questions for yourself.

- How do your enduring vulnerabilities affect your ability to connect emotionally with your coworkers?
- Do you feel that past injuries interfere with your ability to bid for emotional connection with coworkers? In what way?
- Do you feel that past injuries interfere with your ability to respond to your coworkers' bids? How so?
- Do past injuries ever get in the way of your ability to feel included at work?
- Do past injuries interfere with your ability to express or accept appreciation at work?
- Do you sometimes feel that you're struggling too hard to control your coworkers because you feel vulnerable?
- Do you sometimes feel that you're struggling too hard to resist being controlled by coworkers because you feel vulnerable?

## Step 4. Sharpen Your Skills at Emotional Communication with Coworkers

Your ability to read and respond to your coworkers' emotional cues can be a great advantage on the job. In chapter 6, you read about many different forms of communication, from facial expressions to gestures to tone of voice. We introduced the Emotional Communication Game, which gives you a chance to practice your skills in reading and expressing emotions nonverbally. Here's another short version of the game, this one focused primarily on coworker relationships.

You can practice these expressions by yourself, or you can do them with a friend or coworkers. Work groups might find it useful to do the game together to learn one another's emotional communication styles.

## *Exercise: The Emotional Communication Game with Coworkers*

To play the game, silently read each item and its three possible interpretations. Then take turns reading the items aloud, as the other person tries to guess which of the three meanings you're trying to convey.

**1.** Did you get it done?
   **a.** You're pleasantly surprised that the task seems to be finally completed.
   **b.** You're worried that your colleague didn't do what he or she promised to do.
   **c.** You're just asking for information.

**2.** Are you going to the staff retreat?
   **a.** You're not sure you're going to go, and you're trying to decide.
   **b.** You think your colleague should go and not be so isolated from other people at work.
   **c.** You're simply asking for information.

**3.** I completed seven units yesterday by myself.
   **a.** You're proud of the amount of work you accomplished on your own, and you'd like to be acknowledged.
   **b.** You're angry that you didn't get more help from your coworker.
   **c.** You're not feeling one way or another about the workload; you're just giving a tally of what you accomplished.

**4.** Who's going to take responsibility for this project?
   **a.** You're tired of taking the lead on projects you do together, and you want your colleague to do it for a change.
   **b.** You're just asking for information about whose turn it is.
   **c.** Your colleague just naturally takes over. But this time you'd like to have a chance to show what you can do when you're in charge.

**5.** What should we do about including Jane on this project?
   **a.** The two of you want to do the project alone together without having to think about the composition of the work team.
   **b.** Jane is not very competent and is dragging down your team's performance.
   **c.** Jane would be a real asset, and you'd very much like to have her on the team.

## Step 5. Find Shared Meaning in Your Work

As you read in chapter 7, emotional connection requires finding common ground with other people, discovering shared values, and realizing that you derive meaning from the same types of activities. Additionally, it's about honoring one another's dreams and visions. I believe these things are as true in coworker relationships as they are in our marriages, our friendships, and our bonds with our kids and relatives.

In his book *Principle-Centered Leadership* (Summit, 1991), author Stephen R. Covey expresses how important it is for people to believe that their jobs are worthwhile. "People are not just resources or assets, not just economic, social, and psychological beings," Covey writes. "They are also spiritual beings; they want meaning, a sense of doing something that matters. People do not want to work for a cause with little meaning, even though it taps their mental capacities to their fullest. There must be purposes that lift them, ennoble them, and bring them to their highest selves."

What happens when coworkers discover that they derive a shared sense of meaning from their jobs? They connect emotionally, which leads to stronger and more productive relationships. They're more willing and able to work through conflicts that arise, solve problems together, and get things done.

Below is an exercise for exploring the meaning you derive from your work. That's followed by suggested workplace rituals that may help you to strengthen your emotional connections with coworkers.

## *Exercise: What Does Your Job Mean to You?*

Here's a list of questions to consider in your relationships with coworkers. Answering them may help you to clarify issues related to trust, competition, closeness, and so on. As this type of exercise does with other relationships, it may also help to identify what you have in common with your coworkers in terms of your goals, values, and what you find meaningful in life. Discovering common ground in these areas may help you to establish stronger emotional connections, resulting in a better working relationship.

You can answer these questions on your own to gain insight into your perceptions of your relationships on the job, or, if you have one or more coworkers with whom you share a great deal of trust, you can study the questions together and share your answers with one another.

- What does your job mean to you? What does it mean to you to provide your service or product?
- What does it mean to you to be a good coworker?
- What qualities go into creating a good working environment? Does your current job feel that way to you? If not, could things change to make it feel that way?
- What does it mean to you to be part of a team? What are the costs and benefits of knowing that others rely on you to do your job well?
- Are there things you'd like to change about the way you and your coworkers relate to one another? What changes would you like to make?
- What role do ethics play in your job? What does it mean to do your job in an ethical way? What does it mean to treat your coworkers ethically?
- What's the most important thing you'd like to accomplish in your current job? How are your current relationships with your coworkers helping or hindering you?
- What are your future career goals? How do your current job relationships affect your ability to achieve those goals?
- How important is it to be compensated fairly for the job you do?
- How important is it that workers be paid the same wage for the same job?
- How important to you is recognition? How do you like to be recognized and appreciated for a job well done? How would you like for your boss to show that appreciation? How would you like for your coworkers to show that appreciation?
- How is your job performance evaluated? How is that evaluation communicated to you? What do you like or not like about this process?
- How do you feel about being friends with your coworkers? Should friendships at work be different from other friendships? In what way?
- Should people set different boundaries for the friendships they form at work? If so, what should those boundaries be? Under what circumstances might those boundaries be crossed or changed?
- What is the role of intimacy in work-related friendships? How much sharing is enough? How much is too much?
- What about confidentiality among coworkers? Should coworkers have stricter rules about telling and keeping secrets than other kinds of friends have?
- Should coworkers be able to count on one another for emotional sup-

port in times of stress? If you're having a bad day, should you keep your feelings to yourself or tell others and ask for their support?

- How important is it to find a balance amid the demands of work, friends, and family? Should the job be made family-friendly to help achieve that balance?
- What is the role of fun in work-related relationships? Is it okay to be playful or silly on the job?
- How do you feel about expressing negative emotions on the job? Is it okay to tell your coworkers when you're angry, sad, or scared?
- How important is it for you to share your true feelings with your coworkers?
- How do you feel about flirting among coworkers?
- How do you feel about coworkers having romantic or sexual relationships?
- Imagine leaving your current job to retire or to take another position. What would you like for your boss and coworkers to say about you at your going-away party? Are there changes you'd have to make in order for that to happen?

## Rituals of Connection with Coworkers

Workplace rituals can be a powerful way for coworkers to demonstrate their emotional connection. One of the most colorful examples I've heard involves Russian cosmonauts, who like to honor the pioneering spirit of Yuri Gagarin, the first human in space. On the way to the launchpad for his historic 1961 flight, Gagarin got out of the van he was riding in, and peed on its rear tire via a valve in his spacesuit. To this day, Russian space crews always ask the driver to stop so they can repeat the ritual. It's a silly custom, to be sure. But like all good rituals, it sends a significant message: We're linked to something bigger than ourselves, and we're all in this mission together.

Below are descriptions of a few more common (and less messy) workplace rituals. Whether or not they might occur in your job, they may give you some ideas for instituting rituals that can help you improve emotional connections with coworkers.

**Introductions.** How new people are introduced and welcomed into a work group can have a significant impact on their ability to assimilate and perform, especially during the first few weeks on a job. In some positions, the boss arranges to have new employees greeted at the door and escorted through a helpful agenda of orientation activities. The newcomer receives formal introductions, so that all the players can get to know one another and each person's roles efficiently. In other jobs, Day One finds workers on their own, lucky to locate a desk or a working telephone. Obviously, there's lots of latitude between these two extremes, but the more your work group can do to create rituals that make a new member feel welcome, the better.

**Arrivals and departures.**　Hellos and good-byes are simple rituals that can go a long way toward building rapport among coworkers. First, they serve the very practical purpose of letting everybody know who's present and available for business. Second, they can be a time for the type of "small talk" that typically leads to richer emotional connection. So don't be afraid to take a few extra minutes around the coffeepot in the morning or the coatrack at the end of the day. Whether you're just talking baseball, griping about the commute, or swapping photos of your kids, you're doing the important work of building relationships.

**Team meetings.**　Whether you love meetings or hate them, most work groups find it necessary to come together on a regular basis to make decisions, plan projects, and get things done. Organizations often train their managers in how to run efficient meetings, and that's important. But such training rarely addresses the emotional undercurrents that people bring to the table. I believe meetings can become even more productive if the people in attendance can be fully present and emotionally connected as they interact. One way to accomplish this is to take some time at the beginning of the session for each person to "check in" emotionally; that is, to say briefly how they're *feeling* about the way their job or part in a project is going. This may sound risky, especially for teams that are working on tight schedules with limited resources. But it's also a way to bring to the surface problems that can derail projects or cause burnout. As you do the check-in, keep in mind that your ultimate goal is to be able to focus on the shared tasks at hand. So, if workers bring up problems that are too difficult or complex to handle in that particular meeting, schedule another time soon for the group, or for key members of the group, to tackle the issue raised. The important thing is that people feel free to speak their minds *and* their hearts to the group. Then they'll be in a better state of mind to focus on the agenda before them.

**Bulletin boards, staff newsletters, and intranet newsgroups.** Communication tools like these can be a bit of trouble to maintain, but they can also serve an important function in helping coworkers to connect around common interests, including those that are more personal than work-related. They can also be used in fairly simple ways to draw people together emotionally. One office staff, for example, used their bulletin board to post their own baby pictures one month, their high school prom pictures the next, and their most exciting travel snapshots the month after that. The activity was lots of fun, and it gave the workers a chance to see one another from new and different points of view. Imagine seeing your political nemesis as a frightened two-year-old on a pony, or the office tyrant as an awkward teenager in braces and a powder-blue tuxedo. It sent the message that we were all innocent once, we were all vulnerable, and we still carry those parts of ourselves around every day. The vacation shots helped, too, because they gave people a chance to share some of the most thrilling, romantic, and treasured memories of their lives. We certainly don't have to unravel our whole life stories to our coworkers, but it may help to reveal glimpses of our past from time to time.

**Birthday celebrations.** The wonderful thing about celebrating birthdays in the workplace is that everybody has one. Birthday celebrations give work teams an opportunity to show that they care about one another—unconditionally. It doesn't matter whether you're the "employee of the year" or the first person on next month's layoff list; when it's your day, you get to be serenaded by your peers, blow out the candles, and cut the cake.

Here are a few suggestions to keep this common ritual upbeat. Make the celebration short and sweet, while still leaving time for those gathered to offer best wishes informally to the person being honored. Don't dwell on the honoree's age; some folks are quite sensitive about this issue. If you have a choice between planning celebrations for large departments or for smaller work units, go for the smaller, more intimate gathering; it makes the ritual more meaningful. Also, you won't be forced to have so many celebrations each month that participation becomes a rote chore.

**Candy jars, open doors, and other invitations to "face time."** As we become more reliant on e-mail to communicate in the workplace, we're spending less time in the company of one another, getting increasingly fewer doses of what some have come to call "face time." The danger, of course, is that we lose out on all the rich emotional cues that interpersonal contact entails—signals I described in detail in chapter 5. While e-mail is certainly efficient, some people are making a ritualized effort to keep a healthy measure of old-fashioned communication in their work lives. They keep their office doors open. Before sending an e-mail message to somebody across the hall, they stop and think, "Could this be handled in a quick conversation instead?"

One manager at the university keeps a jar of chocolates on her desk as a signal of accessibility. Because her job entails lots of counseling and mentoring, she welcomes people dropping by informally to talk. "They pop into my office and say, 'I'm just here for the candy,' but then they stick around to chat," she says. "So the candy is how I say, 'Come in, sit down, let's talk.'"

**Performance evaluations.** Done poorly, the annual "performance review" can be a source of dread for workers and managers alike. Too often, the boss comes off as a judgmental and punitive parent—the person who holds all the power, arbitrarily deciding who gets raises this year and who doesn't. Unless the evaluation process is designed to truly foster communication about an employee's goals and achievements, workers often walk away from the event wondering if it was just a popularity contest. But some organizations are finding better rituals for evaluating their employees' work—ways that actually enhance the workers' sense of connection to the organization, and may lead to better job performance. One common method is to draft a "performance agreement" at the time an employee is hired. Ideally this agreement, which outlines the employees' annual goals and objectives, draws directly from the organization's goals and objectives. Then, when it comes time for a manager to evaluate an employee's work, the two can sit down together and determine whether the employee did what he or she agreed to do, and see how the work contributed to the organization.

**Holiday celebrations.** In many workplaces, when mid-December comes around, you can nearly forget about getting any work done until after New Year's Day. A problem? For some, yes. But workplace holiday celebrations can also benefit work teams if they allow people to let go of their routines and have a little bit of fun. In the course of decorating offices, exchanging "white elephant" gifts, and hosting potluck lunches, workers may get to know one another better. Holidays can be an opportunity to just relax and connect.

Don't be surprised at how invested people get in such holiday rituals—especially when celebrations become a vehicle for work groups to express feelings of solidarity and affection. A manager I know at one large government institution remembers parties that the organization's physical-plant workers used to hold each December. Staff from each of several facilities would decorate their shops to the hilt. Then a boss would visit each place, awarding prizes for the best holiday spirit, the most bizarre decorations, and so on. Afterward, groups from all the shops would gather for a huge potluck feast of roast turkey, ribs, ham, and side dishes. That was followed by a talent show. It was quite an event.

"Then we reorganized," the manager said sadly, "and the guy who owned the sound system for the talent show was placed in a different work unit. So there was no talent show at the party that year, and it put a pall on the whole event. There was too much silence, too many chairs." And when word got around during the party that the sound-system owner was right upstairs at a little private event his new work group was hosting—well, that put people right over the edge. "It was probably the hardest moment of all for the staff," she says. "There was a lot of grieving over that."

The reorganized groups have talked about creating some new holiday rituals, the manager tells me. "But it hasn't happened yet. And I don't think we're going to have a real sense of connection among these new teams until they do it."

**Recognition for special accomplishments.** Many organizations sponsor rituals like "employee of the month" awards as a way to acknowledge extraordinary contributions. If the goal of such rituals is to foster emotional connection among coworkers, then it's usually best to allow peer groups to select their own winners. This helps to establish a climate of appreciation. It creates an environment in which coworkers are on the lookout for reasons to nominate one another for excellent performance.

Awards and recognition should be given in a public way, if possible. People who work hard deserve to be acknowledged before their peers, customers, and others. One small Web design firm in Seattle, for example, invites employees to submit descriptions of their coworkers' good qualities on the anniversaries of their date of hire. Those comments are then compiled and distributed by e-mail company-wide. Some staff members find the ritual so satisfying that they proudly send the messages along to their parents and friends.

Presentations can also be made at meetings, in the organization's newsletters, on posters, and so on. Riding the city bus in Seattle, it's fun to read the signs inside about the system's "mechanic of the year." It gives you a good feeling somehow to know that this man—who has devoted a good part of his time on earth to this very public service of repairing buses—is getting his due. You want to help pat him on the back.

Of course, some of the most interesting rituals spring from the idiosyncratic culture of various workgroups. Software development teams on the main Microsoft campus in Redmond, Washington, for example, have established this practice: Faced with grueling production schedules, team managers promise to shave their heads if their teams make a difficult deadline. I've even heard of at least one female manager who upheld the promise. It's a crafty solution because it actually allows the team manager to get all the attention. The team meets their goal, but the manager is the one who gets to carry the flag—i.e., appearing in the posh company cafeteria with head freshly shaven as if to say, "I did it! I brought the team along to this difficult benchmark!"

In creating rituals of recognition, don't forget that sometimes the best celebrations are spontaneous ones. Let's say your work group labors overtime three weeks in a row to meet a crucial deadline, and, by gosh, you make it! "Let's go grab a beer," somebody suggests, and you all head for the local watering hole. Once assembled, this would be a great time for somebody—ideally the group leader—to make a toast. But what if there's no leader present? Or what if it looks as if the leader isn't going to do it? I say anybody can make a move. The important thing is not to let the moment slip away unacknowledged. Also, don't be shy about making a good, long, heartfelt speech. Talk about individuals who shone, and the things that they accomplished. Do your best not to leave out anybody who contributed in a significant way. At the same time, don't feel obligated to mention those who didn't pitch in. If you do, you make the whole ritual meaningless. But do lay it on thick for those who have worked hard. Remember, your coworkers give their life energy to their work, and they deserve to be praised for a job well done. They want to be recognized. They want to be celebrated. Let them have it!

# 9

# In Conclusion

*J*ust as we were finishing this book, the city of Seattle was rocked by a magnitude 6.8 earthquake, the strongest the area had experienced in half a century. I was at the University of Washington at the time, sitting in a meeting with three longtime colleagues. As soon as we realized what was happening, we all got up and headed for a narrow doorway in the old two-story, wood-frame building that houses our offices. There we huddled, arms around one another, listening to the building rattle and moan, feeling the floor roll beneath our feet. Terribly frightened, we clung together and wondered what might happen next.

Fortunately, the building did not crumble and nobody got hurt. In fact, the quake caused few serious injuries anywhere. But it was a moment of crisis that few in our community will ever forget.

Later that day, as I remembered how my colleagues and I had reacted, I felt so grateful. I thought about the way we had trusted one another, standing so close in that doorway; how we were able to comfort one another in a terrifying situation. This experience is a metaphor for the way that good relationships work, I thought. We've had ten years of interacting, ten years of offering each other bids for emotional connection, and ten years of turning toward those bids. So now, when there's a crisis and there's no time to think—only to react—we automatically turn toward one another in the kindest way and hang on to one another for support.

That's the way it can be in solid relationships with your spouse, your friends, your children, your relatives, and your coworkers. As my research has shown, strong bonds are not necessarily forged out of earth-shattering events like job loss, irreconcilable conflict, or horrid disaster. Trust doesn't require gut-wrenching conversations that plumb the depths of our souls. Rather, good relationships usually develop slowly over time, growing out of the thousands of mundane interactions we share each day.

"How was your day?"

"A little hectic. You look kind of tired, too."

"I am. Would you like some iced tea?"

"Sure. Here, let me help you . . ."

But when a crisis comes, all that thoughtfulness pays off richly. If you make a habit of turning toward one another's bids for connection, you'll have better access to the healing power of humor, affection, and compassion during times of conflict or catastrophe. By practicing the kind of mindful listening that allows you to understand each other's experiences, you become more sensitive to each other's needs.

Such mindfulness seemed easier in the days after the earthquake. If you've ever experienced a near disaster, you know how it heightens awareness of your own mortality. You're struck by how drastically your life can change in a split second. And you suddenly see just how precious your loved ones are to you.

It helped that friends and relatives from around the country called to check in on me and my family. "We're just fine," I said, delighted to hear from people with whom I hadn't connected in ages. I relished a call from one old friend in particular. He phoned to see if I was okay, but I could hear from his voice that *he* was the one who needed support. Although I had papers to write and a computer glitch to unravel, I stopped working and took the phone to a comfortable chair. It had been a rough year, he said. His new job was not working out the way he'd hoped. We talked for more than an hour. It was a well-balanced conversation, filled with lots of give-and-take and mindful listening. It was the kind of conversation that helps to sustain a friendship over many decades and many miles.

But my research tells me you don't have to wait for an earthquake—or a car accident, a heart attack, or any other near disaster—to start appreciating and improving your relationships. You can begin today in the smallest of ways by extending simple, positive bids for connection and turning toward others' bids in a positive way. I hope this book has given you the fundamental tools and motivation to do that. I believe that if you follow the steps I've described, you will begin to see new and surprising opportunities for emotional connection all around you, and your life will start to change in positive ways.

That's how it's been for a couple I'm now seeing in therapy. The pair likened the gulf between them to the Grand Canyon, until they made a commitment to start listening—*really* listening—to each other's desires. During our last visit, they described a recent weekend as one of the best they'd had together in years. Had they planned a second honeymoon? Flown away to some romantic destination? Not at all. The wife had simply announced that she was going to the grocery store and, uncharacteristically, her husband asked to come along to keep her company. Shopping wasn't what he'd had in mind to do that morning, but he heard the bid for connection in her announcement and, amazingly, offered to join her. Then, at some point during the outing, she suggested that they buy some paint and repaint the kitchen. This task wasn't on the husband's agenda either, but he could hear his wife's enthusiasm for it, and he decided to get behind it. He turned the car toward the paint store and they embarked on the first of many collaborations. They began to revel in noticing bids and turning toward each other. As odd as it may seem, these simple expressions of interest have begun to rekindle the romance in this couple's marriage!

One of the best things about turning toward others' bids for connection is the way that positive responses typically lead to more bidding, more turning toward. Any small, positive effort can get the ball rolling in the right direction. This means you can start anytime, anywhere to improve your relationships and your life. It's simply a matter of becoming a "collector of emotional moments," as Ross Parke suggests, of recognizing all the potential for connection in small, seemingly insignificant interactions—a shy smile, a weak hello, an invitation to the grocery store.

In addition, understanding one another's emotional command systems makes the formation of healthy, strong relationships even easier. Such understanding can help you to see why you feel the way you do and why others may feel differently. Suddenly, conflicts don't seem so confounding or overwhelming. You've got a framework to help you manage your conflicts and achieve more harmonious relationships.

As you apply the principles you've learned in this book, I encourage you to stay observant, patient, and optimistic. If you take every opportunity you can to turn toward the bids of the people in your life, the rewards of this process will become increasingly more evident, and increasingly easy to achieve. It's like learning to drive a car. At first it seems that you have to pay attention to an impossible number of details—the speed limit, the center line, the rearview mirror, and so on. But with time, driving well becomes automatic and you can travel safely and efficiently with very little conscious thought.

Practice these principles of bidding and responding and, in time, bonding will become second nature. You'll feel more deeply connected to those who matter most.

# Index